Mastering Technology Commercialization

By Ste

Copyright 2010–2013 Steven D. Overholt.

No part of this book may be reproduced or transmitted in any form or by any means, electronic or mechanical, including by photocopying or by any information storage and retrieval system, except by express written permission from the publisher.

Published in Erie, Pennsylvania, USA by:

Steven D. Overholt
Erie, PA
soverholt1@roadrunner.com

TABLE OF CONTENTS

INTRODUCTION:
THE REALITY SHOW

Congratulations on your commitment to pursue your dream–the Great American Dream of turning a new-technology idea into a dominant business. You may dream because you have seen others achieve, and perhaps you come here somewhat spurred by envy. Whatever the reason, you have stepped toward quite a journey.

It's an adventure filled with thrills and fraught with danger. I wish I did not have to say the last half of that sentence, but the fact is there are both thrills and danger. Fortunately, you are here to learn the ropes. Knowing the hazards, you can avoid their aftermath, and that makes for a lot more thrills. Many have bogged in the mud, but countless others have achieved their great dream. With the end in mind and a friendly smile, I will be your guide.

In writing this book I am offering to toss my coat onto any mire in front of you. For your benefit I will dig deep into my trove of knowledge and experience, unearthing potent strategies the winners have used to prevail. For my benefit I ask that you also dig deep, revealing potent assets you may not know you have.

Together let's really rock your world!

Your dream is a wonderful thing and it can seem motivational. But a dream is just high-test gasoline–a powerful fuel waiting for the spark of ambition to unleash its power in the engine of persistence. Martin Luther King had a dream, but he got the job done through strategy, planning, and persistence.

Persistence is wrought from unbounded optimism.

Against your aspirations there will always be antagonists–among them doubters, distractions, downfalls, and defeats. Driven by that dream, take to the offense and remain relentless–the goal line; the end zone; the sweet the roar of the crowd.

A sage poet once said: "Hold on to dreams, for when dreams die, life is a broken-winged bird that cannot fly." I want you to hold on to your dream–quite literally. Write that aspiration on the sleek handle of a 12-pound sledge hammer. Then when you need to bust through barriers or break down boulders of disappointment, setbacks, and despair, grab hold of that dream like a convict with the whip at his back and labor away. *That* is how you turn dreams into realities.

Throughout this book I have tried to bring you the best of what you need to know to get the job done, and I trust I have reached my goal. Prepared for you are a variety of little secrets, big rants, and in one instance I have even revealed: "The Secret Sauce." (Really... it's actually a sauce!)

Packed in here are powerful, practical tools and a wealth of advice how to use them. This is counsel that others have used in entering Amazon.com's global contest judging the best business model, pitch, and plan among 2010 technology startups–competing against 1,700 entrants, presenting against six finalists to Silicon Valley's top VCs–and winning it all. Of course it was not solely the advice–it just sits there. It was the acceptance and commitment of those who received it, as it will be for you.

Self-test number one is to really delve into this book–and that hangs on your appointment of time. Foremost from there you must critique your engagement: Do you consult others for help, deliberate your destiny, lay out a plan?

The excitement you feel as you prepare your new business is a connection between us. I have been there and of course while I was there I have also "done that." It's fast; it's furious; it's fun. (Although I must admit that the fun is sometimes like the mirth derived from an icy sidewalk pratfall–not always so fun at the time!)

Surprisingly, progress is very often invented from reversals. Good fortune gathers great momentum as you conquer defeats and from them you learn and grow. I have seen it. Believe it.

Resilience and determination can get you through.

Like Dickens's ghosts of Christmas, both good luck and bad will visit as you work toward your goal. You cannot avoid this; it happens to everyone. Remember that luck flows from elements outside of your control; in this world a great many things are outside of your control. The best response is to take what you get and from it forge triumph.

<u>Inside Scoop:</u> Sometimes good luck comes in streaks; sometimes bad luck comes in streaks. Surviving a tough streak of bad luck puts you in a position to–when the good luck later comes along–revel in it. Persistence matters!

If you are like most who seek to develop a new technology, you have tenaciously mulled the idea for quite some time. In fact, several inventions may hang out in your head, and you could be fretting which to pursue. One thing is certain; you are wondering how to move from where you are to where you want to be.

Fortunately, the pathway for taking an idea from concept to functional technology flourishing on the market–a process known as *technology commercialization*–is well trodden. You must learn from others before launching your own journey. The "early explorers" have drawn the map; use it as your guide.

Early explorers are in more than one way relevant. The most famous early American explorers are of course Meriwether Lewis and William Clark. Noted author Stephen Ambrose wrote a renowned history of the Lewis and Clark Expedition, entitled *Undaunted Courage*. In it Ambrose details how expedition members pushed large heavily laden rafts against the roiling current of the Missouri River in months of grueling labor. Map-less, they then trudged broiling plains and slogged mountains waist-deep in snow, always expecting the ocean in short order but again and again stubbing hard into reality.

Upon finally reaching the sea they framed a rough fort and spent a dismal winter on the verge of starvation. Undaunted courage got them through their three-year journey to triumph and adulation–an excursion that started in Pittsburgh with perhaps the first-ever incarnation of a Great American Dream: "From sea to shining sea."

Another story of an explorer with mind-blowing courage against complete hopelessness–in my opinion far more astonishing than that of Lewis and Clark–is the story of Sir Ernest Shackleton's Antarctic expedition. Read it.

How will reading histories of early explorers help you achieve your fortune-filled dream? Take my word for it; sooner or later you will envy their steel, re-reading their stories seeking solace. How did they, against such odds, hammer their dreams into realities?

Dreams are docile. Reality *rocks*.

After reading histories of those who explored the geographical world, study the most esteemed explorers of the business world. Stories recorded by The American National Business Hall of Fame http://www.anbhf.org/laureates.html, teem with hard luck, hard work, and victory–literally exuding inspiration and better yet: Motivation.

Having climbed the stairway of technology commercialization, I have seen many highs and lows. Straight-up I will tell you I have learned far more from lows than highs. I have guided a host of others travelling the commercialization pathway and in them I have seen both failure and success. Through it all the lines on the map have become clearer. "Terra Incognita" is now laced with superhighways. It's like the Age of Enlightenment!

The good, the bad, the bliss–hang on like a rollercoaster while I reel off the whole story.

The Great American Dream?

No…

Welcome to the Great American Reality Show.

CHAPTER 1:
THE BIG PICTURE

Whether developed by an independent inventor, small business, or major corporation, a great many new technologies have aspects that the developer(s) either can or would like to patent. For this reason, this book details the invention pathway and the book's perspective is focused on an inventor seeking to profit from an invention, whether that inventor is independent or is a principal in a small business. This book will be equally useful, however, to someone developing a technology but who will not seek a patent, as well as to those developing and marketing software products.

So let's start at the top; a very good place to start. This is the so-called "30,000-foot view." Hanging out at 30,000 feet can be very scary and inhospitable... higher than Mt. Everest, bone-chilling cold and leaving you gasping for air. From the shiny warm comfort of a 747, however, it is an awesome view. I'll bring you a bit of both.

As I contemplate the writing of this book, I ask myself what are the overarching concepts that you must firmly grasp–to the point of absorbing into your very soul–if you are to succeed. What are the things that I know that you may not? If I were to go back and start all over again, what do I wish someone had told me? Through the process of assisting hundreds of others in starting and growing their businesses, what have I observed and learned?

First, I have found that people without experience in bringing a new technology to national or international markets usually do not realize how incredibly difficult it is to do so. The process is long, large, expensive, and complex. Many people can handle all of those problems and more, and maybe you can too. However, the real key to your success will be in understanding the "big picture."

THE KEY TO SUCCESS

Basically, the big picture is pretty simple and it is this:

You may have what it takes to succeed in commercializing your new technology, but you must realize that a great technology is *just the start.*

New-technology entrepreneurs succeed by their:

- Market research
- Sales & marketing
- Execution of sound business strategies
- Analysis, judgment, foresight, and adaptability
- People skills
- Financing
- Financial management

- Ability to seek and accept help
- Ability to set and achieve important goals
- Persistence

Of course you need a great technology, but what you do to support that technology is the key.

This book provides a good general overview of the technology development, patenting, business-building, marketing, and financing processes. However, it is no substitute for further research or for expert advice. Many issues are so ponderous that they cannot be fully detailed in any one book. You should do your own research or seek other expert advice on many of these matters.

I wrote this book with the philosophy prescribed in the medical axiom: "First, do no harm." By this I mean that–unlike many authors selling books to entrepreneurs–I will not try to "get you all hopped up" with bravado and feel-good on how rich you will be if you would only follow my sage advice. Instead, my modest but much more important goal is to dissuade you from sinking your hard-earned money into a new technology and later find that you have limited potential to generate a return on your investment.

Yes… I will help you succeed, but often by ensuring that you do not fail.

LEARN THE EASY WAY

On the pathway to success there are many diversions, traps, and pitfalls. I will do my best to point these out to you so that you may avoid them. 90% of your battle will simply be to avoid learning the *hard way* the lessons that have already been learned by someone else through that thoroughly disgusting method.

At the outset, it is essential to be realistic about the time and money required to develop and patent a technology and bring it to market nationally. A good rule of thumb is that it often requires more than a year and hundreds-of-thousands to millions of dollars. You may, however, do it for less if yours is a simple product and you are extremely astute.

Although you may begin the process while working a "day job," eventually you will need to spend full time on your project. Most of the entities that you will be dealing with are only available during business hours. However, do *not* quit your day job based on speculation! Be sure that you have adequate financing already in the bank. Do not depend on investment promises, as they often do not materialize. Realize that you may not just be quitting your job; you may be quitting your *career!* If you are out on your own for perhaps three or five years and then have to go back into the workforce, it can be a whole different world for you by then and not so easy to just jump back in.

It is much easier to contemplate a product than it is to actually produce it commercially and economically–many inventors fall down in this regard. Be sure to take this into account.

There are several companies that advertise on the Internet or late-night television with claims of helping inventors get their product patented and marketed. Be extremely careful about sending your hard-earned cash to one of these companies. Do your research and be sure you are going to get your money's worth. The U. S. Patent & Trademark Office and the Federal Trade Commission warn that an extremely small percentage of inventors ever receive profits to offset the money they spend with invention promotion firms. I have received several complaints from entrepreneurs who felt that they were deceived by such firms, and not so much as one good report.

Also, books are available that claim to help you "patent it yourself." As the patenting process can cost $5,000 - $50,000 or much more through a patent attorney, this is a tempting thought. However, trying to obtain your own patent can be compared to do-it-yourself brain surgery—it saves a lot of money, but the results are generally not worth it. It is very helpful to buy such a book to learn about the patenting process, but you must have an expert write the patent application. I reiterate: You MUST have an expert write your patent application. To do otherwise is foolhardy in the extreme.

WORK THE HARD WAY

No matter who helps you or how much they help, you control your destiny; you are the beast of burden. In this book I have alluded several times to the necessity of hard work—some references covert and others more overt. Well here is where I do not *lay* it, but *smash* it on the line:

> Get ready for grueling, grinding, gargantuan work or get ready for great failure.

Studies show that colossal entrepreneurs did not reach the top by working harder than everyone else. They got there by working *much, much* harder than everyone else. This is absolutely true of the clients I have helped. Some have made it and some have not. The exceptional can show me long email strings from 3:00 in the morning and tickets for back-to-back-to-back bleary plane rides for meetings from San Francisco to London to Dallas.

My highest-achieving client did not attain his success until several years after I began working with him. His first business crashed at the cusp of greatness. Many lost faith. "Ben is a go-getter," I observed. "Never dismiss a go-getter." Unstoppable, nobody now dismisses Ben.

Inside Scoop: Big and bold, brash and brazen—the decisive dominate.

It is my opinion that success in technology commercialization is also largely a result of avoiding pitfalls that could at a minimum lead you astray; at worst, they will swallow your plans and smash them. Of course hard work is required, but you can blow the whole thing up by making mistakes of ignorance or arrogance. If you avoid the landmines, you may be around long enough to succeed. As your guide I am focused on pointing out pitfalls and how to avoid them. By this I am trying to instill for the process not fear, but respect.

IT ALL STARTS WITH SELLING

While we are on the subject of "big-picture" tips on how to scale the mountain, here's some cold, blunt advice from 30,000 feet: In the business of commercializing your technology, you are first and foremost a marketer; a salesman. If you do not accept this, then re-think your plans; you probably don't have a snowball's chance. Why would I say this? As you delve into the chapters ahead, your answer will dawn with a deep sense of discovery.

You will find throughout this book many blunt "blanket" statements such as the above. These are made to drive home a point about the real world. I know about exceptions, and such statements do not apply 100% of the time. However, if you expect to be the anomaly you are depending for your success primarily on luck. Lottery tickets have much better odds and you do not have to expend any effort to lose your money. That to you should sound like a much better proposition!

CHAPTER 2:
SECURING SWEET SUCCESS

Sweet success shines at the end of a long tunnel. Often elusive, it is always difficult.

Yet, would you believe me if I told you that to ensure fruitful technology commercialization you need follow just one overall formula? The problem, however, is that it is an incredibly complicated formula—one that can take years to comprehend and implement. It definitely takes incredible discipline and tremendous fortitude to stick with and actually follow to its fruition.

After many years of insights from having "been there, done that" and from helping others toward their goals, I have created a formula for success that is nearly bulletproof. Unfortunately, my credo is so complicated that many businesses find its implementation to be impossible. Yet you will find it detailed right here in this book. Are you ready? Here it comes:

OVERHOLT'S COMPLEX, CONVOLUTED FORMULA FOR SUCCESS

1) Find out what your customers want.

2) Offer it to them.

I have seen many fancy mission statements that were developed by teams of executives over several days at expensive resort hotels. However, if the resulting statement says anything but the above, then those leaders are on the wrong mission or are more concerned with rhetoric than mission.

The trick is not so much to follow the formula; rather it is to get rid of all the other stuff!

Get rid of the distractions and dead-ends that come from ego and vanity, stubbornness and greed, fear and timidity, laziness and inattention to detail. The result will be a spear-point attack on the goal: Finding out what your customers want and offering it to them.

I will help you do this.

Here is another key point about securing sweet success: It's *sweet!*

Hard work combined with enthusiastic application of the principles laid out for you in this book can produce great success, which many entrepreneurs will tell you can be a whole lotta fun! You should attack this endeavor with the desire to win. Here's a big secret: Winning is fun.

I will help you do this as well.

CHAPTER 3:
WHY RESEARCH MARKETS?

As soon as you have an idea for a new technology, you must start researching the market for it with as much diligence as you put into developing the technology itself. Please read that statement again and truly absorb it, because I have found that no matter how many times I say this to many entrepreneurs, they ignore it.

RESEARCH, THEN DEVELOP

As a matter of fact, you should think of the research & development phase of your project in exactly that order:

1) Research the market

2) Develop the product

It is very easy to put a lot of thought and effort into your new product but not much into the market for it, and most people do this. To illustrate this point, let's take a look at patented inventions: The U. S. Patent & Trademark Office (USPTO) has done studies showing that the percentage of patent-holders who make money on their invention is only 2%. For every 50 inventors receiving a patent, only 1 makes money. 98% of inventors fail to make money on their invention. To drive home the message I have said that three different ways. You now see why it is so important to fully read this book.

Note that in these 98% of cases the inventors did not fail to generate a patent, they failed to generate a *profit*.

Market research and product development can be done in tandem, but be careful how much money you spend on product development before you ascertain that:

1) There is a market for your product.

2) You can capitalize on this market.

Note that 1 and 2 are *not at all the same*.

RESEARCH ALL THAT YOU ARE SELLING

A great many entrepreneurs make the mistake of thinking too narrowly about what they are selling and therefore, which markets to research. Here is a crucial case in point:

Most inventors plan to seek investment capital. Whether they know it at the beginning or not, they will almost always need hundreds-of-thousands or millions of dollars. This means that they will probably at some point be soliciting sophisticated investors.

As is pointed out more fully later in this book, securing large amounts of capital from sophisticated investors requires a strategic sales process. You are selling an *investment opportunity.* As with the market for your product, you must comprehensively research the market for your opportunity. Believe me, there really is a "market" for your opportunity and it can deteriorate or blossom rapidly for many reasons. If you fail to understand the market for your investment opportunity and that market's dynamics, you may well find yourself stuck in the mud for long periods when you try to raise capital or worse yet, you may find there is just no interest among sophisticated investors for your proposition.

Alternatively, you may find in your market research that there would be interest if certain things were done differently than you are initially planning. If so, this information will help to set you on the right track to be attractive to investors when you seek their money.

By the time you reach the end of this book you will have a firm grasp of how to research the market for your investment opportunity.

CHAPTER 4:
INTELLECTUAL PROPERTY

Enough already with those "big pictures!" Let's get down to some nuts and bolts.

Your intellectual property (IP) refers to the ideas or concepts that belong to you. You must take steps to protect your intellectual property or you can lose your right to exclude others from using it. There are several different types of IP that you may currently have or may develop in the future, and the six types of IP that are relevant to technology commercialization are:

1) Patents
2) Trademarks and service marks
3) Copyrights
4) Trade secrets
5) Domain Name (URL)
6) Manufacturing Know-how

These are discussed in general below, but remember that these are complex issues and you must get expert legal advice as you proceed in order to ensure that your rights are fully protected.

PATENTS

I will provide here a basic overview of patents and the patenting process. The information provided is not intended to be sufficient to entice you to attempt to write and prosecute your own patent application. As previously mentioned, I strongly recommend that you hire competent counsel for this purpose.

The Basis for Patents
Patent protection is enshrined as a right in Article 1, Section 8 of the U.S. Constitution. The Patent Act (Title 35) established the U.S. Patent and Trademark Office and governs patents. Through history, there has been a tug-of-war between those who advocate giving inventors exclusive rights to new developments and those who argue strongly against this. This has basically been a conflict between those advocating communal properties vs. those advocating private property rights. Fortunately, the modern world has adopted patents as a means of protecting new developments as the private property of the developer.

However, governments have established a quid pro quo for the inventor and it is this: You tell the public how to make your invention and we will give you the right to prevent them from making, using, or selling it in competition with you. The government's goal here is technological progress. Rather than have new developments shrouded in secrecy, they are out there for all to see, stimulating further innovation.

When you think about it, if you are an inventor you are really in a "Catch-22" situation here–don't patent your invention and be completely vulnerable to theft of your idea, or do patent it but disclose it fully to the public. In the latter scenario you are still vulnerable to theft. The government will not defend your rights; you must do so, and this can require a lot of money in attorney fees.

Should I Get a Patent?
You may have an invention that *could* be patented, but are wondering about the more important question: *Should* I get a patent? The answer to this question is highly complicated and cannot be answered in a book by any author. If you do find someone who answers this question for you without a very thorough investigation and understanding of all of the facts involved in your particular situation, then run–don't walk–away! You must make your own judgment, after careful consideration and input from others, as to the ultimate value of seeking a patent. However, please do not make this decision before you have read this entire book. You should find in the whole of this book the information that you will need to make a decision, but of course there is no substitute for speaking with experts as well.

When to Get a Patent
An ancillary question to: "Should I get a patent?" is the question: "When should I seek a patent?"

Pitfall: Ready; Patent; Aim

I created the above pitfall adage as a take-off on the saying: "Ready; Fire; Aim." If you are familiar with the latter, you know that it refers to a situation in which someone takes an action before they have properly evaluated the situation or prior to preparing themselves for the action.

A great many naïve inventors follow the Ready; Patent; Aim scenario, burning through tens of thousands of dollars and ending up cratering for one or more of myriad reasons, most having to do with lack of understanding of the commercialization process and lack of the preparation that is required on many fronts.

Do not fall into this pit. Read this entire book; know about the process; make a wise choice regarding when to seek a patent.

Patents and Small Business
The USPTO received over 480,000 patent applications in 2010. According to the U.S. Small Business Administration, small businesses not only are the main engine of job growth in the U.S., but they produce about 13 times as many patents as do large corporations. However, the percentage of patents secured by independent inventors has dropped from 21% in 2000 to just over 13% in 2010. Some attribute this drop to the cost of securing patents. Although the USPTO in 2004 cut the basic utility patent application fee, the ancillary attorneys' fees dwarf the USPTO's charges.

For small businesses of under 500 employees, the USPTO maintains a small-entity fee schedule in which most fees are half of those for large entities. Micro-entities get a 75% reduction in most fees.

Types of Patents
There are three basic types of patents: utility; design; and plant.

Utility patents cover inventions that have a utility, such as mechanical devices, software, and chemicals.

Utility patents can cost $5,000 - $50,000 or more including attorney fees, depending on complexity and other factors. The term of a patent is 20 years from date of application. It can take over two years (and sometimes up to four) to receive an initial response from the patent office on a regular utility patent application. As of 2011 the average wait was 35 months.

Design Patents cover the aesthetics or "look" of an item. They do not cover any functional aspect of the item, although the item can have a function.

Design patents can be obtained for $750 - $1,000 including attorney fees. Patent term is 14 years from date of grant. It can take 9 –12 months to receive an initial response from the USPTO on a design patent application. Design patent numbers begin with the letter "D." A product may be marked "patent pending" after the design patent application is submitted.

It is possible to have both a design patent and a utility patent on an invention if both aspects are patentable under the relevant criteria.

Plant Patents cover asexually reproducing plants and will not be discussed here.

Patent Fees
Most of the patent fees listed below are discounted 50% for small entities and 75% for micro-entities.

Basic filing fees for utility patent regular applications are $280, with additional fees added as the application becomes more complex. There are also search, examination, and issue fees of $600, $720, and $1,780, respectively

In addition, patent maintenance fees of $1,600, $3,600, and $7,400 each are required at the 3-1/2, 7-1/2, and 11-1/2 year anniversaries during the 20-year patent term to keep the patent in force. If these maintenance fees are not paid, the patent lapses and cannot be reinstated.

The fee for a provisional patent application (more on this below) is $260.

The basic filing fee for design and plant patents is $180, with additional fees for applications that exceed 100 sheets in length.

See the USPTO fee schedule at: http://www.uspto.gov/web/offices/ac/qs/ope/fee031913.htm

How to Cut Two Years Off of the Patent Process
The USPTO has a program called *Track One*, which, for a fee of $4,800, allows applicants to cut the patent processing time from an average of 35 months to just 12 months.

If you have an invention in a field of rapidly changing technology or in a rapidly changing market, $4,800 may be a very small price to pay in order to cut two years off of the patent process. Having an issued patent will also greatly improve your chances of securing financing for your venture, which is another very large incentive to pay $4,800 for fast-track processing.

Note that the USPTO plans to limit to 10,000 the number of fast-track applications that it will accept in a calendar year. The USPTO received about 5,000 requests for fast-track in the first half of 2013.

<u>The Parts of a Patent Application</u>

The four basic parts of a patent application are the Abstract, Specifications, Claims, and Drawings. In addition, you must provide to the USPTO the results of your prior art search. Each basic part is discussed briefly below, but the best way to understand these parts is to read a number of patents. If yours will be a process patent, be sure to read process patents; if yours will be a composition-of-matter patent, be sure to read composition-of-matter patents, etc., as various aspects of such patents are different. Some applications have drawings and others do not, for instance.

Abstract

The abstract is a brief (one paragraph) general overview of the invention.

Specifications

The Specifications section of the patent consists of several sub-sections:

- Background of the Invention including an elaboration of the Field of the Invention and a Description of the Prior Art. The Field of the Invention could be, for instance: starch-based packaging adhesives. A Description of the Prior Art would then detail the current state of starch-based adhesives in their application to packaging. Included here would be the references found in the prior art search.
- Summary of the Invention is a more-detailed discussion of the invention
- Brief Description of the Drawings gives a very brief general description of each figure in the drawings if drawings are included in the application.
- Description of the Preferred Embodiment including the Claims. The Description of the Preferred Embodiment gives the details of the invention. Here is where you get into the details of what the invention is and how it functions, using the drawings as a reference. This section also puts bounds on various aspects of the invention; for instance, in an adhesive composition, a statement may be made that it may comprise from 20 to 35% corn starch by dry weight. The preferred embodiment, however, may be given as 25 to 30% starch by dry weight. Sufficient detail must be given in this section so that a reader is able to make and use the invention.
- The claims section begins with the words "What is claimed is:" This is the actual patented matter. If it is not in the claims, it is not covered in your patent. Nothing else really matters regarding the scope of your rights. The USPTO will assist you with drafting one claim if you submit your patent application on your own, but I very strongly discourage you from submitting your own application.

Drawings

The drawings must be prepared according to the specifications given by the USPTO. A good summary is provided at: http://www.uspto.gov/web/offices/pac/doc/general/drawing.htm

<u>Patent Attorney and Patent Agent</u>

Both a patent attorney and a patent agent are authorized to practice before the USPTO, which means that they can competently write a patent application and act on your behalf in shepherding it in the long journey through the USPTO. However, a patent agent is not able to litigate patent lawsuits in federal court whereas a patent attorney is able to do so.

Again, you must use either a competent patent agent or patent attorney to prepare your patent application. This is not a legal requirement; it is a common sense requirement. A good patent agent or attorney will keep up-to-date on the latest USPTO or federal-court rulings affecting intellectual property rights. If you have not done so then you will be simply shooting in the dark in trying to write your own patent application. You may, however, save money by writing a draft patent application for subsequent review and revision by an agent or attorney.

At the same time that I emphasize the necessity of hiring competent counsel if you do seek a patent, be aware that patent agents and attorneys make their money by filing patents. They have very little to lose if the patent office does not ultimately grant your patent or if patenting your idea is really not such a good idea. Try to find expert advice on the wisdom of seeking a patent on your invention from someone who is expert but neutral. Such a person could be someone from a government-sponsored economic development agency that assists inventors, for instance.

Can it be Patented?

In order for an invention to be patentable, it must be novel, must not already be patented, must not be an obvious combination of existing patents, and must have utility (usefulness). Expired patents are considered in this analysis. Unfortunately, patent applications that are pending action by the patent office are also considered. The public has limited access to these applications for the purpose of determining if their idea is novel.

The invention also must not be obvious to anyone "skilled in the art" related to the invention.

Inventive Step

The patent office will not grant a patent on a development which is simply an engineering exercise or a series of engineering exercises. There must be an *inventive step* involved. This is rather difficult to define exactly–other than to say that it is not an engineering step. It is actually good if you discovered the invention completely by accident–known as *serendipity*. For instance, if you were conducting experiments and got a completely unexpected result that turned out to be useful, you would have a rather easy time showing an inventive step. If, on the other hand you conducted experiments that led to a result that anyone skilled in the art could have predicted, you may have a more difficult time showing an inventive step.

Getting Around a Patent

You have no doubt heard about the concept of "getting around" a patent by changing something slightly from what is described in the patent. It is important that you understand considerations regarding the ability to do so. One primary consideration is this: If you receive a patent for an invention and someone else can make basically the same invention by leaving out one or more elements in your claims, they can make and use that invention and even get a patent on it. Be sure that your claims include the most basic iteration of your invention. This is one reason that it is essential to utilize a competent patent attorney or patent agent in preparing your patent application.

Inventor Name

The name(s) of each of the true inventor(s) and only the name(s) of the true inventor(s) must be on the patent application. If you want to give someone "credit" that they do not deserve in your application, and it can be shown that the person was not party to the invention, your patent application can be rejected and any subsequent patent can be disqualified. It is exactly like the courtroom principal of: "The truth, the whole truth, and nothing but the truth."

Patentability Opinion

One major advantage of hiring a patent agent or attorney to conduct a patent search is that you can request from the agent or attorney a *patentability opinion*, which is a professional opinion regarding the likelihood that the invention may receive a patent and the expected scope of the claims of such patent. Of course this is merely an opinion, not a guarantee. However, it should give you more comfort in spending the large sums typically required to *prosecute* a patent application, a term which means to move it through the process with the USPTO.

Freedom-to-operate Opinion

You may for some reason know that you cannot get a patent on your new product idea. However, you may not know whether your idea would infringe on somebody else's patent. In this case, you may ask a patent agent or attorney to conduct a search of existing patents that are currently in force and to provide you with a freedom-to-operate opinion which would state that, in the professional opinion of the agent or attorney, your idea would not infringe on the patent of another.

Such opinion may be useful to you if you later are sued for patent infringement. The fact that you sought a freedom-to-operate opinion may assist in your defense against a claim of willful infringement. If willful infringement is found, you may be subject to treble damages to the patent holder.

Utility Patent Coverage

A utility patent may be written to cover both physical entities and processes. Patent claims covering the first are commonly referred to as: *product; apparatus; composition-of-matter, or device claims.* Patent claims covering the second are commonly referred to as *use, process, or method-of-use claims.* There are also a number of other variations of claims which will not be discussed here. Understand, however, that if you perhaps invent a better type of adhesive (composition of matter), you may be able to patent that composition and then independently patent a method of using that composition (for instance to produce corrugated containerboard), as I have done. A patent agent or attorney can explain types of claims to you more fully.

Documentation/Inventor's Notebook

You must document your invention process to establish yourself as the true inventor. This is done by keeping an *inventor's notebook*. To do this, record your development process in a *bound* notebook that has numbered pages. Write down any changes you make in design and why you made them. Sign and date each page. Include a witness statement on the page as follows: "This information was disclosed to and understood by me. (Signature of witness, date)." This witness should not have any stake in the outcome of your invention process.

You should also write in permanent ink and leave no blank spaces. If for some reason you do leave a blank space, cross a line through it and then add your initials and the date.

Drawings should be made directly in your notebook when practical. Otherwise, staple the drawing onto a notebook page and sign so that your signature goes across both the drawing and the notebook page.

Prior to March 2013, the U. S. Patent Office considered the first inventor of a technology to be the true owner of the intellectual property, not the first person to file for a patent. This was known as the "first to invent" doctrine, as opposed to the "first to file" doctrine used in almost all other countries. The America Invents Act of 2011 converted the U.S. to the first-to-file system in March 2013.

In the first-to-file system, the first inventor to file a patent application will be granted the patent if the invention is patentable, even if they cannot document that they are the true inventor. However, if you can show that another person filing a patent has directly "stolen" the technology from you, you may have a chance to maintain ownership and have their patent invalidated. Be sure to consult a qualified attorney if you feel this to be the case. Your inventor's notebook could be invaluable in this case.

In addition to keeping a formal inventor's notebook, you should always have a pen and paper handy to jot down ideas and inspirations as they come to you. It is amazing how easy it is to forget these things, with everything else going on around you. Especially keep a pad and pen by your bedside, as you will find that nighttime is a great time for contemplation.

Non-Recognized Forms of Documentation
There is a common myth that you can document that you are the inventor of a product by describing your invention in a letter, mailing the letter to yourself, and then keeping it unopened. The USPTO and the federal courts do not recognize this as a means of documentation.

Disorganized loose notes and drawings, etc. are also not a recognized means of proper documentation.

Public Disclosure & Offer for Sale
Be very careful about disclosing your invention publicly or offering it for sale before you have applied for a patent. These activities can restrict your ability to patent your invention.

The U.S. allows a one-year grace period in which to apply for a patent after public disclosure of the invention or its offer for sale.

In other countries, you cannot apply for a patent after you publicly disclose, unless you have first applied for a U.S. patent. Once you have applied for a U.S. patent, you can publicly disclose or offer for sale. However, you have only one year after your U.S. patent *application date* to apply for a patent in another country or to begin the PCT process (more on this later) as a first step toward a foreign patent.

Public disclosure can include an article about your invention in a newspaper, showing it at a trade show, public use of the invention, etc.

You should check with the U.S. Patent & Trademark Office (USPTO) at http://www.uspto.gov/, 800-786-9199 or with a patent attorney or patent agent for more details as the rules on these matters are complex.

Non-Disclosure Agreements & Non-Compete Agreements
In a *non-disclosure agreement*, another party agrees that it will not disclose to any third party any information that you provide to them. In a *non-compete agreement*, a party to which you disclose information agrees that it will not use that information to go into competition with you.

A non-disclosure and/or non-compete agreement is typically used to protect yourself when you want to disclose information regarding your invention to another party before you have applied for a patent or while the patent is pending. This other party could be a person from whom you want assistance in preparing drawings or prototypes or a company that you want to hire to conduct market research, etc. It also could be a company to which you would like to *license* your idea.

To license your idea means to give permission to another entity to make use of it in exchange for something of value such as a percentage of their sales, known as a *royalty*.

Note that larger companies will not sign a non-disclosure or non-compete agreement that you provide to them and instead may present you with their own document that offers you little, if any, real protection. For their own protection, many large corporations will not accept submission of an invention idea unless there is an existing patent application on it. Some companies may not accept invention submissions at all.

Certain non-profit organizations that assist inventors, such as government-sponsored or affiliated organizations and economic development agencies, often are willing to sign non-disclosure agreements with inventors that offer real protection to the inventor, although these are normally provided by the organization, not by the inventor.

An example of a non-disclosure agreement is available at
http://www.inventnet.com/nondisclosure.html

Patent Protection Level
A patent simply gives you the right to prevent others from making, using, or selling your invention. The government will not enforce patent protections. You must do so yourself.

If you cannot get an infringer to stop voluntarily, then you must file a patent infringement lawsuit in federal court. These suits can be very expensive, ranging well into the hundreds of thousands of dollars for complicated cases.

When two heavyweights start slugging it out in court over IP rights the amounts can be truly astronomical. Over the course of several years in the late 2000s Mattel Inc. and MGA Entertainment Inc. battled over the rights to the highly successful Bratz line of dolls, which generated $3.3 billion in sales since they were introduced in Europe in 2001. By early 2011 MGA had spent over $150 million in legal fees defending itself against Mattel and an appeal was scheduled, so there is no telling how high the final figure will go before appeals are exhausted.

Some law firms will prosecute patent infringement lawsuits on a contingency basis and if you are lucky you may find one willing to do so for you. However, the firm is going to look at the amount of damages that can be recovered. If you cannot show substantial economic harm, they may be reluctant to take your case on contingency.

Patent infringement insurance is available for the purposes of providing funds to prosecute patent infringement lawsuits against someone who is infringing on your patents. Insurance is also available to protect you from claims by others that you are infringing on their patents.

Patent infringement insurance information can be obtained on the Web by typing "patent infringement insurance" into several search engines.

Provisional & Non-Provisional Application Processes
It is important to understand the concepts of a *provisional patent application* vs. a *non-provisional patent application*. A non-provisional application is also known as a *regular application* and I will use that term for clarity. A provisional application may be made only for utility patents; there is no provisional application process for design patents.

A provisional application can be thought of as a type of place holder until you file a regular application. The regular application is what is used to actually apply for patent protection. I have heard many people say that they "have a provisional patent" or have "filed for a provisional patent," but each phrase is inherently incorrect because there is no such thing as a provisional patent. It is a provisional *application*.

The USPTO developed the provisional patent application process as a means of reducing the costs involved in developing inventions. The provisional application is much simpler and therefore much less expensive to prepare than the regular application. Basically, it provides you a means to "test the waters" in the market before you commit to the substantial costs of a regular application.

You can choose to begin the patent process by filing the expensive regular patent application ($5,000 - $50,000+ in attorney fees), or you can start off by filing a less-expensive provisional application ($130 if self-filed as a small entity) to establish a patent application date; obtain the ability to put "patent pending" on your product, and publicly disclose or test-market your product.

The regular application must be filed within one year of the provisional application in order to receive the benefits of the provisional application. The main benefit is the earlier filing date of the provisional application. A provisional application will lapse in one year unless you file a regular application that is based upon it.

A provisional application can also be used to effectively extend your protection period from the standard 20 years to 21 years. Check with the USPTO or a patent attorney or patent agent for details.

Filing a provisional patent application is much simpler than filing a regular application. Although it is reasonable to attempt preparing a provisional application yourself, you still must be knowledgeable about the process of writing a regular application because the provisional application forms the basis for the later regular application. In order to obtain the benefit of the filing date of a provisional application, the claimed subject matter in the later-filed regular application must have support in the provisional application.

For more information on how to file a provisional application, please check the USPTO web site at http://www.uspto.gov/web/offices/pac/provapp.htm or contact the Inventors Assistance Center at 800-786-9199.

After filing the regular application you will have a wait of typically two-to-three and up to four or more years before you receive your first *office action*, which is the response from the USPTO. The length of the wait varies according to the technology field, some of which are more backlogged than others. You should expect that your first office action will be a rejection, as I have seen figures stating that over 90% of all first office actions are rejections. Note that you will receive no office action on a provisional application.

In its office action the patent office will explain its findings of why some or all of your claims are not accepted and will give you an opportunity to respond.

Eighteen-Month Publication
Unless certain conditions apply, the USPTO will publish your regular patent application eighteen months after submission, making it available to the public. It can easily take 24+ months after the application date for a patent to issue, so this 18-month publication provision often applies. If potential publication of your application concerns you, you should consult the USPTO or a patent attorney or patent agent regarding the rules on publication and how to avoid this. In

general, though, you avoid it by agreeing that you will not seek patent protection in any foreign county.

Provisional patent applications are not published–they lapse in 12 months.

This publication of the patent application can have dire consequences for you if the patent office for some reason does not end up granting you a patent. If this occurs, you have disclosed the details of your invention to the world and will have no recourse against someone who "steals" your idea.

Conducting a Prior Art Search at Reduced Cost
In the jargon of patents, "art" is an antiquated term that is still used, as in: "state-of-the-art technology," but today a more appropriate term would be "science" or "technology."

It is very important to conduct a *prior art search* as early in the invention process as possible. This means to conduct a thorough search to turn up any information related to the patentability of your idea, no matter where that information may reside. Note that a prior art search is far more comprehensive than a simple *patent search* in which only patents are searched.

The information you find through a prior art search could save you a lot of time and money in pursuing an idea that has already been thought of or is already patented.

In conducting a thorough prior art search, you must search a great many sources of information, which is usually extremely difficult to do. These sources include:

- U.S. patents
- U.S. patent applications
- Foreign patents
- Domestic and foreign technical and trade journals
- Newspapers
- Magazines
- Books
- Catalogs
- Websites
- Conference proceedings; etc.

Of course the nature of your invention may eliminate or reduce the likelihood of finding pertinent information in some of the sources. The timeframe of your search is often dependent on the invention as well. An invention for a better type of hand tool could have been developed by someone else many decades ago, whereas cutting-edge-technology inventions of course could not have been.

In doing your prior art search, the nagging problem is always this: How can you be sure that there is not some obscure document out there–even something as obscure as a foreign private individual's laboratory notebook from years ago that is now collecting dust in an attic somewhere–that shows that your invention is not novel? You have to be sure enough of this that you are willing to spend thousands of dollars attempting to get your idea patented.

I will focus my discussion of conducting a prior art search on the subset of patent searching. I will not cover prior-art searching of newspapers, conference proceedings, foreign attics, etc. for obvious reasons. This is also because patent search is facilitated by the USPTO and other entities with online search tools. Other than conducting basic search-engine searches of relevant terms or conducting basic literature searches through tools such as http://findarticles.com/, you should generally focus your initial efforts on patent search.

There are a number of ways to conduct a patent search, one of which is to hire a patent attorney or patent agent at substantial cost.

Alternatively, you can conduct your own initial search, saving the attorney for a more complete search if yours turns up nothing that invalidates your claim to invention. If your search turns up a patent (or an obvious combination of patents) that invalidates your claim to invention, you will not have paid an attorney to receive this bad news. However, if you do not find anything that invalidates your claim, you may want to hire an attorney to do a further search and analyze the resulting information before you spend significant funds on product development and patenting.

Below are several methods of conducting a search without a local attorney:

1) *Hire a patent searcher.* Through the USPTO, you can get a list of qualified individuals who will do a patent search for you. Many are retired patent examiners, etc.

To find a patent searcher: Go to the http://www.uspto website, select "Site Index," and then scroll down to "Agent and Attorney Roster." Select "Listing by Geographic Region," then select a geographic region. You can find them on the following Website: https://oedci. uspto.gov/OEDCI/GeoRegion.jsp. Agents and attorneys are listed. Typically, agents charge less than attorneys. The cost varies greatly by individual and is based on the complexity of the search, but is usually in the low hundreds to low thousands of dollars.

Call several searchers and ask about prices and services, as these vary greatly. You may be able to find a retired patent examiner who does patent searches for a little extra income and who will charge as little as $200 or so for a search. You also may inquire whether the person will conduct a full prior art search and what that would cost if so.

If you hire a local patent attorney or patent agent to do a search, he/she may simply contract with another agent or attorney to conduct the search then mark the price up by double. However, your local attorney/agent should also offer valuable analysis and insight based on what was revealed in the search.

Be sure to properly vet anyone you hire to conduct a patent or prior art search, as there are some shady operators out there who will take your money with no care about whether you years later find out that they did shoddy work. In one case I know of an inventor that hired a patent searcher to conduct a patent search and the searcher stated that there were no similar patents. However, as an exercise, a student intern later conducted a patent search on the same idea and within a few hours found a patent for the exact same invention.

2) *Go to a Patent Depository Library (PDL).* PDLs are often located in the main branch of public libraries in major cities. You can go to a PDL and conduct your own search. General assistance regarding the search process is usually provided at no cost. A listing of PDLs is available on the USPTO website.

3) *Search on USPTO.gov.* The uspto.gov website has a useful search function. To use this, select "Patents, Search" on the uspto.gov home page. You can follow this hyperlink to get right there: http://www.uspto.gov/patft/index.html. You can enter keywords relating to your invention and call up patents that contain those words. Be aware, however, that patents sometimes use legal terms instead of common words that you may think of as keywords.

For a more complete Internet search try the following: If your keyword search brings up patents, look to see what classes/subclasses into which those patents are classified. You can then check the class/subclass descriptions to determine which are relevant to your invention, and then search the patents in those subclasses. Be aware, however, that the U.S. patent classification system has 460 classes and over 150,000 subclasses, so this process can be daunting.

Also, you can review the "prior art" patents that are listed on the patents revealed in your search. Call up those patents, read them, and "follow the thread" of prior art patents that are listed on them, etc. Review all of these patents.

Review the claims, specifications, and drawings of potentially relevant patents; do not rely on the patent title alone.

Be aware that the USPTO Internet database is only "searchable" for patents dating back to 1975. Page images are available for prior patents, but the keyword search function will not search them–this is an important point!

You must also search the patent applications pending action by the USPTO that have been published. This can be done on the USPTO website. The applications search function is on the right half of the page that comes up when you select "Patents, Search" on the home page.

Note that patent applications are not published until 18 months after the application date. This means that there are many applications that are not searchable in this process. This is always a big hole in any search process.

4) *Search on http://www.google.com/patents.* Google hosts a useful patent search function as well. A very important advantage to the Google patents search is that whereas the USPTO keyword search function is only operable on patents back to the year 1975, (prior patents are images only) the Google keyword search function operates on virtually the entire U.S. patent database.

5) *State-funded programs.* Many states have technical assistance programs that provide assistance to entrepreneurs in conducting patent searches. Be sure to check what is available in your area. Usually, a Small Business Development Center can let you know if there is a program available and how to access it if so.

Obtaining a Patent
The complete details regarding obtaining a patent are beyond the scope of this book. However a few general comments regarding the process are pertinent.

A patent can be very beneficial to the success of a company that is marketing a new technology, but a patent is not always essential. A reputation for quality and innovation, brand name awareness, and other factors are important as well. If you cannot patent your invention, this does not mean that you cannot or should not build a company based upon it. Of course that is as long as you are not infringing on someone else's patent.

To illustrate the point of the above paragraph, look at the room that you are in. How many of the items are patented? The desk, the chair, the flooring, the glass, the paper, the pen, your clothing... and on and on and on are not patented. There are many other items or services that cannot be patented: foods, hotel rooms, insurance products, banking, and much, much more. Yet somebody has a successful business selling these items because they are focused on the fundamentals of their business.

If you can potentially get a patent and decide to pursue that course, it is highly foolish to attempt to write your own patent application if you have not had thorough training in how to do so and if you have not kept up-to-date on court rulings, etc. regarding patents, both domestic and foreign. Be sure to hire a competent attorney to do this. You may be able to write an application that results in a patent, but how would it hold up if you were sued in federal court or if you tried to sue someone else for infringement? The federal courts–not the patent office–are the final arbiters of a patent's validity. This is an important point: Even if the patent office grants you a patent it can later be taken away by a court ruling.

It is very important to understand that the law requires you to fully disclose all details of your idea in a patent application. You must disclose how to *practice* the invention, which means how to make use of it. You cannot try to hide certain information in order to keep others from successfully duplicating your invention. If you do so, your patent is subject to invalidation.

Reduction to Practice
Patent law recognizes a concept known as *reduction to practice*. In general, this term means taking concrete steps to develop the invention into a workable product and taking steps to file a patent application on it.

Patent-number Marking Requirements
Once you have applied for a patent, it is important that you mark your product and/or packaging with the term: "Patent Pending." Once the patent has been issued, mark the items with the patent number, such as: U.S. patent number 9,999,999.

Among other things, this protects you from a claim by a potential infringer that they did not know that the product was patented. An infringement then may constitute *willful infringement*. In a case of willful patent infringement, the patent owner may be entitled to collect treble damages from the infringer.

If your patent for some reason expires–for instance due a lack of payment of the patent maintenance fees–you must stop marking the patent number on your goods and packaging. Companies may be liable for a fine of up to $500 per offense for what is known as *false marking*. This means that a fine may be levied of up to $500 for each individual item that is falsely marked.

False-marking suits may only be brought by the federal government or by a party that has suffered a competitive injury as a result of the false-marking violation.

Some false-marking suits have been filed against companies that have licensed patents from another entity. If you license your patent to another firm, you should ensure both that the products are properly marked and also that they are not falsely marked. That concept also flows through to any sub-licensees that your licensee may allow.

Foreign Patents Primer
Be very careful to do thorough research before applying for foreign patents. You must be sure that your technology has a real market in the target countries and especially that you will have the resources and expertise to capture that market. You must also evaluate the actual level of protection that a foreign patent may give you. Also, will you have the resources to prosecute patent infringement lawsuits in foreign countries?

Although someone can make your product in China or another country if you do not have a patent there, you can prevent them from selling that product in the U.S. if you have a U.S. patent.

International Patent Search

Searching of foreign patents has become much easier, of course, with the advent of the Internet. A central site that is quite useful for searching European patents is provided at: http://www.espacenet.com. Information on how to search Japanese patents in English is available at: http://www.jpaa.or.jp/english/patent/how_to_search.html. The Canadian patent database is available at: http://brevets-patents.ic.gc.ca/opic-cipo/cpd/eng/introduction.html. Information on how to search Chinese patents in English, as well as other information regarding IP rights in China, is available at: http://www.epo.org/patents/patent-information/east-asian/helpdesk/china /faq.html.

Filing International Patents

There are several international bodies and conventions that govern intellectual property protection cooperation between countries. Concepts of international patent protection were initially solidified in 1883 in the Paris Convention. Today we have The World Intellectual Property Organization (WIPO), a United Nations agency. It is dedicated to developing a workable international IP system. WIPO was established by the WIPO Convention in 1967 and is headquartered in Geneva, Switzerland.

The Patent Cooperation Treaty (PCT) was concluded among many nations in 1970 and has been amended several times. The Treaty provides a means to seek patent protection for an invention simultaneously in many countries by filing an *international patent application.*

In filing foreign patents, you have three basic options:

1) File separate applications simultaneously in each country (or perhaps region) of interest
2) File in one Paris Convention country and then have up to a year to file in any other
3) File an application under the PCT. This is the easiest option and it also saves money.

Following is a brief discussion of option #3:

Generally, patent applicants wishing to use the PCT process will first file a patent application in their home country. They then have up to 12 months to file the international application under the PCT, claiming the priority date of the home-country application.

It is important to note that this international application will never result in actual patent protection in any country. It is merely an optional intermediary step that conveys certain advantages, prior to filing patent applications in individual foreign countries.

One of the primary advantages of filing the international application under the PCT is that the application undergoes an *international search* by one of the world's major patent offices designated as an International Searching Authority (ISA). Within four or five months, that office then prepares an *international search report* citing documents that may affect patentability, as well as an opinion on the patentability of the invention. This is quite useful information to have prior to making a decision on whether to file patent applications in foreign countries, which is a very expensive proposition.

You may make amendments to your PCT international application in response to information discovered by the ISA. If so, you may then request an *international preliminary examination*, in which the amended application undergoes review. You will then receive an *international preliminary report on patentability.*

After receiving the international search report and patentability opinion, or the international preliminary report on patentability, as the case may be, you may decide to proceed or to withdraw the application. If you choose to proceed, you then will enter the *national phase.*

In the national phase, you will submit individual applications in each country or region of interest. In most cases, you have 18 months from the date of the PCT application to file applications in the individual countries or regions. Note that this can be up to 30 months from the date of the initial patent application filing in the home country (12 months to file the PCT application + 18 months to file the application in an individual foreign country).

There are fees ranging from about $1,500 to $3,000 for the PCT process, but the "big money" comes if you decide to submit applications in the national phase. This can cost well over $5,000 per country.

Note that your PCT application will be published for the world to see 18 months after you submit it.

You can see that it is essential to obtain competent legal assistance throughout this process.

If you choose not to pursue foreign patents, you can still obtain a measure of protection of your intellectual property by requiring non-disclosure and non-compete agreements from any foreign entity with which you conduct business, such as foreign manufacturers or distributors, etc. Of course, the real protection is only as good as your ability to enforce the agreement in court, the same as with foreign patents.

New Uses of Old Products
Many new developments come simply from using an old technology in a new way. Just for a little fun, here is an amazing example to both blow your mind and get your creative juices flowing.

Inkjet printers, only recently having revolutionized the printing industry, are now being used by the Armed Forces Institute of Regenerative Medicine in collaboration with the Wake Forest Institute for Regenerative Medicine (WFIRM) to print new skin onto mouse burn "victims." The "ink cartridge" is loaded with mouse skin cells, which are then sprayed onto the burned areas of the mouse's body, where they take hold and heal the wound. As of early 2011 this has been done successfully in mice and it is only a matter of time until humans will find similar relief from the horrifying aftermath of burns.

More incredible–and never before conceived even by science fiction writers–researchers at WFIRM have successfully printed a mouse heart using an inkjet printer, depositing multiple cell types in a specific order onto a platform that allows the structure to build up vertically, forming the 3D shape of a heart. The heart produced has even been made to beat!

In *my* book, (and this is my book), this has to qualify as the most astounding new use of an old product in the history of mankind.

Be careful, however, if you come up with a new use of a product that is covered by an in-force patent. You may need to get the permission of the patent holder in order to practice your invention.

TRADEMARKS AND SERVICE MARKS

The USPTO defines a *trademark* as "any word, name, symbol, or device, or any combination, used, or intended to be used, in commerce to identify and distinguish the goods of one manufacturer or seller from goods manufactured or sold by others, and to indicate the source of the goods."

The USPTO defines a *service mark* as "any word, name, symbol, device, or any combination, used, or intended to be used, in commerce, to identify and distinguish the services of one provider from services provided by others, and to indicate the source of the services." It is basically the same as a trademark, except it is for services instead of physical goods.

The term trademark is often used inclusively of the term service mark, (It is not called the U.S. Patent, Trademark, & Service Mark Office); again, however, a trademark is for physical goods, whereas a service mark is for services.

Trademarks and service marks are intended to prevent confusion among the public as to the source of goods or services. For example, when I see the trademarked name "Coke®" on a can of cola, I know that the product came from the Coca Cola® Company and not from a vat in your basement.

Claiming Your Rights

At its simplest level, you can claim a trademark merely by using ™ with the word(s) or symbol(s) that you would like to protect. However, you should conduct a trademark search or have a search conducted before doing so. The USPTO Website provides a convenient search tool for searching trademarks which can be accessed at this address: http://tess2.uspto.gov/bin/gate.exe?f=tess&state=4008:fmjgh5.1.1. However, it is very unwise to rely on this tool entirely. Various states also have trademark registration systems, for instance. There are also foreign registrations to consider if you plan to market internationally.

There are a number of for-profit entities that facilitate or conduct trademark searches. One of the best of these is Thomson CompuMark at: http://compumark.thomson.com/do/thomson_compumark. The service is described on the Website as follows: "Thomson CompuMark delivers comprehensive solutions for global trademark and brand protection powered by the most extensive trademark and copyright research sources in the world."

Once you have registered your trademark with the USPTO, you may use the ® symbol instead of ™. Registration with the USPTO is the differentiator between the two. You must use the trademark in interstate commerce in order to be able to register it with the USPTO. Marks used solely within one state are not permitted registration.

If you intend to use the mark in interstate commerce, but have not yet done so, you may file an "Intent to Use" application for the Principal Register. This will give protection, but will also give you a limited time period in which to begin using the mark in interstate commerce, although time extensions are permitted.

A service mark is designated by the "SM" symbol before registration of the mark with the USPTO, whereas the designation ® is used after registration, same as with a trademark.

Protecting Your Rights

Although it is not legally required, you should use the SM, TM or ® symbol consistently in order to notify others of your rights to the trademark. You should include the proper symbol on each piece of marketing material that you create, on your letterhead, on your packaging, in articles that you may write, etc. You do not have to use the symbol each time the name is used in each document, just the first time; that is sufficient to notify anyone seeing the document that you are claiming the mark as yours.

It is also very important to prevent others from using your trademark in a generic manner. There are many examples of trademarks that have lost their protection: linoleum; stainless steel, etc., because they came into general public use as synonymous with the product–i.e. the term became "genericized."

It is interesting to note that "aspirin" was an exclusive trademark of Germany's Bayer Co. until after WWI when the Allies forced the company to relinquish it in the U.S., U.K., France, and Russia as part of the terms of the Treaty of Versailles that ended the war. The name remains trademarked in many other countries.

If you see your trademark or service mark used by others in an improper manner, you should send a letter to the offending party instructing them to refrain from doing so and keep a copy of the letter for your records. This will show that you have attempted to protect your property.

For example, Kimberly Clark Inc. monitors for generic use of their Kleenex® brand name and diligently sends letters to offending parties. For instance, if I were to write a story and say: "The woman reached for a Kleenex to wipe her tears," I would probably receive a letter from Kimberly Clark instructing me to instead use the term "facial tissue" or "Kleenex® brand facial tissue." This is how they protect their brand name even though it essentially has become generic.

It is interesting to note that for some reason, Google does not seem to care that its name has become genericized as a verb meaning "to conduct a search on the Internet."

Duplicate Trademarks
A certain word can be trademarked by more than one company if the markets for the products from the companies do not overlap. For instance: Delta airlines and Delta faucets. If I purchase an airline ticket, I am unlikely to be confused and think that it came from a faucet company. (Remember that the purpose of trademarks is to prevent confusion as to the source of the goods or services.) So when you are conducting a trademark search, remember that just because a name is already "taken" for one product does not necessarily mean that you cannot use it for your product if your businesses do not overlap. See the USPTO website for more information on this.

The exception to the rule in the above paragraph is the concept of a *famous mark*. A trademark can become so famous that it cannot be used by others for any other product or service whatsoever. For instance, I would not be permitted to start the "Coca Cola Airline Company."

Distinctiveness Defined
A trademark or service mark cannot be: 1) descriptive or 2) deceptively mis-descriptive of the product or service. The former is to prevent the government from granting exclusive use of common language and the latter is for obvious reasons.

A trademark must be distinctive and may only be granted either because the mark has *inherent distinctiveness* or it has *acquired distinctiveness*. An example of a trademark that is inherently distinctive is a completely made-up name such as Kodak. Because the name is made up it is unique, or distinctive. Another inherently distinctive name could be "Eagle" if it is a brand of condensed milk, for instance. Since the word has no inherent relation to the product, it is assumed to be distinctive–or unique–in its application to the product condensed milk.

Surnames, geographic names, and descriptive terms are in general not permitted to be trademarked, because they are non-distinctive. For instance, if a bottle of water is labeled "California Water," there could be many different producers of that water, so "California Water" would not indicate to the public a particular source of the product. The exception to this rule is if the name has been previously marketed to such an extent that the public has come to associate the name with a particular source of certain goods or services; thus, the name has acquired distinctiveness in the market. An example of a trademark that has acquired distinctiveness is Ford, which would otherwise be rejected from registration because it is a surname.

To reiterate, the concept of acquired distinctiveness can be described as such: A term that would otherwise not be distinctive may acquire distinctiveness over time by virtue of its use in the market. For example, a company has marketed the name to the public to the point that the public perceives the name as indicating a particular source of goods or services.

Two Trademark Registers
The USPTO has two trademark registers: The *Principal Register* and the *Supplemental Register*. The principal register is for registering marks that are distinctive–whether they are already in use in interstate commerce or whether there is intent to use them in interstate commerce. The supplemental register is for names that are non-distinctive and is described below.

Trademark Supplemental Register
The USPTO has a process by which non-distinctive names may be considered for distinctiveness in the market and thus be allowed for registration. The name can be essentially "parked away" for a number of years (the number varies, but could be three to five or more) and then brought forth for consideration as having acquired a distinctiveness in the market and eligible for full registration. This process is based on the *Supplemental Register*.

The following information regarding the supplemental register is excerpted from the USPTO *Trademark Manual of Examination Procedure*: "An application requesting registration on the Supplemental Register should state that the applicant requests registration on the Supplemental Register. If no register is specified, the USPTO will assume that the applicant is requesting registration on the Principal Register. The mark must be in lawful use in commerce on or in connection with the goods/services before the mark can register. An intent-to-use applicant is not eligible for registration on the Supplemental Register until the applicant has filed an acceptable allegation of use."

Geographic Area Protection
As mentioned previously, you are not required to register your trademark with the USPTO. However, unregistered trademarks are only enforceable in geographic regions in which they are actually used in commerce. For instance, if I have a Pufferbelly Pizza Shop chain and operate it solely in CA, WA, and OR, I have no right to exclude someone from opening a similarly named restaurant in any other geographic region. In fact, if I have only one restaurant in OR, I may not be able to claim rights to the entire state, just the city in which my restaurant is located.

Once I register the name with the USPTO, it is protected throughout the U.S. in any geographic region in which it was not already being used at the time that I registered it. This concept is known as *presumptive rights*. However, if someone was using the name somewhere before I registered it, I could not use the name in competition with them just because I registered it. For instance, if someone had a Pufferbelly Pizza Shop chain in NY at the time I registered the name, I could not use the name there even after I register it. (This of course assumes the NY chain has never registered the name–which they could not have done, because if they had, I could not have then registered it.)

If you have not registered your trademark, you will not be able to use the federal courts to enforce it. You can, however, register the trademark after an infringement and then use the federal courts to enforce it if your right to it is legitimate.

The federal government will proactively enforce infringement of trademarks and copyrights by foreign entities that ship such infringing products to the U.S. This enforcement is carried out by Customs & Border Patrol (CBP) at the border, or by the Department of Justice (DOJ) if the products make it past the border. The primary means that CBP uses for enforcement is impoundment of the shipment at the border. More enforcement information is provided later in this book. Note that no governmental agency proactively enforces patents.

For more information on trademarks and service marks please go to: http://www.uspto.gov/web/offices/tac/tmfaq.htm

How to Register a Trademark
You must register a trademark in each of the international classes in which you would like protection. Goods are grouped into 34 classes. These are usually sorted by the material from which the goods are made and the use to which the goods are put. Services are grouped into 11 classes that are usually sorted by service type. This classification system allows trademarks to be searched and compared for conflicts. In the U.S., international classes are assigned to a trademark under the International Schedule of Classes of Goods and Services. The Schedule is provided at: http://www.uspto.gov/trademarks/notices/international.jsp.

Trademarks are best filed through the USPTO's Trademark Electronic Application System (TEAS). Information is provided on the USPTO site at http://www.uspto.gov/trademarks/teas/index.jsp. Electronic-application filing fees are $325 per international class of goods or services and there are other fees such as a $100 publication fee and a renewal fee every ten years of $400. If this renewal fee is not paid the trademark registration will lapse.

COPYRIGHTS

Copyrights are administered by the Library of Congress, not the USPTO, and provide protection to "original works of authorship." This can include software code. Copyright is an inherent right. You own the copyright by virtue of having created the "work of authorship" unless you have granted this right to another–for instance, in exchange for receiving pay for your work from your employer.

Like trademarks, you are not required to register your copyright with the government (Library of Congress in this case). You may simply use a statement such as: Copyright Steven Overholt 2003. All rights reserved. If you have not registered your copyright, you will not be able to use the federal courts to enforce it. You can, however, register it after an infringement and then use the courts to enforce it. Filing fees for a copyright in 2013 are $35.

The term of a copyright is the life of the creator plus 70 years.

You are not required to include a copyright notice, but it is highly recommended, and is required if you want CBP and DOJ to enforce your copyright for imported materials.

A copyright will not protect you against independently created works. If someone else comes up with the same creation, and did not copy it from you, they have their own rights to it.

International copyright protection is available through the Berne Convention. Through this Convention, many countries recognize the copyrights of others, unlike the case for patents and trademarks. This means that if you register your copyright in the U.S., you do not need to separately register in other countries signatory to the Berne Convention.

For more information please go to: http://www.copyright.gov/

PROTECTION OF SOFTWARE INTELLECTUAL PROPERTY

Software may be protected by copyright. Each software update is independently copyrighted. This is why you will see, for instance: "Copyright Microsoft Corporation 1985 –2001", which denotes that there are multiple copyrights on the material as of the year 2001.

It may also be possible to protect the functionality of a software program through a patent, although this is becoming more difficult to do as the USPTO and courts take a harder stance against too-easily granting such "business method" patents. The Supreme Court in 2010 did affirm the validity of business method patents, however.

A software patent would cover the actions that the program would take, such as (very simplistically) to go to a register X, return a value Y, and use that in a formula Z to create result R. The computer language in which these instructions are written is not really relevant, just the actions taken by the program.

LICENSING OF INTELLECTUAL PROPERTY

You may transfer or sell to others the right to utilize your patents, trademarks, and copyrights. Typically, in order to transfer these rights, you would grant a *license* to the other entity allowing them to make use of your IP under the terms and conditions of the *licensing agreement*. In such a relationship you would be the *licensor* and the other entity would be the *licensee*.

This license may be exclusive (you will grant the right to no others) or non-exclusive. In return for this permission to use your IP, you would typically request a royalty, which is typically computed as a percentage of the revenues that the other entity generates through the use of your IP.

When you license your IP to another entity, you may or may not allow that entity to *sub-license* the IP to a third party. Typically, you would want to receive a portion of the revenue that the licensee receives through a sub-licensing agreement.

ASSIGNMENT OF INTELLECTUAL PROPERTY

You may transfer the actual ownership of your patents, trademarks, and copyrights to another entity through the *assignment* process. Unlike licensing, in which you retain ownership and are simply granting another entity the right to use your IP, you are actually giving up ownership through assignment.

Assignment of IP is done through filings with the USPTO or Library of Congress. In contrast, no filings are made with these entities in licensing agreements, as licensing is considered a private transaction between two parties of no interest to the USPTO or LOC.

Once you assign your IP to another entity, you no longer have the right to use it unless you license it back from the assignee or make a similar arrangement with them.

WHAT TO WATCH OUT FOR IN ASSIGNMENT AND LICENSING

There are a number of reasons why patent-holders either assign (sell) their patents or license (sell the right to use) their patent. There are a number of reasons why entities purchase patents or patent rights. On each side of this equation, some players are in it for sound business purposes and other players are in it for reasons much seamier, even if legal.

A sound business purpose, of course, would be a transfer in order that the purchaser may make, use, and sell the invention and so that the seller of the IP may benefit financially either in the short term or the long term.

Seamier purposes would include a purchaser buying patent rights in order to "shelve" the innovation and keep it off the market and out of competition with the buyer's existing or planned products.

Also, there exist what are known as *patent-licensing companies* whose sole purpose is to buy up rights to patents for various purposes other than to make, use, and sell the invention. Some of these firms are quite large. For instance, the *defensive-patent-aggregator* firm RPX Corporation filed in 2011 for a $100 million public stock offering. The company has 72 dues-paying members–including many of the elite of the technology world–that pay for RPX to purchase patents so that they may not be used in patent-infringement claims against member companies.

Another firm, MPEG LA, manages a *patent pool* of 1,700 patents covering high-definition video encoding under the H.264 standard. Members of MPEG LA include tech heavyweights Microsoft Corp. and Apple Inc. MPEG LA collects royalties from companies such as YouTube and Netflix that stream video via the Web, as well as from video-device manufacturers. The concept of such patent pools is to provide companies with a one-stop-shop to license all of the patents necessary to provide their goods or services to the market.

RPX was formed in 2009 as a reaction to *patent trolls*, the bane of legitimate technology companies for many years. A patent troll is a firm that buys up patent rights solely to use them as a weapon against other companies. The trolls do not make and sell products based on the patents that they hold; they simply file patent-infringement suits against other companies that actually make and sell products. The trolls seek to carve off large chunks of the profit that the other companies have generated through their hard work and marketing. Trolls may know that these suits are frivolous but that the prey company would rather settle out of court that spend the hundreds-of-thousands or millions of dollars and thousands of man-hours defending themselves.

Fortunately for entrepreneurs, Google and NetApp in April 2013 formed Unified Patents (www.unifiedpatents.com), which allows smaller patent-holders to pool resources with each other and major corporations to fight off the trolls. This service can be free for small entities and is definitely worth checking out!

TRADE SECRETS

A trade secret is a secret that is kept for purposes of conducting commerce or trade. There is no provision for governmental registration of trade secrets in any manner similar to patents, trademarks, and copyrights. It is possible to protect trade secrets through the courts if, for instance, you have been diligent in protecting the secret and an employee with knowledge of it leaves and then tries to use it in competition with you or use it in his/her employment with one of your competitors.

It may sometimes be appropriate to keep details of an invention a trade secret rather than to obtain a patent on it, as the whole point of the patent system is to encourage public disclosure of new technology. However, keeping a trade secret requires a high level of diligence and you have no recourse against someone else who reverse-engineers your product. It is very important to have employees sign documents that prevent them from disclosing or profiting from your trade secrets. If you choose the trade secret route, you should consult an attorney on how to protect your rights in this manner.

If your invention is not patentable, but it does not infringe on another patent, it still may have certain aspects that are worth keeping as trade secrets.

One advantage of a trade secret over a patent is that a trade secret is good for as long as you can maintain secrecy, whereas a patent has a term of 20 years.

Trade secrets are protected under state laws, not under federal law.

DOMAIN NAMES & URLS

Following is a brief description of domain names and URLs in reference to these items as akin to intellectual property.

Wikipedia defines a *domain name* as: "an identification label that defines a realm of administrative autonomy, authority, or control in the Internet. Domain names are also hostnames that identify Internet Protocol (IP) resources such as web sites. Domain names are formed by the rules and procedures of the Domain Name System (DNS)."

URL stands for *uniform resource locator*, which is what is commonly thought of as a Web address. Wiktionary.com defines URL as: "the address of a web page, ftp site, audio stream or other Internet resource; for example, http://en.wiktionary.org/. More technically, a URL is a subset of a Uniform Resource Identifier. The URL acts as an item's address on the Internet."

A URL such as that of my blog: http://www.inventyourcompany.blogspot.com actually refers in turn to an IP address number assigned by the Internet Corporation for Assigned Names and Numbers (ICANN). This number is the actual Internet address of my blog, not the name itself. It is obviously much easier for someone to remember a name than it is the long string of address-numbers to which it refers.

Domain names are organized in a hierarchy of subordinated levels. Top-level domains are, for instance: ".com," ".org," ".biz," etc. and the various country codes such as ".uk". The hierarchy descends from right to left. For instance, in my blog address, blogspot is a subdomain of .com and inventyourcompany is in turn a subdomain of blogspot.

ICANN authorizes certain *domain name registrars* through which you may secure your URLs. You can find many such entities by searching the term: "register url."

In the early days of the Internet, it was possible for someone with no connection to a business or celebrity name to register a URL based upon it and then demand from the company or person who would naturally be thought of as the rightful owner of the URL a payment for the use of the URL. A law has since been passed preventing such practice.

The registrant or "owner" of a domain name or URL is the entity that is given by ICANN the exclusive right to use the name or URL as a Web address. This does not convey any other legal rights to the name.

MANUFACTURING KNOW-HOW

There is a type of intellectual property not often thought about by inventors and entrepreneurs that falls generally under the category of trade secrets. This is the concept of *manufacturing know-how*, which refers to the knowledge of how to manufacture the product. Very often I hear successful inventors say: "Yeah, someone could look at my product and reverse-engineer it, but let them try to actually make it! I spent years on that."

In fact, I am one of those entrepreneurs. This was definitely true of my own product line. The concept details and general product construction and layout came to me rather quickly–about two months or so–and I was able to work through these issues by myself. However, working out the specific manufacturing processes and steps took much longer and involved several other people who helped to figure out critical steps. The product was quite unique for its industry and required certain very tight tolerances and precise placement of parts relative to each other. We found that certain production processes had to be done in a certain order and very specific types of tooling and jigs had to be created to properly locate the parts during assembly. Also, I conceived of a unique way to form a certain part that was far more effective than the more obvious method.

If you think that you may plan to claim manufacturing know-how as a trade secret, be sure that you have good solid agreements in place with all who will be working on your project regarding ownership of any developments, keeping them secret, and competing with you or using the development for the projects of others. In my case my agreements stated that any such developments would be my property.

Since manufacturing know-how generally consists of a set of engineering-type steps it is often not patentable. However, it is certainly possible that some aspect may be patentable and it would be good to discuss this with a patent agent or attorney.

It is possible to license manufacturing know-how separately from a patent. This will be discussed further in the chapter on manufacturing.

INTELLECTUAL-PROPERTY STRATEGY

You must approach the intellectual property assets and potential assets of your business with a plan and a strategy. As with everything else about your business, you cannot just "wing it" or drift with the currents and eddies. If you require assistance, of course you may speak with your IP attorney, but sometimes they are not really qualified to advise you on your overall strategy. Also, remember that they have a vested interest in suggesting that you apply for patents.

Advice may also be sought from other entrepreneurs and from economic development agencies; but again, be sure that they truly have the expertise you need.

Many firms crowd the field of intellectual-property consulting and a Google search on the term yields 4,780,000 results, so you should have plenty of them to evaluate if you decide to go that route!

CHAPTER 5:
BUILDING A BUSINESS

TRAPPING MICE

What does trapping mice have to do with building a business? Well just *hold your horses* and you'll see!

We have all heard the adage: "Build a better mousetrap and the world with beat a path to your door." What a *dream* that is! I almost want to laugh when I hear that.

> **Pitfall**: *"If I build a better mousetrap the world will beat a path to my door."*

If this is what you think, then wake up from that dream and take some advice from the reality show. I came across the following quote many years ago and it is the essence of bringing new technologies to market: "The goal is not to build a better mousetrap, but to build a better mousetrap *company*."

That famous mousetrap adage should say: "Build a better mousetrap and then beat a path to the world's door." If you adopt this philosophy then you are *taking control of your destiny*, not depending on the world to serve it up.

> **Inside Scoop:** *Build a better mousetrap and then beat a path to the world's door.*

THE BEST IP PROTECTION OF ALL

In the previous chapter we spent considerable time studying a number of ways–patents, trademarks, etc. –to protect your idea so that you may profit from it. Unfortunately, all of them are useless.

You read that correctly: All of them are useless.

> **Pitfall: Assuming that patents, trademarks, copyrights, or trade secrets have value**

These items have no value because not one of them can stand on its own. Nor can any combination of them stand alone. A patent, trademark, copyright, or trade secret has no inherent value. They are simply a means to protect something–regardless of the value of that "something." If you do not build a successful business around your idea, then all that your patent will be is bragging rights framed on your wall.

If you do not build a successful business around your idea, many bad things will happen—one of which is that you will likely end up without the funds to pay the required patent maintenance fees—thus watching your patent lapse. (Don't worry; it will still be there on your wall.)

Inside Scoop: The only way a patent, trademark, copyright or trade secret can have value is if it protects something that has value.

Even if you intend to sell or license your technology to another entity, you still need to build a successful business. Successfully licensing your IP and then ensuring over the years that you are able to profit from the arrangement is typically no easy task. In this case the process of finding and screening potential licensees, selling them on your technology, negotiating a favorable contract, and then ensuring adherence to that contract constitutes "building a successful business around your idea."

In fact, if you plan to license your idea, you may very well find that you will generate little or no interest from potential licensees unless you first produce your product and demonstrate that it can be profitably sold in commercial quantities. This means that it is very often true that you will have to first build a successful business making and selling your technology before you will be able to license it to a large company.

Inside Scoop: The best way to protect your idea is to build a successful business around it.

Building a better mousetrap company is no small feat. Lucky for you, the Small Business Development Centers (SBDC) http://www.sba.gov/aboutsba/sbaprograms/sbdc/index.html and the SCORE organization http://www.score.org/index.html are great resources that you can tap into for assistance in building a business. In the meantime, below is some general information to get you started in creating your company.

THE BEST FIRST DOLLAR YOU CAN SPEND

I am constantly amazed at how many entrepreneurs will spend thousands of dollars on invention promotion scams; advertising that they don't need or understand; unnecessary inventory; business filings, and many other large expenditures, but they just will not open up their wallet to pay an attorney.

Inside Scoop: Paying an attorney is the best first dollar you can spend.

Before you spend all of your money on all of that other stuff, why not make sure that you are doing it right? A competent attorney is expensive, but can be well worth it. Just be sure that you are hiring someone who really knows what they are doing. Ask for references and get referrals from other businesses, then interview at least three attorneys before selecting the one to assist you.

I have had several business attorneys state to me that they make the bulk of their money by fixing messes that entrepreneurs got into because they did not come to the attorney beforehand.

38

BUILDING A BIG-LEAGUE BUSINESS PLAN

As there are hundreds, if not thousands of references available on how to write a business plan (BP), I will not detail the entire process here. I would like to give you a few very important pointers, however, that are sometimes not properly addressed in many business plan guides.

Goal

To borrow a question from a source that I do not recall: "What is your big hairy goal?"

To borrow a phrase from a source that I *do* recall–that source being Theodore Roosevelt: "Dare greatly!"

Set audacious goals in your business plan and then lay out a plan to achieve them. Swing for the fence. Sophisticated investors do not want to invest in meekness; they want to participate in greatness.

Why Bother?

One of the primary advantages of writing a business plan, other than the fact that this process has been shown to increase the odds of entrepreneurial success by 300%, is to force you to learn. To write an excellent BP you must learn about your business and your *market space*, which is the market within which your business will operate.

Also, a BP gives other people something to critique. You want as much expert advice as you can get your hands on and this is how you get it: Have people review and comment on your BP. Your BP should be of such quality that someone reading it would think that you had been in that business for many years, not a newcomer to it as is often the case for an entrepreneur.

Tools and Assistance

I and other business consultants I know recommend that you do not use the business plan software packages available for substantial cost, such as Business Plan Pro. There are so many free sources available that this does not make sense. Also, I have never once seen anyone use these programs and develop a good solid plan.

You may contact an economic development agency that provides low or no-cost assistance with business plans, such as the SBDC or SCORE. These entities typically will not write your BP for you, but they may provide one-on-one individualized consulting to guide you through the process. Note, however, that few economic development personnel are qualified to help you write a business plan powerful enough and meeting all of the requirements for approaching sophisticated investors such as VCs. This is truly a specialized skill and you must find someone who has written such plans that have been successfully used to *actually receive* VC investment. Mere attempts at doing so do not count in this regard!

Many college-level marketing classes take on business-plan-writing assignments as class projects; be sure to check into opportunities. Be very careful, though, as the students may require considerable guidance from you to develop an excellent plan. Check with professors in the business school for opportunities. Note that it is not likely that a group of students or even a business professor will create a BP of the quality necessary for soliciting investments from sophisticated investors, but they may give you a good start.

Be sure to also get assistance from high-caliber people in the industry, successful entrepreneurs, etc. This is especially true when it comes to your business model and revenue model. You really need the input of *seasoned experts* on these; you absolutely must not make assumptions here.

I have written–separately from this book–a detailed business plan outline and instructions. If you would like me to email these to you at no charge, please contact me through my blog at: www.inventyourcompany.blogspot.com

A Real Business Plan
Warning: Get ready for some "tough love," because we will now be slogging into the morass of one of my biggest pet peeves as a business consultant.

Here is a little pre-test for you: The operative word in the term: *business plan* is what word?

No–it's the word PLAN!!! (Shame on you.)

Pitfall: Writing a "business dream"

Of the many business plans that I have reviewed, (including some written by MBAs from top business schools), I have not once seen a first draft of a BP that clearly defines an actual PLAN. Instead, the entrepreneur simply makes general statements regarding his business, makes unsubstantiated claims, and tells what he is going to do rather than telling that which is most important: *how* he is going to do it, how much that will cost, and how much revenue that will produce and when.

I call such BPs a: "Magical Mystery Tour." In such BPs everything is going to happen magically; it is a mystery exactly what will happen or how it will happen, and it is simply a tour around the business. Especially weak are the product development and marketing sections of all first-draft BPs that I have ever reviewed.

A BP cannot be written straight out of your head. It takes research. Writing a top-notch business plan is hard work that usually takes months to accomplish.

I once had two MBA entrepreneurs submit a 40-page BP for my review. They were starting a technology company and anticipated raising $5 million or more from VCs, so I knew the BP had to end up as a good one. Unfortunately, their BP did not start out as a good one. We worked on it for a period of over four months, going through at least six sessions of review followed by their re-writing, adding, clarifying, etc. to make it not just good, but excellent. During the final meeting, when I finally gave them my thumbs up and congratulated them for a job well done, I asked them to describe the process they had gone through to produce the plan. The word they chose was: "Grueling."

And it was. It was grueling even for me.

A proper BP does not need to be, nor should it be very long. Few people will actually read the entire business plan, so you probably should limit it to under about 30 - 40 pages. You may have considerably more information as attachments and backup material in case anyone asks for more information.

You must prepare a concise *executive summary*, typically of three pages or less.

A BP must include financial projections for three to five years into the future. VCs typically will want to see five years, whereas banks will typically require only three years.

Targeting a Market

The crux of your business plan will be to identify your *target market*. This is the narrow subset of the global market for all goods and services on which you will focus your marketing efforts. You will learn much more about target markets as you read further in this book, but for now I will tell you this:

Your target market comprises those who are *desperately seeking* the benefit that your product or service provides. It may also include those that you know for certain you can *cause* to desperately seek your benefit through your innovative and dynamic marketing campaign.

Business Plan Lamentations

I empathize greatly with those who have to write BPs. Before I started my first business the task seemed hugely daunting and the thought of it actually inhibited me from starting a business for several years. However, I and others have found that if you just get started and take the attitude of chipping away at it gradually, you can get it done. Don't think of writing a business plan; think of writing the operations section, then of writing the marketing section, etc.

How do I Know?

One of the most common laments I receive from those preparing a BP, especially when it comes to preparing the financial projections, (known as *financial pro forma statements*), is "How do I know?" They wonder: "How do I know what my sales of product X will be in year Y?" The point is that you *don't* know and everyone knows that you don't know. What you must do is conduct thorough research and make your best educated guess. (Yes, that is also known as a SWAG.).

The best philosophy in writing a business plan is to determine what you want to do, then how you are going to do it, followed by an analysis of how much that will bring in revenue. Once you have a conception of what you want to do, it is then easiest to start your financial projections with the expenses. If you need to rent certain space, go find out how much that space rents for. If you need to hire a certain person, go find out how much you will need to pay them, etc.

Start with the easy parts. It is rather like having a 2000-piece puzzle dumped out in front of you. You start putting it together by building the border because all of the pieces have a straight edge and this makes them easy to place. Next, you put in all of the blue-sky pieces, etc. The more of the easy pieces you get in the easier it is to put in the difficult pieces, until that glorious moment when there is only one piece left and you slap it down with triumph.

Change is Bad?

Another common lament is: "As soon as I write it down, things will change." The point is that as soon as you write it down things *will* change. When a savvy businessperson reads your BP they know that the likelihood is that things will not play out exactly as laid out in your plan. However, when that businessperson reads your plan they should think to themselves: "Yes, I can see that if they follow this plan they will have a very solid chance at success." The question to be answered is whether you know enough about the business to lay out a credible path to success. If you can, then investors also know that you likely are capable of adapting as necessary while you march toward your goal.

How to Write Powerfully and Convincingly

Your business plan must be written in language that is powerful.

People will be far more inclined to invest in your company if they feel that you are in control. One of the ways to sound like you are in control is to write in the *active voice* rather than the *passive voice*. In the active voice, the subject of the sentence is the entity that is taking the action. In the passive voice the subject of the sentence is the receiver of the action. Here is an example that both explains the difference between the two and shows why the use of active/passive voice is important in powerful writing:

Let's say I am at a party with my wife one evening and some drunk comes over and starts trying to "hit on" her and will not stop despite my warnings. So finally I get right in the face of the drunk, grit my teeth and snarl: "If stopping isn't accomplished by you, you will be punched in the nose by me." I doubt it! Of course I would say: "You better stop or I'll punch you in the nose."

In general, you should in your business plan use the active voice, although there are certain reasons for exception to this rule.

Also, instead of writing long lists in paragraph form, break them out into bullets. Understand that the most powerful positions in a sentence are the first and last words, and words preceding a pause such as a comma. In a paragraph, the most powerful positions are the first and last sentences.

To write convincingly, avoid unclear or imprecise words or terms such as "large," "work with," "align with," "partner with," "intend to," etc. Do not say what you intend to do. State what you *will do* once you assemble the tools and resources necessary to do it. For important facts, figures, and other information, provide sources that are reputable. Clearly differentiate fact from opinion.

Also, do not make absolute statements that you have no way of knowing, such as: "Nobody else is addressing this problem." You have absolutely no idea of what a couple of geeks in Silicon Valley may be working on in their garage, so don't say that you do.

Follow the Money
In your business plan you must define a clear path to revenue. Exactly what are you going to sell, how will you sell it, how will people buy it, how often will they buy it, etc. There is a phrase for this and it is: *Follow the money.* Related to this is the fact that it is generally bad to depend on only one source of income; for instance, one product or product line. A change in the market environment can have devastating consequences if you only have one leg to stand on.

Unsubstantiated Statements
Be sure to back everything up with authoritative sources. If you quote market statistics, add a footnote giving the source.

Especially do not state that you will offer better customer service or higher quality than your competitors unless you can clearly and authoritatively define the exact level of customer service and quality that your competitors offer. The last time your competitor did a survey of its customers regarding its customer service, what did it find? How do your competitor's most recent survey results compare with their previous ones? Answer: you probably don't have a clue!

Your opinions about your competitors mean *nothing* here.

Also, you must define exactly how you will offer, for instance, better quality. Will you implement Six Sigma practices, whereas your competitors do not? If you cannot lay out a plan to accomplish these things, as well as tell how much they will cost and what exactly they will produce, you are simply writing a business *dream*.

When You Wish Upon a Star...
Isn't that just the most inspiring song? How lovely that we just wish and it comes true!

Pitfall: *"If we get just 1% of this $5 billion market by Year 5 that will be $50 million in sales."*

Inside Scoop: You won't.

Q. How do I know that you won't?

A. Because you said that you would.

I also know that you will send packing any investor that has a lick of sense if you fall into the pit of making a statement like that. You seriously will, so do not do it!

The proper way to estimate sales is from the grassroots up, not the blue-sky down. Lay out a solid marketing plan showing that you understand the market. Demonstrate that you know how to generate sales within that market. Then show that you have or can secure the tools required to generate those sales. *Now* I believe that you can generate $50 million in revenue!

Give a Business Tour
One way to think about starting the process of writing a business plan, especially regarding the operations section, is to imagine that you are giving a tour to an important visitor. Lay out how your business will operate. Include information on your facilities, manufacturing processes, distribution methods, personnel, etc.

Tour your operation at the following stages: startup; year 1; year 3, and year 5 (if you go out this long). What would you show visitors and what would you tell them about your operation and how everything works as you are giving them the tour? You should be able to quote important statistics to your visitor, such as how many people you have in various positions, how many pieces that you pick and pack, and how many cartons you ship per day, etc. Give this "tour" to the reader of your business plan.

Of course, as we saw above, your plan must comprise much more than this tour!

Use of a Business Plan to Raise Capital
If you plan to raise equity capital (covered later in the chapter on finance) you may need to provide potential investors with a *private placement memorandum (PPM)* or *prospectus*, which are legal documents that detail the investment opportunities and risks. Often the company's BP forms the core of the prospectus or PPM. You may find yourself constantly revising your business plan and prospectus or PPM due to the fact that they must contain the most up-to-date information at the time they are given to the prospective investor and at the time the investment is accepted.

Be aware that you cannot simply offer your business plan out to potential investors for purposes of soliciting investments, unless you are dealing with accredited investors (covered in the chapter on finance) *and* the offering meets certain criteria defined by the SEC. This means that if you ask your neighbor or your uncle Bob about investing in your business, you cannot simply give them your business plan from which they will make their investment decision unless you understand the rules that would allow this.

Typically, unsophisticated investors or investors of relatively small amounts of money will require a three-year BP, whereas VCs will require a five-year BP. Entities making loans will typically require a three-year BP.

Hiring a Professional to Write Your Business Plan
Many consultants will offer to write a business plan. The cost of a truly great BP can easily run $8 – 10,000 or more. Be very careful in hiring someone, however; thoroughly vet their work. There are many consultants claiming the ability to create a BP that do shoddy work. The reason that it costs so much to hire this out is because of the time and expertise involved.

Some CPA firms will offer to write a business plan. Personally, I would shy away from this, because the money is the *result* of your plan, not the basis for it. But there are of course exceptions to every rule and you may find a CPA competent to write a thorough business plan.

Often, the cost of having the plan written is only part of your overall cost. For instance, if you are planning to raise investment capital you will likely require a private placement memorandum or prospectus. These documents may be based on your BP, but they require other elements that are typically composed by an attorney, to whom you will pay additional fees.

Win Cash Through Business Plan Contests
Many state and local government entities, economic development agencies, and colleges or universities conduct business plan contests, often with valuable prizes–usually monetary. Coaching is also often provided to contestants in preparing their plans. There are various other entities that hold such competitions, such as Invent.org, with its Collegiate Inventors Competition offering a $25,000 grand prize.

Often the monetary prize is the least valuable aspect of entering such competitions. The true and lasting value comes because you can build very important connections. The judging panel very often includes members of angel groups, VCs, or employees of economic development agencies that have money to disburse. You get a great showing in front of these people even if you do not win. I have often seen entrepreneurs that did not even place in the top three who were later approached by these people with interest in their company. The judges may see value in what you are doing, but just feel that you did not present it in the best possible manner. Be sure to ask for a debriefing session with the judging panel in any case, even if you win. Check online for competitions for which you may be eligible.

Here is a very motivating story regarding entering such competitions: I know of a couple of entrepreneurs that were preparing a business plan to enter a competition covering 38 counties in one of the most populous states in the nation. The grand prize was $35,000. The entrepreneurs made it through the preliminary rounds and were invited to travel to the state capital–a five-hour drive–to present live to the judging panel in competition with five other finalists.

Neither of the entrepreneurs had much self-confidence, and they had had a number of business setbacks in the weeks prior to the final live presentation. This situation conjured up that hideous monster of motivation killers: Dejection. The morning of the contest the two woke up early and spoke by phone regarding whether to travel the five hours to the competition, considering the fact that their finances were low and the price of gasoline was high. Expecting that they did not have a snowball's chance of winning, they decided to just stay home.

An hour or so later one of them changed his mind, called the other, and they decided: "What the heck?" Scrambling now because they were late, they jumped in their car without breakfast and tore down the highway, arriving just in time for their presentation. Of course you can probably guess that I would not be telling you this story if the ending was any but this: They won the $35,000!

SITE SELECTION

Be sure to thoroughly evaluate the potential locations for your company headquarters or manufacturing facilities prior to making a decision on this very important aspect of your business. Every state and some municipalities have incentive programs to encourage businesses to locate in certain areas, as does the federal government.

HUB Zone Tax Incentives
At the federal level, *Historically Underutilized Business*, or *HUB Zones* are designated geographic regions in the U.S. that have been set up to confer advantages to small businesses located within. The primary benefit is preference in selling to the federal government or military. You can find where HUB Zones are located at: http://map.sba.gov/hubzone/init.asp

State and Local Incentive Programs
Check with your state economic development agency or with local economic development entities to find out what is available near you. You also may want to check with neighboring states and consider moving if the incentives are great enough to make it worthwhile. The typical advantages conferred by state and local governments are tax advantages for a certain period of years and/or perhaps access to special grant or loan programs, including low-interest loan programs.

Business & Technology Incubators
Check on the availability of manufacturing, business, or technology *incubators* that may provide valuable in-depth startup assistance. A true incubator will provide a very high level of advice and mentoring services, and sometimes access to special loan or equity funds. Because incubators often implement a selection process and do not let just anyone in, location within an incubator often conveys a measure of respect when you approach investors. The success rate of businesses "hatched" from incubators is much higher than others as well.

Many incubators provide a shared receptionist and/or secretary and also provide office furniture and phone and Internet services, utilities, etc.

One of the primary benefits of locating within an incubator is the fact that there will be other entrepreneurs with whom to bounce ideas around, commiserate, and socialize.

Usually such entities will expect you to "graduate" out of their facility within five years or so.

Be aware that some entities calling themselves incubators provide little more than space and perhaps some secretarial assistance. Thoroughly check out any incubator and interview current and former tenants prior to signing any lease.

The trade association for business incubators is the National Business Incubator Association (NBIA). More information is available at: http://www.nbia.org/. NBIA has a "Find a Business Incubator" tool at: http://www.nbia.org/links_to_member_incubators/

University and Trade School Assistance

You may also want to consider locating near a university or trade school from which you may recruit interns for part-time positions in your company. Such schools may also provide opportunities for you to use their facilities for research or they may conduct research for you. This includes both scientific/technical research and market research. Marketing classes may take on a market research project for your company.

Trade schools and engineering schools with manufacturing technology programs have manufacturing equipment and may be able to prepare CAD drawings, rapid prototypes, machined prototypes, molded parts, etc. They also may conduct engineering work. I have had clients utilize such programs to very great benefit. Be sure, however, that you thoroughly understand the intellectual property policies of any such entity you work with. Some of them claim all developments made while working on your project as their own.

Regardless of your location, you should contact these entities to see what opportunities they may hold for your company.

Zoning Considerations

Be sure to check whether the location that you are considering is zoned for the use you contemplate. This may seem like a no-brainer, but I have seen entrepreneurs that have had a great big "Oops" on this one.

Home Office Advantages/Disadvantages

Many entrepreneurs start out in their own home. This conveys certain advantages, such as: reduced cost; the potential ability to deduct certain expenses such a percentage of the rent or mortgage payment; proximity to family; etc. For instance, if your office utilizes 10% of your home's area, you may be able to deduct 10% of your mortgage payment, electric bill, real estate taxes, and more. The space must be used exclusively for business, however. Be sure to consult a tax advisor.

If your home is located in an area zoned residential only, or if there are covenants against operating a business in your neighborhood, remember that these rules were set up to prevent you from being a nuisance to your neighbors. They are to prevent you from putting up a sign and to prevent customers from parking in front of your home, etc. They are not normally intended to prevent you from having an office in your home or from conducting other "light" business from your home if you do not impact your neighbors.

If you feel that using your home address as the return address for your business would convey an "amateur" image (123 Primrose Lane, for instance), consider using a post office box.

BUSINESS STRUCTURE CONSIDERATIONS

When you decide to start a business you are creating from scratch something that never before existed–a brand new entity on the face of the earth. There are a number of different types of entities that you can create, however. The choice that you make here is extremely critical and must be well considered.

There are several business structures from which you may choose. Among the common structures are:

1. Sole proprietorship
2. General partnership

3. Limited partnership (LP)
4. Limited liability company (LLC)
5. S Corporation
6. C Corporation

A complete discussion of each structure and the advantages/disadvantages of each is beyond the scope of this book. Also, these structures are governed by the various states and the processes to set them up and the rules governing them vary between states. You must hire a competent business attorney to guide you in setting up your business structure.

In general, though, here are some points to consider regarding business structure to help get you started:

Sole Proprietorship

A sole proprietorship (SP) is a very informal business structure and it can have only one owner. You cannot raise investment funds and remain as a sole proprietorship. This is because if someone invests in your business, they are purchasing a partial ownership, which violates the term "sole." However, a sole proprietorship may receive loans from individuals or banks, etc. The IRS will require you to keep your personal and business funds separate from each other and accounted for separately. You will need to set up a separate bank account for the business in order to accomplish this.

With a sole proprietorship, the business and its owner are one and the same. Therefore, profits and losses are recorded on the owner's personal income tax return via Schedule C. In addition, the owner is personally liable for the debts and liabilities of the business, including damage awards against the business.

General Partnership

A general partnership (GP) has shared ownership among the partners. If you want to bring in a partner, the partner(s) can put money into the business, but they are not "investing" in the sense that most people think of the term. When the partner comes in with money, he/she will have direct management responsibilities controlling the performance of the business unless he/she gives up those rights in a partnership agreement. The partner has far more control than, for instance an investor in a corporation, who can only influence the course of the company by voting for directors.

It is usually a bad idea to set up a business so that two partners have 50/50 control. This can (and often does) lead to paralysis if the two disagree on an important point and each refuses to budge. One person should have a superior position and be able to say to the other, if necessary: "I have considered your opinion and respect it, but I have decided that we must [do X] in order to succeed."

In a general partnership, the profit or loss of the business is apportioned to the partners according to their ownership percentages and reported on their personal income tax returns. Each partner bears *joint and several liability* for the debts and liabilities of the business. This means that a claimant can recover from any one partner or any combination of partners the total amount owed by the business. Also, one partner can commit the others to obligations by, for instance, going out and getting a loan for the business without telling the other partners.

It is possible to start up as a SP or GP and then switch to another entity later. SPs and GPs are relatively inexpensive to set up. It is cleaner and less expensive in the long term if you set up the proper organization from the start, though, if you can afford to do this in the short term.

Just because you have chosen one of the less formal business structures such as SP or GP does not relieve you of the responsibility to keep a good accounting of your business finances. Of course, even if you choose one of the more formal structures below, it is still imperative to keep good financial records, but this will affect the finances of the business entity, not your personal taxes directly.

Note that just because taxes from sole proprietorships and general partnerships flow through to the personal returns of the owners, this does not mean that the businesses are not required to file any tax reporting forms with any governmental agencies. Be sure to consult a qualified tax advisor regarding any filings that you must submit.

Be sure to keep a good accounting of your expenses related to developing your technology and business, even prior to having a prototype or sales. This includes travel, training, purchase of items for R&D, attorney fees, office supplies, business use of your home, and more. These costs may be deductible from your personal taxes. Your time, however, generally is not. If you are using your home, etc. in your work for a corporation or LLC, you may also be able to deduct these types of expenses if you are not receiving compensation from the company. Consult a qualified tax advisor.

Limited Partnership
Limited partnerships are not often used to form new-technology startup companies. A limited partnership has both general partners and limited partners. The difference is that the general partners have management duties and unlimited liability for the debts and liabilities of the partnership whereas the limited partners do not have management duties and their liability is limited to the amount of their investment into the company, i.e. they can lose their investment but no more than that.

When you bring on a general partner, you are not subject to U. S. Securities Exchange Commission laws and regulations due to the fact that general partners have management control. If you however create a limited partnership and bring on a limited partner, the limited-partner's stake may be considered a security regulated by the SEC due to the limited partner's lack of management control.

The profits and losses of the business are reported on the partners' personal tax returns.

Limited Liability Company (LLC)
A LLC is a type of hybrid business structure that gives its owners various options on how to be taxed: as a corporation or with pass-through taxation as in a partnership. In pass-through taxation–the usual choice–the profit or loss of the LLC is apportioned to each owner (known as a "member") according to his/her percent ownership and reported on his/her personal income tax return.

Members are not liable for the debt or liabilities of the LLC. However, a bank will not loan to a small LLC unless each member with more than 20% ownership signs a document agreeing to pay off the loan if the LLC does not (known as a *personal guarantee*). This will be a joint and severable guarantee.

In general, a venture capital group does not like to invest in LLCs, preferring corporations instead. You may want to take this into account if you plan to seek VC funding in the future.

Corporations

There are two basic forms of corporation: C-corporation and S-corporation. Stockholders in a corporation are not responsible for the debt or liabilities of the corporation. You can think of the "S" as standing for "small" although it actually refers to Sub-chapter S of the Internal Revenue Code, which deals with small corporations.

Both forms of corporation are complicated to set up and operate, requiring a board of directors, shareholder meetings, tracking of stock issuance, etc. The following is a *very brief* review of the two corporate structures. Again, (you guessed it), seek competent legal advice in setting up a corporation.

You can find on the Internet various sites that will help you incorporate for some low amount of money. I do not recommend that you use these. You want to have a relationship going forward with a competent attorney who has assisted you along the way and understands what was done and why. As you grow, you will encounter a great many more legal issues than just setting up your business, some of them related back to the setup of your business. The attorney knows the history.

C-corporation

The C-corporation structure allows an unlimited number of shareholders and has no restrictions on who may purchase shares. The amount of money that can be raised is unlimited. This corporate structure is usually necessary if you aspire to be a large national or global company and need to raise large amounts of capital.

The biggest disadvantage of a C-corp is double taxation. If the corporation earns a profit, it has to pay taxes on that money. If the corporation distributes the remaining profit to its shareholders as dividends, the shareholders have to pay income taxes on that money, so the money that the corporation earns gets taxed twice. This a major reason why the Bush administration in 2003 reduced the income tax rate on dividends from that of ordinary income (up to 35%) to a set rate of 15%.

Stock in a C-corporation may be *privately traded* or may become *publicly traded* through an *initial public offering (IPO)*. "Privately traded" means that the stock is sold through means other than stock exchanges like the NYSE or non-exchange markets such as over-the-counter networks. Typically, this means that it is sold to and through the limited business networks of the founders and existing stockholders and perhaps through individuals or firms representing the company. Stock sales to angels, angel groups, and VCs are almost always private sales.

S-corporation

A corporation is automatically a C-corp unless a special election is made to be an S-corp when setting up the corporation. This election may also be made at a later date if for some reason that is necessary. There are certain eligibility requirements for becoming an S-corp. For instance, an S-corp may have no more than 100 shareholders and there are a number of restrictions on whom these may be–for instance: no nonresident aliens and only natural persons or qualified trusts and estates. Another business cannot own shares in an S-corp.

The principal advantage of an S-corp is that the profits and losses can pass through to the individual shareholders. The corporation does not pay federal income taxes. The ability to pass losses through to shareholders (subject to conditions) can be very advantageous during the startup years when the corporation may sustain substantial losses. The shareholders can deduct these losses against their other income on their tax returns.

S-corporation stock is always privately traded–not publicly traded–due to the restrictions on the stock ownership. If you do not ever expect to grow to the point of needing more than 100 shareholders, a S-corporation may be suitable. It is possible to switch to a C-corporation at a later date if you end up needing to do so. Seek competent legal advice, as this is only a brief overview of the highlights.

Liability
As I mentioned, owners of LLCs and corporations are not responsible for the debt or liabilities of the LLC or corporation. For instance, if the corporation is sued, the owners do not have to pay damages. There is an exception to this rule, however, and that is in the case of fraudulent activity. If the owners conduct fraudulent activity, the courts can *pierce the corporate veil* and recover damages for victims from the owners of the LLC or corporation.

BOARD OF DIRECTORS

Below are a few relevant comments for entrepreneurs regarding boards of directors.

Necessity
Several of the above business entities require a board of directors, which is the top-level governing body of the entity, such as the corporation.

Corporate Governance
The responsibility of the board is *corporate governance*. This is the long-term management and oversight process by which the board protects the interests of the shareholders and creates shareholder value. In carrying out this duty to shareholders, the board must consider the balance between itself, the management, the shareholders, and other stakeholders including the employees and the community within which the business will operate. The board must ensure that the company meets all of its legal and ethical obligations, and the board sets the governing principals and values for the company.

Board/Management Duties
Often some boards or board members may want to meddle in the day-to-day operations of the company, but this is not their role. If the board does not like what is occurring, their route is to work with the executive management (CEO), not to conduct the management themselves.

The CEO reports to the board of directors and may be fired by the board. The chairman of the board may be a *non-executive chairman*, who has no special powers–he or she simply runs the board, or may be an *executive chairman*–he or she has a management role in the company in addition to running the board. The *president* is an officer of the company, not of the board. One individual may hold more than one title, and it is possible for company management to serve on the board.

It is usually wise to have an odd number of board members to prevent tie votes. Initial terms should be staggered in length so that everyone's terms do not expire at the same time. For instance, various members would start off with terms of one, two, or three years. Each renewal would then be for a set term.

Board candidates may be nominated by shareholders and may be elected by those holding qualified stock. Note that a C-corporation may issue both voting and non-voting classes of stock and LLCs may be able to have voting and non-voting members. An S-corporation, however, can issue only one class of stock.

Whom to Ask
Recruiting a board of directors is *serious business*. Typically, the entrepreneur has the primary role in selecting the initial board members, often by default because he or she is the majority shareholder. At a very early stage the entrepreneur may not need board members other than himself and perhaps a spouse.

You will want to have people on your board that are well respected, competent, and personable. Many investors will request or require a seat on your board, but be careful of whom you let serve. Just because someone is a successful dentist, attorney, or local businessperson with money does not mean that they have a clue how to run a fast-growing technology company with national or international markets and that must raise significant private-equity capital.

Try to find people with experience in your market space and especially in entrepreneurship. Also, you should recruit people with "connections" that will be valuable in your company's progress on various fronts–especially financing and sales, as these are the two areas where personal connections have the most impact. Having a high-quality board will make your company more attractive to future investors. Thoroughly consider your choices for your board members. These are among the most critical "hires" you will make.

How to Find Directors
Finding high-quality board members can be a difficult process. Like many other aspects of being an entrepreneur, finding good board members is a sales process that involves networking. The obvious first places to look are your acquaintances and investors. Encourage your initial board members to find other board members. You may want to contact your local chamber of commerce or economic development agencies to get suggestions of good nominees. The business writer for the local newspaper may be a good source of references as well. Be sure to have potential board members submit a resume for your review.

Unofficial Duties
Make it clear, if necessary, to your board members before they come aboard that one of the duties that you will expect from them is to assist the company in raising capital. If they are not comfortable with this, think long and hard before you nominate them to serve. Another duty of the board should be to find other good board members.

D & O Insurance
Shareholders can sue board members if they feel that the board is not properly protecting their interests. Be sure that your nominees understand this. Some people that you speak with about serving on your board may be reluctant to do so because of the liability involved.

The company can have a written agreement with the board to protect, indemnify, and hold harmless, but if the company does not have the money to defend the board member in court, that agreement is pretty worthless. Therefore, you may want to consider directors' and officers' (D&O) insurance for your board members. This is a policy that will defend the members if they are sued by a shareholder. If you feel that the company cannot afford such insurance, try asking your board members if they would be willing to contribute toward the policy premiums. Of course for fairness it would probably have to be an all-or-none situation among the members; either all contribute or none contribute.

Managing a Board

If you will be the CEO of your company, then the board of directors is technically your boss. However, you should actively manage your board so that it does not go in directions that are not for the good of the company. Of course the first step in managing a board is to put together a manageable board. By this I mean a board that will not require much management because they understand their role and are highly competent both in governance of a startup and in your market space. The key to this management process will be the application–by you–of the fine art of persuasion. You may not be able to tell your board what to do, but you surely can influence them to do the right thing.

Robert's Rules of Order

The board chair should run the board meetings and shareholder's meetings according to *Robert's Rules of Order*. The Website is: http://www.robertsrules.com/

BOARD OF ADVISORS

In addition to a board of directors, you may want to set up a board of advisors. This may be a way to secure the participation of someone who does not want to commit to the responsibilities of a director position or it may be a way for you to give someone a "trial run" to check them out as board-member material.

A board of advisors can be especially valuable in the fields of financing, operations, and marketing. If your advisors have the right connections, they can be invaluable in these areas.

You want to find at least some advisors with big-business experience who can point out wise business practices that can assist you in avoiding pitfalls. If you have not previously worked in a big-business atmosphere you may dismiss their practices as staid and innovation-killing, and indeed some of them are. But there are a great many of these practices that have been refined over many years based on finding out what works and what does not work when it comes running a successful business.

If nothing else, look at your board of advisors as job security for you, providing you with the guidance you need to grow with the company.

NETWORKING/PEOPLE SKILLS

In the process of inventing, prototyping, developing a manufacturable product and especially in marketing, it is essential that you build large and strong networks of individuals and businesses that you can call on for assistance. The broader and deeper your reach, the more successful you will be.

Note: In the paragraph above and later in this book I use the term *manufacturable* to mean: "able to be produced at a cost that allows you to receive an adequate profit from its sale."

Your ability to work well with people and to get them to genuinely want to assist you will be critical. Your business will not succeed based on what you can do, but based on what others do for you. It takes a strong leader for a business to succeed, but that leadership must be directed toward getting a team to pull together.

The "Luckiest" Man I Ever Met

When I think of the value of great networking, one entrepreneur comes to mind as the shining example. I will call him Bob. Everyone who knows about what happened to Bob thinks he is lucky; but luck is a strange animal and good fortune has this great anomaly: It smiles adoringly upon those who hunt it down with a shark-like vengeance.

Although he is a vegetarian, Bob hungers to rip the meat from the bones of opportunity. The result—as you will see below—is a rather full plate.

Bob developed a new technology, filed a patent application on it, and then started talking to anyone and everyone about what he was doing. He had built a small pilot facility to demonstrate his technology, but was still in the phase of conducting trials to further refine the process. One day he was attending a funeral for his uncle and he met a "long-lost" cousin that now lived in New Mexico. Bob told the cousin about his technology. Guess what? The cousin worked at Los Alamos National Laboratory and knew the head of the group working on the technology field pertaining to Bob's process. Well, a couple of days later Bob was on the phone with that program manager, who was impressed enough that he invited Bob to submit for research funding.

A couple of months later, Bob attended a local seminar related to his technology. He met the director of a local non-profit organization and Bob began speaking to him about what Bob was doing. It turned out that the non-profit had been funding research in the same technology arena at companies located many miles across the country and was pleased to find that there was someone locally working on a project that they may be able to fund. Additionally, the non-profit already had a working relationship with the university that Bob was partnering with in his research.

And I have saved the best for last regarding Bob's "luck."

Prior to either of the two above events, while Bob was using space at a local science consortium laboratory to conduct "bucket trials" of his process, a visitor came in and Bob started talking to him about the big picture of what he was trying to accomplish, including launching a business based on his technology. After about 15 minutes this man—whom Bob had never before met—asked Bob: "How much money do you need to do that?"

Unprepared and not wanting to push his luck, Bob replied: "Oh, maybe $50,000." "Naaa," said the visitor. "You're going to need a lot more than that. At least $300,000." Bob stammered an affirmation. That was three years ago. The visitor not only invested $300,000 into Bob's company, but he continues to provide funding for certain projects. This was definitely a stroke of unfathomable good luck, but good luck happens to those on the prowl!

Good luck happened to Bob. It can happen to you.

I know many more examples of the phenomenal power of networking, including personal ones. There is a paradox in good luck: You must depend on it, but you must not depend on it. I trust that you can figure out what I mean by that. If you cannot, you may contact me via my blog for an explanation.

Inside Scoop: Get out there and get the good luck that you are due!

How to Get in to See Influential People

One of the biggest challenges of networking is simply getting the attention and consideration of influential people with whom you wish to network. Of course there are quite a number of reasons that you may seek the attention of influential people: soliciting board members; soliciting investments; soliciting strategic partnerships; making sales calls; soliciting licensing deals, etc.

Each of these situations presents a similar challenge and in each case the solution is the same:

Inside Scoop: Do your homework and then get creative!

Simply sending a proposal in the mail, sending an email, or attempting a phone call very rarely works in getting through the bustling clutter of an influential person's life. For instance, I have spoken with marketing managers at major corporations and VCs at major firms that report receiving thousands of unsolicited proposals a year. They simply cannot possibly look at or properly consider every one of them.

Instead of blindly sending out proposals, you must first find out as much as you can about the business and personal life of your prospect: Where did he/she go to school; what are his/her favorite causes; to what organizations does he/she belong; whom does he/she look up to; what is his/her favorite movie; etc.? Once you have this information you can put on your thinking cap and develop a creative, entertaining, or intriguing way to get the attention of your prospect.

You also may be able to come up with a more universal creative, compelling way to gain the attention of the large majority of your prospects by relying on more general traits of human emotion or behavior. A couple of these could be curiosity or humor, for instance.

How a Brainstorm Saved the Day

As an example of the use of humor to gain the attention of busy prospects, I once heard a talk by Bill Rancic, the champion of the first year of Donald Trump's television show *The Apprentice*. Before he appeared on the show, Rancic had already created a highly successful enterprise, Cigars Around the World. Early in the process of developing this business, Rancic had of course found it difficult to get the attention of various important prospects simply by sending proposals to them through the mail.

One day he got a brainstorm and kooky though it was, it worked like a charm. He went out and purchased all of the Groucho Marx glasses/mustache sets that he could find and then sent out his proposals in a box instead of an envelope. The first thing the prospect saw on opening the box was a set of the glasses with the note: "Take a closer look at my proposal." Although he was sending to powerful business professionals, even those people are subject to their basic human emotions.

Who is Number One?

The necessity of great "people skills" is especially true in your management of employees. This will be your "tightest" team of all. Your employees are typically the ones who deal directly with your customers.

I am always a bit perturbed when I hear a CEO say something along the lines of: "At XYZ Company, our customers are Number One." To a company's management, the customer should be second. To a company's management, the employees should be Number One. If employees feel valued, empowered, responsible, and incented, they will treat the customer like Number One when management asks them to do so. If the employees instead feel helpless, ignored, hopeless, and frustrated, they are highly unlikely to treat the customers like Number One when management asks them to.

Pitfall: Thinking that your customer is Number One

Again, a bit of balance is in order, in that you cannot run your company completely by "What *they* said." At times you may need to do something that goes against your employees' wishes or thoughts on the subject. But if you do, be sure that your employees feel that their views were seriously and thoughtfully considered and then be sure to take the time to explain why you are doing what you are doing. Be sure also to follow up with employees at later intervals regarding their thinking and their continuing acceptance of your decision.

A great example of this philosophy in motion is the story of Andra Rush, who in 2010 was featured in *Reader's Digest*. Andra started a trucking business in the 1970s and later started an auto parts business that in 2009 generated $370 million in revenue. Neither business is typically thought of as a woman's domain! When *Reader's Digest* asked her "What is the key to your success?" she responded: "You have to be service-driven. You think of customers every day, every minute. You think about what would make their lives or their businesses more successful. And you have to be focused on who's serving them. *If we don't look after our drivers, they won't look after our customers.*" (Emphasis added.)

Managing Expectations
One thing is very important in working with others and especially in soliciting ideas from employees, and that is the concept of *managing expectations*. This means to be sure that others do not overestimate the potential outcome or have unrealistic views of what is within your power to achieve.

For instance, if you solicit employee suggestions, be sure to make it clearly known up front that you probably will not be able to implement all suggestions, but you are sure that you will be able to implement some of them. Be sure that everyone understands the "odds" of their idea being acted on and encourage them to keep submitting even if their first few did not get implemented.

You may want to consider conducting monthly prize drawings from among all suggestion submissions, awarding a prize to persons who submit a suggestion that is implemented, or a combination of both.

Admit That You Are Wrong?
We have all heard how important it is to be able to admit that you were wrong, and indeed it is. Lack of an ability to do this is perhaps one of the most destructive forces in interpersonal relationships. However, I have learned over many years that the rule: "Always admit when you are wrong" has a corollary, and it is this:

**Inside Scoop: Never admit you are wrong to someone
who cannot handle the information.**

You probably already know what I mean by this, but just in case, I will explain. Some people use information as a weapon. There are in fact people out there with ill intent. (Hitler, Hussein, Stalin, Castro, Manson ring a bell?) If you are dealing with a person such as this, (though hopefully not the same order of magnitude), it is my opinion that it is probably counter-productive to hand them a big weapon to wield against you. This is especially true if you know that they are going to swing that weapon around and create a circle of destruction that is as wide as possible.

As with anything, think before you speak. Err toward the side of admission, but remember that there is an exception to every rule.

PERSONNEL PRIMER

Again, a few pointers are all that are germane to a general overview such as this book. There are many books on personnel management, because to thoroughly cover the subject takes an entire book. I suggest that you read at least one such book.

Your Only Asset

It's no secret that people are critical to your business. In my opinion people are a business's *sole asset*.

Accountants want to talk about the value of the company's fixed assets. Accountants want to count things like buildings, money, equipment, and inventory as assets, but these are not assets because they have absolutely no value to a company. They are simply *tools* to be used by the company's one and only asset–its *people*–who build value into them. That value is not fixed! It takes only a very cursory look around to see the truth in these statements. In the late 2000s General Motors' management trashed each and every one of the "assets" on its balance sheet. It was not the "asset" that did this, it was the people who did this. In the meantime, Apple Inc.'s people were properly using that company's tools to build into them incredible value.

How to Hire Great People

Hiring is a very difficult and scary subject for an entrepreneur. There are myriad rules and regulations to follow, taxes to withhold, etc. Fortunately, there are payroll services and accounting firms that know all about this and can help you through all of it. An accounting firm should also be able to assist you in determining how the hire will impact your bottom line.

Be sure to consider alternative forms of compensation such as stock options, commissions, performance bonuses, etc. to reduce your cash outlay.

Also, be sure that you do not try to call someone a "contractor" if they are actually functioning as an employee, in order to try to avoid paying payroll taxes. Learn the laws in this regard and comply with them.

In your hiring decision, do not get too focused on the resume. Ensure first that the person will be a great addition to your team and has the right attitude. All of the experience and contacts in the world can mean nothing if the person has a "bad attitude." It is very rare to come across such a person, but if you do, they can really cause problems that far outweigh their resume. Be sure in the interviewing process to ask open-ended questions to try to find out about these things. Such questions would be, for instance:

- Tell me about your favorite job and why it was your favorite.
- Discuss the subject of "difficult people."

- What do you feel are the biggest detriments to a teamwork environment?
- Tell me about your most-favorite and your least-favorite supervisors and why this was so.
- What is important to you in your employment and in your employer?
- What are your long-term goals?
- Whom do you admire or look up to and why?
- If you were to hire someone for this position, what would you look for?
- Why did you leave your last employer?
- What do you feel are your most important attributes when it comes to performing the duties of this job and contributing to the organization? (If the answer does not go much beyond experience or resume, watch out!)
- Have you ever worked to improve something about yourself, and if so, how did you go about it?

PRODUCT-LINE MANAGEMENT

It is very difficult to build a successful business based on only one product. The reasons for this are many, but a couple of them are:

1) It is difficult to get attention in the market over a long period of time for just one product.
2) There is a major trend among corporations to reduce the number of suppliers that they have. If you can only offer the corporation one product, you are asking them to set up a new vendor in their system for just one product, write relatively small and numerous payment checks, etc. This is inefficient for them.

You must think about what new products you can introduce and when you can introduce them. Such products do not need to be simply more iterations of your existing product. However, they would need to be something else that you can sell to your existing customers or through your existing channels.

THE CRITICAL IMPORTANCE OF VENDORS

I would be remiss in writing this chapter on building a successful business if I did not mention the importance of finding good vendors. So much focus is placed on finding good customers, but poor vendors can prevent you from serving the needs of those great customers you so diligently sought. These vendors include business advisors such as accountants, attorneys, and insurance agents. In the case of these advisors, be sure to interview several and then choose the one that you feel can best serve your needs and at the best price—remembering, however—that you get what you pay for.

Finding good vendors for raw materials is very important because any cost savings you may receive from a less-expensive vendor falls right to your "bottom line," meaning that it directly results in higher profits for you. Of course price is not always the only consideration. You may find through ThomasNet that Vendor A sells bolts at 20 cents each and Vendor B sells the same-spec bolt for 16 cents. However, if you do your research and talk to people, you may discover the vital intelligence that Vendor B is known for poor quality and late shipments; however, there is a Vendor C selling the bolts for 18 cents and that has great customer service.

Prices can vary considerably among vendors for the exact same product or service. Think about the price differences you see between—for instance—brand-name grocery items at Wal-Mart Inc. vs. a traditional full-margin grocer. Wal-Mart's efficiencies allow it to provide the same item at a lower price. These relative differences in operating efficiencies pervade the business world and are not limited to retailers!

HOW TO FIND GREAT CUSTOMERS

I will discuss customers later in much more detail in the market research and marketing chapters of this book, but there are a couple of aspects of customers that do not fall into those categories. Let's take a look at them here.

<u>Pitfall</u>: **Selling to anyone who says they will buy.**

<u>Inside Scoop:</u> **Pick great customers. In fact: Pick great customers, personnel, and vendors– excellence all around you!**

Most entrepreneurs have a very difficult time picking great customers. They simply chase whatever sale they can get. However, *your customers can kill you.*

Some customers are highly and unreasonably demanding; some have a habit of non-payment; some are wishy-washy, never knowing what they really want; some are too big for you to handle; some will cut you out if they can find a slightly lower price; some will try to reverse-engineer your product and give it to one of their more-preferred vendors; some will try to go into competition with you; some will... well, the list is endless, really.

This is one of the reasons why the saying: "It's a dog-eat-dog world out there" was so astutely conjured up. Be careful out there, folks!!!

Be sure to vet your potential customers as thoroughly as you vet your potential employees and vendors. The quality of each is of great importance to your business.

Just as you may need to fire an underperforming supplier or employee, you may need to fire an underperforming customer. Each is a very difficult decision, but who said this would be easy? (Certainly not me–at least not that I recall!)

As important as it to pick great customers, be sure that you do your homework by checking references, running a D & B report (more on D & B later), etc.

CRITICAL COMPONENTS OF YOUR DISTRIBUTION CHANNEL

The means by which you provide your product to the consumer is your *distribution channel*. Traditionally, distribution channels involved: master distributors; distributors; wholesalers; buying groups; retailers; catalog companies; shipping companies; door-to-door; in-home parties, etc. Today the distribution channel may include: streaming via the Internet; *cloud services*, which simply refers to software services delivered via the Internet, and cellular phone services, for instance for mobile applications or *apps*.

A distribution term you should know is *Software as a service (SaaS,)* which is a general term for software that does not reside on the users' device and is accessed via the Web or cellular phone service. A mobile-phone application, or *app*, can be a type of SaaS.

As its traditional distribution channel has been exploded by Amazon.com Inc. and others with their e-readers, the publishing industry has recently gone through wrenching change. Traditional brick-and-mortar bookstores, such as big-box giant Barnes & Noble Inc.–which only a decade before was pilloried for causing the demise of small independent bookstores–was nearly forced into bankruptcy in 2010. Borders Inc. did declare bankruptcy in February 2011.

Amazon's pioneering and domineering distribution system for books first included the ordering of physical books via the Internet and shipping to customers, then expanded into digital distribution to its Kindle e-reader and other e-readers via methods such as: hard-wired Internet connection, Wi-Fi wireless Internet connection, and cellular phone service.

Considerations in selection of the proper distribution channel are very complex. You must do your proper research before choosing one or more channels that are best for your overall situation. This is where it is particularly important to speak with people in the industry who can give you critical advice and insights.

I will provide you with information regarding pricing levels throughout a common retail distribution channel later in this book in the section on pricing.

PAYMENT TERMS AND SYSTEMS

Typical terms for payment of invoices on credit are 30 days from the date of the invoice. The invoice date should be the date the product was shipped or the services delivered. It is relatively common to offer a 2% discount for payment within 10 days of the invoice date. Such terms are abbreviated as: *2% 10, net 30*. I.e. the net (full) amount of the invoice is due within 30 days and the customer may deduct 2% of the invoice amount if they pay within 10 days. You will almost certainly have customers that will pay beyond 10 days yet take the 2% discount and you must be diligent in not allowing this.

It may be advisable to accept credit cards. To do this you will need to set up a *merchant account*. This is a relatively easy process. You do not go through the credit card companies themselves to do this. You can get set up through your bank to accept credit cards, but banks are typically an expensive option. If you belong to a warehouse club such as Sam's Club or Costco Inc., check on such services offered to their members. It may be worth the membership fee just to participate in their credit card program. You can also check online for offerings. There are of course various fees to the merchant for accepting credit cards; be sure that you understand them and evaluate them in the context of how you will do business, such as expected order size and frequency, etc.

COLLECTIONS

When you signed up to be an entrepreneur, you probably did not think that you were signing up to be "Guido," but you were. Although collecting debts from your customers is an unpleasant task, the inability to do so has sunk more than one aspiring mogul. If you let your accounts receivable pile up, you may need to borrow or bring in additional investment to carry your deadbeat customers' businesses–not a wise business practice, to say the least. Let's take a minute here to discuss this bit of unpleasantry.

Should You Offer Credit?
Of course the need to perform collections comes only from the fact that you have sold something to someone on credit. The best way to avoid collections is to avoid offering credit. The next best way is to be very careful about offering credit. Be sure to run a *Dun & Bradstreet (D & B) credit check* on any company to which you are considering offering credit. D & B collects data on the payment history of companies. It will cost you to get this information but it may be worth it.

It is usually best to require first-time customers to pay cash up-front before you offer them credit terms on later orders.

Be sure that your invoices clearly state your payment terms and the consequences of late payment, such as interest penalties of one or one-and-a-half percent per month. Some entrepreneurs have found it effective to highlight the penalty provision with a yellow highlighter.

Understanding Collection Procedures

It is very important that you develop, write down, and then actually follow a clearly defined set of collection procedures that escalate in firmness with each step. A typical procedure would be as follows:

If the full amount is not paid by the due date, call the account on that day and speak with them about the need to pay. Ask them if they dispute the amount and document the details of your conversation, especially the fact that they did not dispute the charges, if so.

If the full amount has not been paid by the time that you set in your first conversation, send a letter requesting payment. Offer to accept partial payment toward a payment plan, even an amount as small as $5 or $10. This will establish legally that they acknowledge the debt.

If payment is not made according to the terms of the letter, send another advising that you will be sending the account to a collections agency and then do so if the debt is not paid by the timeframe you set in this letter.

In no case should you wait beyond 90 days past the due date to send the account to collections. This is a very difficult policy to stick with, especially for customers that could represent large volumes of future business. However, you really need to think about whether you are "seeing the writing on the wall" with these customers.

Large corporations can often treat small vendors with disdain. When it comes to big corporate clients, try to get to know the accounts payable clerk that has the responsibility to pay you and develop a rapport with them. This may help to influence their decision as to when you get paid.

Collection Agencies

Collection agencies typically keep half of the amount that they recover. You can find collection agencies listed in phone books or of course online. Interview several before you choose. The agency does not necessarily need to be located close to you.

CREATING GREAT CONTRACTS

Pitfall: Doing business on a handshake

**Inside Scoop: That went the way of the handshake
(It's now the fist bump... haven't you noticed?)**

A former partner in one of my businesses used to say all the time: "Good contracts make good friends." Keep this in mind because it is very true.

IT'S NOT WHAT YOU KNOW, IT'S WHAT YOU DO

Get things done!

Success in business is not determined by what you know that you need to do, it is determined solely by what you *actually do.* Too often, business owners make a statement that goes much like this: "I know that I need to _____, but I _____"

Pitfall: Of course, pretty much anything can go in the blank spaces above, but the sentence is unfortunately sometimes completed as follows: "...but I'd rather fail miserably because I'm doing other things instead of that."

Determine what is important, prioritize it, and don't procrastinate or approach it with half-measures.

In this regard, it is critical to be goal-oriented, rather than activity-oriented. By this I mean that it does not matter, for instance, how many sales cold-calls that you have made today; the only thing that matters is whether you have made a sale today.

The bank will not put money into your account out of sympathy for the amount of effort that you have expended!

If your efforts are not producing results, you may need to re-think what you are doing and develop new approaches to those efforts or undertake different efforts that do produce results.

It is very helpful to keep lists of what you need to do and cross off the items as they are accomplished. Considering the amazing complexity of the process of new technology commercialization, it is hard to imagine how someone could succeed without so doing. You cannot just "wing it."

HOW TO CONSERVE CASH

In starting a business it is vital to conserve cash and use it only for those things that are absolutely necessary. Many large companies started out this way. I remember reading a story about a highly successful Silicon Valley startup (I think it was Yahoo) that in its early days used old doors across sawhorses as desks. They did not really need actual desks, so that is not where they spent their money.

You should also consider leasing anything that you can lease, including computer equipment, phone systems, office space and furniture, manufacturing equipment and facilities, employees (through temp agencies), etc.

I don't think I have ever seen a startup that did not run very short of cash at some point in its early development. Be sure that your money is working for you—not paying for unnecessarily expensive office space or furniture, unjustifiable salaries, or any other use that is not truly essential.

I cannot stress enough the importance of cash conservation. This must be at the top of your mind for every decision. Spend the money if absolutely necessary, but find an alternative if not—use that creativity of yours here as well!

Dun & Bradstreet (D & B)
One of the ways to conserve cash it to purchase on credit rather than pay cash. If you plan to purchase on credit, it is advisable to register your company with Dun & Bradstreet to get a *DUNS number* as soon as possible. This will allow potential creditors to run a credit report on your company so that they can make a credit decision. Of course there will initially be little or no

data on your company. As you pay invoices on time, be sure that this activity gets reported to D & B so that you establish a payment history profile with D & B.

CREATING WINNING PARTNERSHIPS

Later in this book I give several examples of major companies such as Microsoft Corp. and Google Inc. that were put on the map by the strategic partners that they secured very early in their development.

I also have mentioned previously that your business will succeed based largely on what you can get others to do for you. You hopefully understand how critical it is to secure partnerships with other entities that have strategic value to your company, known as *strategic partnerships*.

What Value do You Bring to the Table?
One of the first things you must do is to determine how your business would benefit another entity. What is in it for them? This value must be validated, detailed and concrete.

To do this, you must research the entity's business, customers, and even its employees. For instance, if you know that a certain influential manager has certain goals, you may be able to show that a partnership with your organization may assist that manager in meeting those goals.

A Whole Lot of Audacity Goes a Long Way
Be big and bold in seeking strategic partnerships. Once you have determined that you have value, present that value to those that can really assist your business. Go ahead and ask that *Fortune* 500 company about a strategic partnership. The answer will probably be "no," but if you do not even ask, the answer is definitely "no." I like the former odds much better than the latter. Of course you must protect your IP and plans through non-disclosure and non-compete agreements if necessary. It is also possible to get "burned" if you are not careful. But in order to generate audacious greatness you must be audacious.

Inside Scoop: Swing for the fence!

OPERATIONS

I have seen many entrepreneurs become overwhelmed by various aspects of operating their business as their business grows. Be very vigilant for this in your case. Often, various aspects of operations can be contracted out, such as order fulfillment, answering customer-service calls, payroll, etc. Be sure to evaluate how you are spending your time and whether you are focusing on its highest and best use. Although you cannot take your thumb off of operations, there are various aspects of it that you may be able to take your fingers off of!

Quality Control Considerations
I also have seen that early-on, many entrepreneurs struggle with quality control. Internal or external quality (e.g. that of vendors) is often initially lacking. Dealing with these issues usually cannot be contracted out and typically requires substantial time. Developing and implementing solid QC procedures may be among those highest and best uses of your precious time.

SHORT-TERM VS. LONG-TERM ISSUES

Changing gears a little bit, I would like to point out another pitfall into which I have seen entrepreneurs fall with regard to building a business.

Pitfall: Being too focused on the future.

It is important to consider the long-term aspects of your business, but it is much more important to attend to today's issues in order to ensure that you can make it to the future. (This does not, however, mean that you should be in constant "fire-fighting" crisis mode.)

A good analogy is a receiver in a football game who is wide open at the 30 yard line, with just two defenders between him and the goal. The quarterback makes a perfect pass headed right for the receiver's breadbasket. In thoughts of glory, and planning how he will run like the wind and dodge the defenders, the receiver takes his eye off the ball, only to have it slip through his hands.

It was important that the receiver plan how he was going to shake off those defenders. The receiver probably would never have achieved his long-term goal of scoring a touchdown if he had not thought about and prepared for this issue. But because he did not take care of the short-term issues, he never even got the chance to employ those long-term plans.

Inside Scoop: The long term only matters if you can make it there!

Focus on building a solid business today and the long-term issues will have a way of taking care of themselves. You need a balance, of course, but which would you rather be absolutely certain is being properly taken care of?

An actual example of the pitfalls of excessive focus on the future is the following story: In the year 2000 a small company introduced an innovative new product to the sporting goods market. Things were tough the first couple years, but slowly the product began to gain acceptance and sales. The product was manufactured overseas and air-freighted to the U.S. in shipments of around 1,000 units at a time.

In the spring of 2002, the company gained entry to a prestigious national chain of sporting goods stores. However, it was on a trial basis in only nine of the stores. Based on the results of the trial, the store's buyer would make a decision whether to expand the product into all stores.

Upon receiving the order for several hundred units of product for the trial, the CEO of the company immediately began preparations for the surge of business that she expected from this chain and all the other chains that she thought would follow suit once the product was a smash hit in the first chain. In addition to her normal CEO duties, this CEO also had direct responsibility for the sales and marketing functions of the company.

The CEO spent her time looking into how to import product by ship in container loads instead of by air freight 1,000 at a time. Each container would hold 250,000 units of the product. She planned for the relocation of company headquarters into larger facilities–how many employees would be necessary and in what positions, how much office and warehouse space would be needed, what it would cost to build a building, etc. She investigated new overseas manufacturers that would be able to produce larger quantities than the current manufacturer was able to produce.

She also contacted economic development agencies in all of the major U.S. ports to see what economic development assistance would be available if company headquarters were to be moved to their city. She checked into costs associated with unloading shipping containers in the various U.S. ports compared with one another. She investigated trucking companies and their rates to move the product from the port to warehouses and stores.

For weeks in advance of the sales trial at the national chain, the company's COO (who was not responsible for marketing) pleaded for the CEO to create point-of-purchase displays for the stores. The COO pleaded for the CEO to conduct product education and sales training for the store management and sales clerks in the trial stores. Since the trial would be taking place just before Father's Day, and it was well known that Father's Day is a big sales period for the product, the COO pleaded with the CEO to send the product's inventor to stores for Father's Day "meet the inventor" promotions. In fact, one of the stores requested that this be done as well.

All of this the CEO failed to do, instead focusing on the long-term issues that would confront the company once massive orders started rolling in.

Of course the trial failed miserably; the buyer did not put the product into any more stores; other store chains did not purchase massive quantities of the product, and the issue of how much it would cost to import the product 250,000 units at a time instead of 1,000 at a time was completely moot.

The company headquarters did not move to the port offering the best economic development package. Instead the company quickly became insolvent and was forced to move in with a company owned by a relative of the CEO for free rent, in the center of the country far from any port.

Such is the cost of long-term planning at the expense of taking care of today's real needs.

THE POINT OF NO RETURN

Regarding your business, there is of course never a guarantee of future prosperity. Anything can happen. Many thriving firms were taken down by unfortunate events, mistakes, malfeasance, or shear bad luck. Living life on this edge can be exhilarating to some, unnerving to others.

There is to be had, however, a Nirvana. In Buddhism, *Nirvana* is freedom from an endless cycle of reincarnation. In business the corollary would be to sell the enterprise you have so diligently built–cashing out, mellowing out, and retiring gracefully to the virgin white sands of that oh-so-seductive tropical isle.

This is the point when dreams mold reality, and it's time now to slow down for some dreaming practice. Please set a minute aside to take a nice mental journey with me and envision Nirvana:

First, envelop your entire being in a serene state of mind. Relax… relax… relax every muscle.

Close your eyes now. Lay back your head and breathe three times slowly.

Delve deep into your dream, moving your mind to a more laid-back locale. Squish luscious white sand as you stroll the beach barefoot in ruby-tinged twilight. The seabirds pirouette and drift off to roost. Tranquil and glistening, a multi-hued seascape absorbs the sun's quenching ember–backlighting slender silhouettes of palms gently swaying, ruffling their feathers before the dewy softness of night. Hand-in-hand now, escort your lover back to your beach house, and there you will open the finest of wines.

Imagine it. Dream it.

All this can be yours…

But first you've got work to do, and it's back to cold, hard reality for you!

Hey, I said to *snap out of it!!*

I refer to the sale of a business as the point of no return because of course once you have received cold hard cash your fate is de-coupled from that of the firm. Maybe this scenario should actually be your goal, not just the profitable business itself–that is simply one of the steps toward Nirvana. (Don't drift off on me again now!)

In fact, a primary means by which business owners profit from their business is via its sale. It is quite obvious that critical to success in such a transaction is having a valuable business to sell. Not so obvious are the factors that a savvy buyer uses to judge value when purchasing an enterprise. Be sure to understand and emphasize these criteria as you build your business.

CHAPTER 6:
MARKETING RESEARCH

Marketing research and marketing–here is where it starts getting fun!

First, I would like to point out that this marketing research section is presented prior to the section on product development, although some initial aspects of product development may be pursued in conjunction with or even prior to some of the steps listed here. Marketing research is presented first to emphasize its relative importance vs. product development.

Because marketing research is information based, it can often be conducted for less money than can product development. This is important because you can save yourself the substantial costs of product development if your marketing research shows that you for some reason will not be able to make money on your idea.

Your marketing research also ensures that you develop the right product for the market, and what could be so wrong with that?

START BY RESEARCHING MARKETING

If you are not already well-versed in marketing through years of actual experience, then the first step in your marketing research must be to research marketing. You must understand marketing tools and strategies if you are going to be able to determine what aspects of the market that you need to research and how to make sense of what you find. Reading the chapters in this book on marketing research and on marketing are a great start in your process of researching marketing, but you must carry the process much further by reading other books, talking to experts, etc.

No matter what you may read or hear elsewhere, the roadmap of marketing is *strategy*. To build my case for that statement, a few definitions from higher authorities are appropriate. *Dictionary.com* lists several definitions of strategy, the first being: "The science or art of combining and deploying the means of war in planning and directing large military operations." It also says: "In military usage, a distinction is made between strategy and tactics. Strategy is the utilization, during both peace and war, of all of a nation's forces, through large-scale, long-range planning and development, to ensure security or victory. Tactics deals with the use and deployment of troops in actual combat."

Princeton *Wordnetweb* defines strategy as: "an elaborate and systematic plan of action."

The concept is key because the ultimate goal of marketing research is gather the information and intelligence necessary to allow you to develop a winning marketing strategy. You cannot win without a winning strategy; ask any successful general about that one.

Two great ways to begin researching various marketing strategies are:

1) Contact the Marketing Research Association at http://www.marketresearch.com/?SID= 59099716-496167201-504832869 for more information on marketing research strategies, tools, and techniques.
2) Subscribe to Marketing Experiments Journal at http://www.marketingexperiments.com/ (for Internet marketing–available online only)

FIND OUT IF YOU ARE FIRST

<u>Pitfall</u>: A hole in the market does not equal an opportunity in the market.

It is unwise to assume that just because you can look around and not see your idea on the market that:

1) You were the first to have the idea.
2) There is an opportunity to profit from your idea.

<u>Inside Scoop:</u> Others may have tried and died.

Later in this marketing research chapter I will discuss the importance of talking to players in your industry, especially those who have been around a long time. This is one important example of that necessity. It is of course possible that the reason your idea is not on the market is because somebody else tried to market such a product and was unsuccessful. Fortunately, there are a great many reasons why the person could have been unsuccessful, and it is not automatically true that all other persons trying to market a similar product will meet the same sad fate.

However, it <u>may</u> be true that all other persons trying to market a similar product will meet the same sad fate. Later in this book, in the chapter on manufacturing a product, I give an example of a product idea that three entrepreneurs have brought to me over the years but that will certainly produce failure for anyone attempting its commercialization.

You must do your research to find out if a similar product has ever been offered to the market and if it is no longer there; why?

CONSUMER NEED VS. MARKET DEMAND

My clients often ask, after showing me their new product idea, whether I think that there is a market demand for it. My answer is always the same: The big fat N – O!

Marketing texts talk about how to research consumer demand for a new product, but there is none, so do not bother trying to do that.

You can and must research the *need* for your new technology, however. I am not trying to set myself up as smarter than the authors of all of those marketing textbooks, but I find that many of my clients do not understand the difference between market need and market demand and this always hurts them greatly. They assume that need and demand are equivalent.

Most entrepreneurs are far too focused in their market research on determining whether potential customers have a need for their technology rather than on determining how to create a demand for their technology in the market. It is important to determine whether consumers have a need for your product, but much more important to determine why people buy products like yours.

Here's a great way to think about this: Have you ever known someone who bought something that they did not need? Of course you have!

Q. Why did that person buy something they did not *need*?

A. Because they *wanted* it!

It is only when a large group of people want something that they create a market demand. Need is only one small element of want, and subsequently, demand. Need is only one of the myriad reasons why people want something.

Think about the opposite case to the question I asked above: Have you ever known someone who bought something they did not for some reason want? Of course not! Think about which is more important in the purchasing decision: need or want. When you go into business, is it not more important to determine what it would take to get someone to actually purchase your product rather than to simply determine what that person needs?

I need a car, but I want a Ferrari. I need to slake my thirst but I want Evian bottled water. I need to stay warm, but I want a fashionable coat. I need running shoes but I want Nike shoes. I need an MP3 player but I want an iPod. And the list goes on and on.

Do you notice anything in common among these choices? I do: The product that I really want comes at a much higher price than the product that I simply need. It also provides me with *emotional comforts* in addition to the rational ones that are based on need.

Inside Scoop: You can charge a much higher price for products that people want than you can for products that they simply need.

How, you may ask, can there be a need for a product but no demand for it? Well, the most obvious answer is if the market is not even aware that the new technology exists. If I invent a simple inexpensive device that converts lead into gold, would there be a huge number of people who need that product? Of course—everyone who can't pay their rent, is in foreclosure on their home, needs a new car, etc.

However, what if I do not tell anyone that I have developed this technology; will there be a market demand for it? Of course not. How about if I attempt to tell the market, but nobody listens? How about if people listen but nobody believes me?

If you think about it, you can see that the last two of the above scenarios are just as bad for me as the first. And if you think more deeply, you will see that the last two are actually far worse than the first, because at least the first does not cost me money!

Which would you rather try to build a business around... a technology for which there is a need but no demand, or a technology for which there is a demand but no need? To take it further: How would you like to build a business around a technology for which there is both a need and a demand? That sounds like fun!

I will focus this market research chapter on the last of those three choices.

69

Inside Scoop: *A market need for a technology exists on its own merit. A market demand for a technology must be created.*

HOLISTIC APPROACH

It is important to take a holistic approach in bringing new technologies to market–especially in researching the overall environment into which your new product will be born.

The viability of a new technology in the marketplace is directly linked to its:

- Manufacturability
- Economics
- Marketing
- Use by the consumer
- Market size and market growth rate (This is sometimes the weakest of these links–it is possible to create new markets or to turn them in a different direction, but this is exceedingly difficult).

The above factors must be considered as a whole. For instance, a new product idea may have marketable features and benefits, but it may not be feasible to manufacture it, and vice versa. A new product could be manufacturable, but at too high of a cost to be marketable.

New product developers often overlook or give short shrift to a thorough analysis of the use of the product by the consumer; this is at the developers' peril. The section below entitled: "Good Ideas, Bad Products," showcases several examples of this issue in order to help you to understand its importance.

The factors in the above bulleted list should be researched together, as they are tightly interwoven. If this seems too overwhelming, then research them separately, but *be sure to research them all.*

PROTECT YOUR IP

Remember to protect your intellectual property through non-disclosure agreements, non-compete agreements, etc. as you are conducting marketing research.

Also remember that in order to get good advice, you have to give good information. This means that if you are expecting an expert to give you good advice, you must fully disclose what it is that you are planning to do.

Think of it this way: Let's say you find yourself in a high-stakes poker game, but you don't know how to play poker. You have an expert whom you can ask how to play your hand. When you ask the expert, he requests to see your cards. You hold them close to your chest and tell him: "Well, there's some red ones and some black ones." When the expert says he needs more information, you say: "Well, some of them have diamonds on them and some have hearts."

How much actionable advice is that expert able to give you? You must fully disclose your entire hand in order to get good help. It is sometimes difficult for entrepreneurs to balance this need with the need to protect their new technology and plans for it.

TAKE THE RIGHT APPROACH

Be careful about relying on your family, friends, and co-workers to tell you what they think of your idea–often they are reluctant to burst your bubble. Also, approach the entire process of marketing research with the attitude of trying to find the weak points in your technology or your plans for it. You probably already know what is great about your idea. What you need to find out is what's not so great. The latter information is out there and will affect you whether you know about it or not, so you might as well know about potential drawbacks so you can deal with them if they exist.

Instead of simply asking someone what they think of your new-technology idea, try asking them to "critique" it. This signals that you are open to an honest appraisal and this is what you may get.

COMPETITIVE ADVANTAGE

It is very important to assess your *competitive advantage*–the advantage that you have vs. your competitors. Much has been written in marketing texts about the importance of determining your competitive advantage. It is typically recommended that this be done during the marketing research phase.

If you want to determine what your competitive advantage is, here is a great little exercise to help you do so: Take ten minutes to write down your competitive advantages. Take longer if necessary and really think about it.

Now, consider what you wrote. How much of it deals with your technology's attributes such as unique product features, product benefits, product quality, etc. and how much of it deals with the resources you will assemble, the business you will build, and your marketing strategies?

You are going to think that I can read your mind, because I can tell you that you concentrated on your product attributes and ignored your business and your marketing strategies.

Inside Scoop: Reverse this!

As you may know, there are many product-innovation award or quality award competitions that you can enter. If vying for one of these awards is how you define competition, then your product's attributes are critical to your competitive advantage.

However, if you intend for your product to compete in the *marketplace*, then your *marketing* is critical to your competitive advantage.

The point here is that the competition is not about *having* the best technology; it is about doing the best with it. It is important to have the best technology, but you don't make any money just by *having* it; that is just your starting point. Once you have the best product, then you can enter the race.

You should be looking around at the various competitors and wondering: "How can I out-market those guys?" Then develop a plan to do just that.

Need proof? Take a look at technology giants IBM Corp. and Apple Inc. IBM was awarded 5,896 U.S. patents in 2010 and has received the most U.S. patents of any company for 18 years in a row. Apple received 563 patents in 2010 and only 186 in 2008. Yet from 2006 through

2010, IBM's stock price increased by 77%, while Apple's increased 316%, a rate more than four times greater than that of IBM. Apple is a marketing maniac, whereas IBM has long been perceived as much more staid.

Take a look as well at Nortel Networks Corp. Wireless-networks and fiber-optics-company Nortel was in the late 1990s and early 2000s one of the biggest hits of the technology world, yet in 2009 it filed for bankruptcy protection in the U.S., U.K. and Canada. Beginning in 2009 Nortel was ripped apart and auctioned off in a most horrifying manner. Its CDMA and Multi-Service Switch businesses were sold off along with its enterprise unit, LTE access technology, and Metro Ethernet Networks. In 2011 one of Nortel's last remaining assets went on the auction block: Its huge and innovative suite of patents covering some of the basic foundations of wireless technology.

A sad, sad fate for a company founded in 1895 building phones and fire-alarm boxes, then becoming a Titan of the early innovators in the recent technology boom that could not survive its rapidly changing market space.

Inside Scoop: Plan to totally dominate your market and your competitors!

AWARD-WINNING TOAST

There are quite a few different product-innovation awards that are presented by a host of entities, some of them quite prestigious. It may be advisable to submit your product for such awards.

But if you do submit, be advised that scorching in the netherworld of marketing infamy are the high hopes and dreams of entrepreneurs enthralled by their "big win" in a product-award competition. The market being an equal opportunity destroyer, those infernal regions also swirl with the incinerated expectations of major corporations–dreams now crispy and black.

For example, the Palm Pre wowed judges and grabbed the 2009 Consumer Electronics Show's prestigious *Best in Show* award. But it then went out to face the cold cruel world and hurtled down into that hot, fiery hangout that ceaselessly claims the recalcitrant slackers of free enterprise.

As well, digital music players from Creative Technology Ltd. racked up major awards at the Consumer Electronics Show for three years running in the mid-2000s. But then one-by-one they shuffled out to the market and stumbled into the grave.

A distinguished award from an esteemed authority is a momentous achievement, and if you should score one, then please party down. But refuse your champagne to the market's Grim Reaper.

MARKET STATISTICS AND MARKET RESEARCH

Many people consider "market research" to mean gathering statistics on the size of the market for a product or gathering demographics on potential customers, etc. One of the major reasons people tend to focus on this is that it is the *easy* part of market research. It is also by far the *least important* part.

Market statistics are essential, but of little importance relative to the organizations, systems and procedures employed to capitalize on them.

A good analogy is air as it relates to your life. Air is essential, but unless you have lungs to take advantage of it, the existence of air means nothing. In your marketing research, you need to find out how the "lungs" work in your industry. In fact, you need to understand how the entire "respiratory system" works!

Determining that there are 1,000,000 potential customers with a certain demographic profile within a certain geographic area does virtually nothing to put profits into your bank account. *How* will you capture that market?

True marketing research cannot be done in a library; only one small component of it can be done there.

Below is a look at statistics for the automobile market that serves as a great illustration of the folly in relying on market statistics that have been gathered by others and published for consumption by the lazy... those too lazy to go out and talk to the buyers, sellers, distributors, trade organizations, technical journal editors, bloggers, government regulators, competitors, etc. in their industry.

Beware Statistics Gone Wild
In October 2010 the most well-respected automobile-market research firm J.D. Power and Associates released a study on the future of the global combined hybrid and electric car markets. The study predicted that in 2020 these types of vehicles would comprise only 7.3% of all automobile sales worldwide. This report was widely picked up in the national media and ran under headlines such as *Slow Takeoff Forecast for Electric Cars*.

If you were a company looking to launch a product dependent on a strong, dynamic hybrid and electric car market over the next decade, this headline should certainly give you reason for concern.

However, if you were to read another research report issued by the also-highly-respected market research firm The Boston Consulting Group, you would find that the sales of these vehicles will total not a measly 7.3% of the market in 2020, but a robust 26% –a factor of 3.5 times greater! Then there's the study by research firm PRTM, which predicts a market penetration of a whopping 30% in 2020–over four times greater than the J.D. Power study. The difference between the high and low predictions is over 16,000,000 vehicles a year. If you were selling a $100 product into this market, that represents a difference of $1.6 billion in potential annual revenue. Of course hybrid/electric cars cost around $40,000, (Chevy Volt's announced price in 2011,) so the variance between the high and low projections represents a difference in hybrid/electric car sales of around $640,000,000,000!

The sad thing is, these firms typically charge $4,000 - $5,000 and more for their research reports.

Mark Twain is credited with saying: "There are three kinds of lies: Lies, damned lies, and statistics." This is as true today as it was in Twain's day.

So what is an entrepreneur to do?

Inside Scoop: Do not simply rely on statistics for your marketing research. That is *the lazy way out* and when that method is applied to any endeavor, it often leads to unpleasant results.

Determining Total Available Market

The term *total available market* (TAM) refers to the total size of the market for your product or service. This market size may be given in one of three ways:

- Number of customers in the market
- Number of units sold per year or in total, or
- Total annual revenue generated in the market

It is usually best to list all three of these. Be sure to specify whether the data is for the U.S. only or is a global figure. If global, do you truly mean global or only certain developed countries; and if so, which ones?

It is very important to determine the total available market. However, realize that the size of the market may be influenced (read: expanded) by effective marketing, although this requires extraordinary expertise, favorable general market trends, or just plain luck. For instance: Initially the total market for home computers was quite small. Practically nobody predicted that even grandmas would eventually be using the Internet, email, etc., but indeed they now are.

Pitfall: *"My total available market is all small businesses in the U.S."*

Sometimes it may seem that the total available market is "everyone." However, do not fall into this trap. This is an instant turnoff to savvy investors, and for good reason. As you read the chapter ahead on marketing, the reason for this will become starkly clear.

Total Available Market is important if you plan to seek investment capital. As you approach more sophisticated investors and as you ask for more money, the size of the TAM becomes commensurately more important. If you are asking for $10,000 from your uncle Joe, he may not care that the total market size for your reverse left-handed rubber-band invention is a mere $1,000,000 per year, of which you could at most hope to capture 10 – 20%. If, however, you are approaching a VC firm for a $10 million investment, your TAM must be in the multi-billions, as VCs typically want to invest in companies that have the potential to themselves generate revenue in excess of $1 billion.

THE RIGHT WAY TO RESEARCH

First off–notice that I keep using the term: "marketing research" rather than the much more common term: "market research." There is a very good reason for this, and I think you can figure it out.

It is advisable to buy a marketing book if you plan to do your own marketing research, but until then, here is a summary of steps you can take:

1) *Talk to people!* People have more in their head than just statistics; they have experience, insight, analysis, and advice. This is what you need. At the end of each conversation, remember to ask: "Do you know anyone else I can talk to?"

2) Talk to sellers, not just customers. Sellers need to understand the market; customers do not. For instance, talk to sales reps, VARs, distributors. Visit stores and talk to sales people, store managers, or store owners. Again, sellers know how the market works, and this is what you need to know.

3) Go to trade shows.

4) Call trade organizations.

5) Talk to merchandisers or buyers for stores or catalogs that may purchase your product. For example, call the catalog toll-free number and ask to talk to the buyer for the product line of interest.

6) Research the competition. Start by going to their Website and reviewing their SEC filings if they must make filings such as quarterly and annual reports. Study their: place in the market; strategies; ads; packaging; customers; pricing; profit margins, etc. You also need to learn about their *distribution channels*, which is the set of "pass-through" entities through which a product flows to reach the consumer or end-user.

7) Find out all of the ways that people are currently coping with the problem that your innovation purports to solve. What are the true advantages/disadvantages of each solution, as seen by the customer?

Inside Scoop: Realize that one very popular way of coping with a problem is to *ignore it*!

8) Conduct *focus groups*. This is a group of typically six to eight people representing elements of your target market. A moderator asks the group relevant questions and leads discussion. You may be able to do this at relatively low cost through a college marketing professor or class in your community. A focus group is a great way to discover the thoughts and behaviors of consumers with regard to your idea. Any college marketing professor will want to focus on customers, but you need a focus group of "sellers" as well. Do not let the professor or students dissuade you from this!

9) Get ad rates for newspapers, radio, TV, magazines, websites, etc. that reach your potential customers. Brainstorm creative advertising strategies with their salespeople. These advertising personnel–if they have experience in designing and running ads in markets similar to yours–could be considered "sellers" as per item no. 2 above.

10) Go to the public library and ask for assistance at the reference desk. These personnel know how to research and can assist you for free.

11) Contact economic development entities such as a Small Business Development Center (SBDC) near you. These entities have many resources available and may even do some of this research for you, though usually that research is highly focused on industry or consumer statistics.

12) Search the Internet. Two good sites are provided by the U.S. Census Bureau, http://www.census.gov/ and the American Marketing Association, http://www.marketingpower.com.

13) Talk to people at various entities that set standards for your industry or people at regulatory agencies for your industry.

14) Talk to people at groups known as "consumer watchdogs," as they may have information regarding issues your competitors may be having with their products, etc.

15) Talk to angel groups, VC firms, investment banks, and others that specialize in investing in firms in your industry. They must remain very comprehensively up-to-speed on the industry if they are to be successful investors. Note, however, that sometimes these entities will try to extract as much information as they can out of you regarding your plans. Imagine the reason for this!

16) Talk to former employees of relevant entities. However, be sure that they are authorized to disclose the information that you request. (e.g., no trade secrets)

17) Subscribe to relevant blogs.

18) Review corporate news releases on Web consolidator services such as PR Newswire, http://www.prnewswire.com/news-releases/.

The above steps 1, 2, and 5 warrant further discussion below:

1) *Talk to people.*

Here's a question: How can you determine the most effective way to market to your potential customers?

Here's the answer: Ask them!

Why struggle trying to guess which will be the most effective tools and strategies to cut through the clutter and grab the attention of your target audience? Why speculate on what it will take to cause your audience to believe your message? Find these people and ask them.

This is true in general regarding your market research. People have the information that you need and can add information that you may not think to investigate. In fact, the large bulk of your research should be conducted in this manner. Often it may be necessary to contact someone that you suspect may not have the information that you are seeking, but whom you suspect could refer you to another who does have that information. The process is rather like being a detective trying to solve a crime. Gather as many leads as you can and then follow up on them to "solve the crime." Be creative and analytical in the process as well.

Remember though, that everyone has different opinions and different experiences. It is usually necessary to talk to a considerable number of people so that you can discern commonalities or patterns on which you can act.

Also, it takes finesse to be able to talk to strangers and elicit information from them. You must first: create a personal rapport; create credibility for yourself; realize that the person may be busy; get past their natural suspicion of strangers asking them questions, and sometimes settle for ballpark data rather than specifics. With practice and the right attitude you can improve dramatically in this area through experience. Do not forget to say "Thank you," and try to offer something in return, even if that is simply some information you have that you feel may be valuable to them, but is not proprietary to you.

When I started my second business, my partner and I spent the first six weeks on the phone four to six hours a day calling various entities within our market space and asking questions as I am suggesting that you do. Out of the hundreds of calls–many answered by that abominable voicemail–one produced a literal goldmine of information. I hate to think of what would have happened had I not made that particular call to that particular individual on that particular day.

I had a partner assist me in these calls because I already knew how incredibly time-consuming it would be to do a thorough job at it. Just getting past the secretaries and voice mail systems is more than 50% of the battle. This is a task for which it is necessary to apply a great deal of persistence.

Inside Scoop: Be goal oriented, not task oriented.

It does not matter how many calls you made today. If you did not get the information that you set out to get, you have done *nothing* all day. Do not stop until you reach your goal.

2) *Talk to sellers, not just buyers.* Most market research texts and courses, etc. focus almost entirely on researching the customers in a market. However, most customers for a technology know very little about the market for it or about effective overall marketing strategies for the technology. Think about it: just because someone purchases a product does not mean they know anything about the manufacture, distribution, effective marketing, industry players, etc. for that technology and the entire industry in which it competes.

One good example of this fact is laptop computers. You probably have purchased a laptop computer–but do you really understand the myriad intricacies regarding the history, rapid changes, and future of the market for them, including the complex dynamics of their actual sales and marketing? Certainly not, if you have not previously been a player in the industry.

Pitfall: Excessive consumer focus in marketing research

**Inside Scoop: The consumer is the <u>dead end</u> of the marketing effort.
What you must learn about is the marketing effort!**

5) *Talk to merchandisers or buyers for stores or catalogs that may purchase your product.* This is easier said than done, but then who said this would be easy? You must be persistent and somewhat aggressive to be able to get through to these people, who are very busy–especially the successful ones. But it can be done and it is critical to do so.

You want to ask them, for instance, if they have ever seen similar products on the market or products that have attempted to solve the same problem that you are attempting to solve. They are often a wealth of information just sitting there for you to mine! They often can answer most of the questions below, although it is unwise to depend solely on them for the answers.

18 Key Questions to Answer in Your Marketing Research:
1) Who is likely to buy your product?
2) How fast is this group expanding?
3) Why would they want to buy your product?
4) Where and how do they want to buy it?
5) How much are they willing to spend?
6) How can you target these people?
7) How can you innovate in marketing to these people?
8) What is the most effective advertising message?
9) What is the best vehicle for getting this message to your target audience?
10) What is the likely response rate to your advertising message? (Response rates can be 0.5% or less.)

11) For how long will you need to present your message, considering the response rate, to generate the number of customers required?

12) *How much will it cost to present your message to enough people to sustain your business?*

13) What are the potential channels of distribution and terms of sale for each?

14) Will you need to conduct both trade and consumer marketing?

15) Who are the players in the industry–top-to-bottom; corporate and individual?

16) Who are the innovators, early adopters, heavy users, opinion leaders?

17) Which niche should you focus on for your initial product launch?

18) How will people interact with your product after they have purchased it?

GATHERING INDUSTRY STATISTICS

Despite the amount of "dissing" I have done regarding industry statistics, they are important–but more, I feel–as a backdrop for what you will need to do with your marketing, not as the main stage production. Following is a primer on industry statistics:

It All Starts With NAICS and SIC

Before you attempt to gather industry statistics you must understand NAICS and SIC codes. *NAICS* is an acronym for *North American Industry Classification System* and *SIC* stands for *Standard Industrial Code*. These codes were developed by the U.S. Department of Commerce as a means to keep track of data that the Census Bureau collects regarding various industries; they are a numbering system and each industry sector has its own unique number.

You will need to know the codes for your industry in order to search the U.S. Census Bureau statistics and the statistics provided by many other public and private data collectors and compilers.

Note that SIC is no longer officially in use but you will still find statistics compiled based upon it. The NAICS system is updated periodically. You can find the NAICS for your industry on the Census Bureau Website at: http://www.census.gov/eos/www/naics. SIC code information is available at: http://www.osha.gov/pls/imis/sicsearch.html.

U.S. Census Bureau–A Wealth of Free Information

Many people do not realize it, but the Census Bureau conducts an economic census, from the national to the local level, every five years. Some of the data is quite specific, such as the number of skid steers (a common brand name is Bobcat) sold annually in the U.S. This data includes foreign trade statistics such as import and export figures. You can learn more about the economic census and access its data at: http://www.census.gov/econ.

U.S. Commercial Service Statistics

The U.S. Commercial Service provides valuable international trade statistics at: http://trade.gov/cs/ under the Data & Analysis tab.

Corporate Intelligence From U. S. Securities Exchange Commission

All companies that issue stock to the public, and those with more than 500 shareholders-of-record and $10 million in total assets must file quarterly and annual reports to the U.S. Securities Exchange Commission (SEC) that can be a good source of industry statistics and other information. For instance, the company must disclose its revenue in these reports. The annual report is much more comprehensive than the quarterly report and contains narrative that often gives clues regarding the status and outlook of the industry and the particular company.

These and other filings must be made with the SEC. The SEC has set up an electronic database for searching these reports, known by its acronym EDGAR, which can be accessed at: http://www.sec.gov/edgar.shtml. Note that the corporate annual report is Form 10-K. You can search the database for a wealth of information on public companies. You can find information on companies planning a public offering of stock by reviewing their prospectuses filed with the SEC.

Another source for finding free corporate annual reports is The Public Register, available at: http://www.prars.com/.

U.S. Bureau of Labor Statistics (BLS)

The BLS publishes the Producer Price Index, which is described on the BLS Website as follows: "The Producer Price Index (PPI) program measures the average change over time in the selling prices received by domestic producers for their output. The prices included in the PPI are from the first commercial transaction for many products and some services." The Index may be accessed at: http://www.bls.gov/ppi.

Business Publications

General business publications such as: *The Wall Street Journal; Forbes, Fortune; Inc; Fast Company; Harvard Business Review*, and many others often disclose statistics when they run stories on certain industries or companies. Often they quote data from private data-collection or market-research firms that would otherwise cost you thousands of dollars to access directly from the research firm. It may be useful to subscribe to the online versions of several business publications so that you may search their back issues as well.

There are also a large number of publications that specialize on a certain industry, known as *trade publications*. These are published both by for-profit publishers and by trade associations. Various data is available from these publishers and of course it may be useful to subscribe to the publication. Some of the publications are free to the subscriber, paid for fully by the advertising. When reviewing the trade press, think broadly about your market. It may be wise to review publications of suppliers and members of your distribution channel, etc., not just for your technology itself.

A useful Website for searching for articles on specific topics or industries is FindArticles.com at: http://findarticles.com/.

Market Research Firms

There are many firms that research markets and/or compile information on markets. Some firms are generalists and some focus on certain industries. A number of generalists are the following firms: Standard & Poor's (S&P); Dun & Bradstreet (D&B); Moody's; Hoover's; Forrester Research; DataMonitor; General BusinessFile ASAP; LexisNexis; Ward's Business Directory; Risk Management Association (RMA); Barron's; Nielsen; comScore; ThomasNet; iSuppli; eMarketer.com; Gartner Inc. and Institute for Supply Management (ISM).

All of these entities charge for their information and reports. Detailed industry reports may cost into the several thousands of dollars each, whereas more limited information may be less expensive. Following is a brief review of the above-listed firms:

Standard & Poor's industry surveys are described by the firm as follows: "Each report is authored by a Standard & Poor's industry research analyst and includes the following sections: Current Environment, Industry Trends, How the Industry Operates, Key Industry Ratios and

Statistics, How to Analyze a Company, Glossary of Industry Terms, Additional Industry Information References and Comparative Company Financial Analysis." The reports may be accessed at: http://sandp.ecnext.com/coms2/page_industry. Another S&P online research tool is NetAdvantage, available at: http://www.netadvantage.standardandpoors.com/NASApp/NetAdvantage/servlet/login?url=/NASApp/NetAdvantage/index.do.

Dun & Bradstreet operates its *Million Dollar Database (MDDI),* which provides revenue information, listings of corporate officer names, and other information on over 1,600,000 global companies. It can be accessed at: http://www.dnbmdd.com/mddi/sample.aspx#Company.

Moody's Corporation provides financial research on many companies, available at: http://v3.moodys.com/Pages/default.aspx.

Hoovers is owned by D&B and provides general business information described on its Website as follows: "From customer analysis and segmentation to identifying new and expanding markets, Hoover's powerful list-building tool provides quick and easy access to targeted data on organizations and key people needed for successful, impactful campaigns.

"Dig into your prospects' trends, challenges, and opportunities with expert industry overviews to enhance strategic planning and execution for collateral, websites, newsletters, and presentations."

"With information about more than 32 million companies, you'll spend less time searching and more time selling." Hoovers is available at: http://www.hoovers.com.

Forrester Research collects both consumer and business data. For instance, its Forrsights service is described on the Website http://www.forrester.com/Forrsights as follows: "Forrester's Forrsights for Business Technology helps you understand how and why businesses — ranging from small to enterprise-level — budget for, purchase, and use technology both today and their plans for the future.

"Forrester conducts surveys in 12 countries on five continents spanning North American, European, and emerging markets. We target specific job functions and titles of respondents for each survey population and set quotas across several categories, including industry, firm size, and geography."

On the consumer side, Forrester for instance offers its Consumer Technographics service, which the company describes on its website http://www.forrester.com/rb/consumerdata/Overview.jsp? cm_re=Navigation_010710-_-consumer_data_tab-_-consumer_data as: "Forrester's Consumer Technographics Data & Services provide detailed survey data on consumer adoption of digital devices, channels, and services, and on technology's impact on consumer behavior. Our unlimited client service gives you the ability to tailor our syndicated data to your company's markets and needs on-demand.

"Consumer Technographics surveys include: North American; European; Asia Pacific; Latin American; Canadian; and Russian consumers."

Datamonitor describes its services on its Website as follows: "At Datamonitor, we are market analysis experts. We don't just deliver top quality data; we interpret it, combining an insider's market expertise with the objectivity of an outsider to give you the best possible insight into your competitors' strategies and tactics.

"Quality Data: Our emphasis on primary research ensures that we provide a complete, accurate picture.

"Market Profiles: provide all the information you need on key markets including:

- Market Values
- Market Volumes
- Market Sectors
- Competitive Analysis
- Market Shares
- Distribution and Market Forecasts data

"Country Profiles: Country dynamics decoded. Country Profiles are designed to give users real time appraisals of over 50 countries. Each profile contains a description of the country's economic performance, GDP and potential for development along with detailed market and industry analysis of the country's business environment and forecasts based on advanced modeling techniques and historical data."

General BusinessFile ASAP describes its information as follows: "The right content for comprehensive business research, General BusinessFile ASAP provides not just more data, but the right content for business research. Covering practical business issues in every business-related area, this database integrates a wide variety of sources unmatched by any competing database: local-area business titles such as Crain's Detroit Business; national magazines such as Forbes and Inc.; trade journals like Tax Executive, full-text investment reports on thousands of private and public companies; full-text listings from Ward's Business Directory; Graham and Whiteside's Major Companies of the World, full-text PR Newswire releases; and indexing of several major national newspapers."

LexisNexis maintains statistical databases described as follows: "LexisNexis Statistical DataSets is a Web-based research solutions tool that provides fast and easy access to more than 14 billion data points from licensed and public domain datasets within an easy-to-use interface. With this dynamic new tool, you can scan the contents of the collection, select subjects and variable of interest, and view your data in side-by-side tables and charts." Many libraries subscribe to LexisNexis. Its Web address is http://www.lexisnexis.com.

Ward's Business Directory describes itself as follows: "*Ward's Business Directory of U.S. Private and Public Companies* is a comprehensive, one-stop resource for information on thousands of companies active in the United States. The most detailed resource of its kind, *Ward's Business Directory of U.S. Private and Public Companies* provides invaluable, up-to-date information on public and private companies, including full contact details, rankings and analysis.

"Each edition of this long-standing resource features more than 112,000 company entries, approximately 90% of which covering privately held companies. Multiple editions are available by standing order, ensuring access to the most up-to-date information as well as historical data. Entries typically include: company name; full contact details, including e-mail and Web site URL (when available); type of company; operating revenue; number of employees; SIC and NAICS codes; a description of the company; and much more."

The Ward's Business Directory hardcover edition is listed on Amazon.com at $3,075, so you may want to check its availability in a library near you.

The Risk Management Association (RMA) publishes its *Annual Statement Studies*. This guide provides general financial ratio information for various industry sectors. For instance, you can learn what the average percentage net revenue is for a certain business segment. RMA describes this guide as follows: "RMA's Annual Statement Studies is the only source of comparative data that comes directly from financial statements of the small and medium-size business customers of RMA's member institutions." The link is: http://www.rmahq.org/RMA/RMAUniversity /ProductsandServices/RMABookstore/StatementStudies/default.htm.

Barron's provides valuable analysis of business in general, industry sectors, and individual companies. It is available online at: http://online.barrons.com/home-page.

The Nielsen Company conducts a broad range of market research, not just the TV rankings for which they are famous. For instance, the company surveys retailers for sales data on consumer packaged goods, described on its Website as follows: "Nielsen's broad range of consumer packaged goods analytics and consulting services are specifically designed for, and with, top CPG manufacturers and retailers, to ensure they have most accurate view of the consumer and the marketplace.

"Whether it's insight into private label growth, consumer confidence, volume, pricing, promotion, demand, or emerging markets, Nielsen's industry expertise can be trusted again and again to improve bottom-line profits and maximize ROI.

"With our constant focus on the consumer, Nielsen helps clients understand shopping and purchasing habits and how to innovate during every stage of their product cycle, from product testing to product placement.

"Nielsen's integration of retail and consumer panel information helps clients identify the right customer, the right market and the right marketing mix."

More information on The Nielsen Company may be found at: http://www.nielsen.com.

comScore focuses on research related to the online world and describes its services as follows: "Measuring the Digital World: From emerging markets to converging media, comScore is the one global source of digital market intelligence that truly measures the digital world. Clients turn to comScore for objective, accurate and reliable insights into consumers' online behavior and for details into their demographic characteristics, attitudes, lifestyles and offline activities. Spanning across nearly every region of the globe, comScore provides comprehensive international solutions, helping clients get answers to the questions that matter most to them." The company's Web address is: http://www.comscore.com.

ThomasNet may be used to determine how many competitive firms there are in your industry space, including within certain geographic boundaries, but be aware that this is not necessarily a comprehensive listing. ThomasNet is available at: http://www.thomasnet.com.

iSuppli bills itself on its Website as a market intelligence firm "helping technology companies achieve market leadership with market research that's rigorous, reliable, and relevant." The site offers free signup for sample research reports on 13 subject areas such as contract manufacturing, electronic component supply and demand, and supply and demand for large TFT-LCD panels. You can also choose from among 45 areas of technology interest and sign up to receive free newsletters on the topics. iSuppli also publishes Market Watch and you can receive a free 30-day trial subscription. You may sign up at: http://www.isuppli.com/Pages/Free-Research.aspx.

eMarketer.com gathers and compiles statistics about online business. The company's Website states: "We refine raw data and perspectives from more than 4,000 sources and transform them into the digital marketing intelligence clients need."

There are also a number of specialists in the market research space. For instance, *Plunkett Research, Ltd.* specializes in research on the automobile industry, which can be accessed at: http://www.plunkettresearch.com/automobiles%20trucks%20market%20research/industry%20and%20business%20data.

Gartner Inc. conducts customized research and makes market projections. For instance, the company in early 2011 said it expects global shipments of PCs to grow by 10.5% to 388 million units for the year. (In a previous projection, however, Gartner had predicted that the PC market would grow by 15.9% in 2011.) Information is available at: http://www.gartner.com/technology/research.jsp.

Institute for Supply Management (ISM) is a trade group promoting the profession of supply management across all business sectors. It publishes a monthly *Report on Business* detailing growth trends among various manufacturing and service sectors, such: as pulp and paper; apparel; transportation equipment; electrical equipment, and much more.

Other market research specialists may be found through search engines. You can also find useful information on various companies by simply typing into a search engine the term: "history of X company." Be sure to do this, as you will often find very enlightening information regarding the company.

Be sure to check with your public and university libraries to see if they maintain subscriptions to any of the market research statistics sources.

COMPILING CONSUMER STATISTICS

Pitfall: *"Wow; there's millions and millions of people who would buy this!"*

In general, consumer statistics inform you about potential customers. As with industry statistics, consumer statistics are a necessary stage backdrop for your marketing efforts, but they are not the main production. All of the action takes place in front of these statistics. (It is interesting to note the similarity between the word *static* and the word *statistics*.)

Inside Scoop: Most businesses do not fail from lack of *potential* customers; they fail from lack of *actual* customers.

Double Scoop: Success is yours for the *making;* it's not there for the *taking.*

There; now that I have hammered on that subject a few times again to ensure that you have gotten my message, let's get on with some actual information about consumer statistics, shall we?

There are two general categories for which you may want to collect data: demographics and psychographics.

Demographics deal with the physical aspects of the consumer such as:

- Age
- Gender
- Race
- Income
- Education
- Location
- Student status
- Which products they purchase
- Which car they drive
- Home ownership
- Employment status
- Licenses and certifications
- Diseases suffered
- Disabilities
- Spending habits
- Debt levels
- Pregnancy, etc.

Psychographics deal with the emotional or rational aspects of the consumer–what is going on in their mind. For instance:

- Interests
- Activities
- Opinions
- Lifestyles
- Attitudes
- Values
- Desires
- Beliefs
- Religious conviction
- Personality types

There are two basic means of collecting consumer statistics: Primary research and secondary research.

1) *Primary research* denotes research in which the data was collected directly from the consumer, typically by the entrepreneur or by an entity hired by the entrepreneur.
2) *Secondary research* denotes research in which the data was collected by some third party–often a government entity, trade group, or market research firm–and was simply accessed and used by the entrepreneur.

Primary research may be gathered through focus groups or by communicating with potential customers or other interested parties through many means, including: Speaking with them directly, sending out surveys, or even watching consumers as they go about their business or their lives.

Common sources of secondary research include the U.S. Census Bureau, through its American FactFinder, which has a wealth of free information available at: http://factfinder.census.gov/ home/saff/main.html?_lang=en.

The U.S. Department of Labor Bureau of Labor Statistics (BLS) also has considerable demographic data available, including: characteristics of the workforce, work-related injuries and illnesses, and consumer spending profiles. The latter is especially interesting for companies marketing to consumers. The BLS Consumer Spending Survey program consists of two surveys: The quarterly Interview Survey and the Diary Survey, that provide information on the buying habits of American consumers, including data on their expenditures, income, and consumer unit (families and single consumers) characteristics. The survey data are collected for the BLS by the U.S. Census Bureau. The demographic data is available at: http://www.bls.gov/bls/ demographics.htm.

There are many private sources of consumer statistics including The Nielsen Company, Symphony IRI Group, and Mintel International. Some of these companies simply repackage government statistics and some collect the data themselves. An Internet search for the term "consumer demographic data" will reveal many sources for you to evaluate.

BE REALISTIC

You need to be *objective and realistic* in marketing research. Again, if there is bad news, you are much better off identifying it, accepting it, and making rational decisions regarding it. You must ask the right questions to the right people and not let your love of your technology influence your perception of the answers you get. Why bother doing the research if you don't properly use the results?

Be aware during your research that it is one thing for a person to express a willingness to purchase your product, but often quite another to get them to actually purchase it. Try this: if you show your prototype to someone and they tell you how great your product is, ask them to sign an advance order for it. If your product is complete, ask them to buy one at full retail price. This is when you may find out how they really feel! If they perhaps say "I don't use that type of product" as an excuse to not purchase, then why did you ask their opinion about it?

The good news is that there are many examples of people who did things that the "experts" said couldn't be done. The cautions listed throughout this document are not meant to discourage you, but rather to help ensure that you are among the 2% of inventors that profit from their invention. You can be sure that successful inventors had a positive outlook, but they also confronted cold, hard reality head-on rather than ignoring it.

Success can also be defined as realizing that you will be unable to market your new technology idea–if that is the reality–thus preventing the loss of your money in vain attempts to do so. You should be able to discard a bad idea and spend your valuable time in coming up with a better one. You may have a great technology idea but find that the market is such that you lack the resources to properly market it.

Inside Scoop: One alternative approach would be to look around for a market that you can play in and then develop an innovation there.

GOOD IDEAS, BAD PRODUCTS

Let's face it: Sometimes inventors get patents for good ideas that are bad products. This is a major reason why only 2% of patents are profitable for the inventor. In turn, a major reason that inventors get patents for bad products is perhaps that they do not go deep and wide enough in their market and manufacturing research.

A person developing a new product must consider not only the idea, but its implementation in manufacturing and in use by the consumer.

Manufacturability Matters

A simple example that comes to mind of poor manufacturability and product-use research is a patent I once saw for a three-pronged barbeque fork that had a hollow handle for holding marinade. The idea was that the marinade could be squeezed out through the tips of the hollow, pointed prongs, similar in concept to a baster. The user of the product could inject marinade into meat using the same utensil that is used for flipping the meat during grilling. Initially, this may sound like an interesting idea.

However, from a manufacturing standpoint, the device as drawn in the patent illustrations requires that three separate hollow, pointed metal prongs be joined and then connected to a single reservoir of marinade. How would this be accomplished? It can be done, but at relatively high manufacturing cost, considering the intricate welding necessary to join several small, thin-walled metal tubes.

The problems with the product include:

1) Its high cost of manufacture relative to the cost of a standard BBQ fork, when compared to the benefit of using the product. A standard BBQ fork is extremely inexpensive to produce.
2) The added cost of the invention may not be worth the benefit it provides.
3) There are many competing methods of marinating meat.
4) Commercially available marinades at the time the device was patented included spices, garlic, etc. that would plug the hollow tines. In the many years since, the process of deep-frying whole turkeys became popular. Along with this came the popularity of injecting flavorings and marinades into the turkey with a large syringe and needle specially made for the purpose. Special marinades were also developed that had no solids to plug the needle. Once these special marinades were developed and became widely available, the BBQ fork product would be more viable, (excluding manufacturing cost) but by then it was too late for the inventor.

This invention may be a good *idea*, but not such a good *product*. A developer of a new product must clearly evaluate both aspects before getting a patent.

Ask yourself: If you were aware of the product drawbacks listed above, would you spend $5,000–$10,000 getting this product patented? Why do you think that the product's inventor did so? Could it be because he did not do his homework before going to the patent attorney?

Consumer-implementation Consequences

In another case illustrating the importance of thoroughly considering the consumer-level implementation of a potential new product, many years ago I read a newspaper article about an inventor in Montana who received a patent for an idea that would allow users to clean their teeth in the shower using his device, which is similar to a Water Pik. The inventor's device was designed to attach above the shower head, draw water from the household plumbing, and emit a thin stream of water from a small nozzle. It utilizes water at household water pressure.

Again, this may (or may not!) sound interesting at first glance. However, in this case, the inventor not only needed to learn everything there is to know about people's teeth cleaning habits; he needed to learn everything there is to know about people's showering habits. Unfortunately, the inventor failed to recognize the fact that showering habits are just as important to his product as teeth cleaning habits.

For instance:

- Does everyone shower every day? What is the normal schedule?
- What percentage of people rarely takes a shower at home because they shower at the spa or at work, take baths, etc.
- Do people shower with the same frequency and at the same time of day that they would want to clean their teeth?
- What product use concept is the inventor trying to sell: "Use my product only when you shower, and use dental floss the rest of the time," "Change your teeth cleaning habits to align with your showering habits" or "Change your showering habits to align with your teeth cleaning habits"?
- Is the water pressure from household systems sufficient to properly clean teeth?

This invention could probably be manufactured at relatively low cost. However, its usage issues severely restrict the market.

The inventor paid $10,000 to an invention promotion firm for which he had seen television ads. The firm prepared a patent application and sent out several slick proposals to licensing prospects. However, 3 ½ years later the inventor decided it was not worth it to pay the maintenance fee of several hundred dollars to the USPTO that was required to keep the patent in force.

Big-time Consumer-use Fiascos
It is not just the little guys who focus on the technology and ignore the consumer's interaction with it; you'll be delighted to know that corporate giants do the same.

For instance, Frito Lay developed–at great expense–a new bag for its Sun Chips line of salty snacks, introducing it in January 2010. The bag was fully compostable and plant based–an attempt to capitalize on the hype for "green" products and packaging. A technical masterpiece, the package triumphantly donned its "green" moniker, generating high-fives of self-approval in the executive suites and boardroom.

Then along came the kill-joy.

There was massacre in the marketplace. Consumer reaction to the sack was so negative that, according to the *Wall Street Journal*, they "posted videos on the Web poking fun at the new bags and lodged fierce complaints on social networking sites."

The problem was the mighty crackling of the bag when handled–an incredible 95 decibels–a din louder than most lawnmowers. This is so loud that many countries require workers to wear ear protection in such noise. Startled consumers refused the abuse, prompting Frito Lay to euthanize the bag after ten months of plunging sales. Attempting to save face, the company retained the sack for the "original" flavor in the Sun Chips line.

The *WSJ* designated the Sun Chips package fiasco as one of the five worst marketing "bombs" of 2010.

Here's the kicker: Just a year prior to this, PepsiCo–owner of the Frito Lay brand–had pulled its new packaging for Tropicana orange juice due to consumer complaints about the design. This debacle is reported to have cost the company upwards of $35 million, and sales of Tropicana Pure Premium juice was reported to have dropped 20% before PepsiCo yanked the new package and reverted to the old. The re-design had been an attempt to give the product an updated, more trendy and youthful aura. I wonder if PepsiCo considered the desires of its best customers before setting off on that course.

Also, PepsiCo in summer 2010 re-packaged its Trop50 low-calorie brand of orange juice, switching to clear carafes instead of paperboard cartons. Sales for the product then increased 50% in less than a year. This resounding re-packaging success drove PepsiCo to again re-package its Tropicana orange juice in February 2011, this time in a clear plastic carafe. All of this clarity in the market for orange juice was driven initially by the Coca Cola Co., which in 2001 launched its Simply brand of orange juice and put it in clear plastic carafe containers that took the market by storm.

Media reports quote a PepsiCo spokeswoman as saying that the company had done extensive consumer research prior to the carafe packaging initiatives and that "the biggest insight was that consumers like to see the juice."

Google Inc. is another large company that has found that consumer-use issues not only are important, but they also vary among different consumer groups. The large majority of Google's $24 billion in revenue is derived from its AdWords technology, in which businesses pay for clicks on search-result listings on Google's search engine. For instance, a firm selling computers may bid a certain price to pay Google to get Google to place the firm's information high in the search results for the word "computer." Whoever offers Google the highest price to pay each time a searcher clicks on that bidder's listing will appear at the top of the search results when someone types in the word "computer." (This is a simplification–it is actually somewhat more complicated than that.)

Google has found that it has had great success getting large businesses to advertise via AdWords, but it has had very poor success with small businesses, meaning that Google is missing out on many billions in potential revenue each year. The problem is that although large companies have the resources and expertise to figure out the relatively complicated bidding process, small businesses do not. Therefore, in 2010, Google began a campaign of hiring salespeople to call small businesses, explain the process, and assist them through it.

Google found that large businesses could interact with its technology but small businesses could not. Because of this, it found that it must sell its technology to one customer group in a completely different manner than it does to another customer group. The costs of hiring a sales staff are considerable and therefore the profitability of the small-business clients is likely to be substantially lower than the large-business clients. I wonder if Google anticipated this in its plans when it launched AdWords.

Understanding Product Life Cycle
Another reason that a good idea could be a bad product is that the product would not last long in the market for one reason or another. This could be due to rapidly changing technology, a rapidly changing market, the entry of numerous competitors which may introduce versions

better in some way than yours, or the fact that the product will be simply a fad or capitalizes on a fad. If yours is such a product, you had first better understand this and then second be very aggressive and nimble so that you are able to profit before the opportunity evaporates along with your investment.

<u>Will Others Give Away What You Are Trying to Sell?</u>
If yours is a software product, you must be particularly concerned in your market research with determining whether some larger company may be able to give away a product similar to that which you will be trying to sell. This is less important with regard to physical products due to the cost of producing real goods, which makes them much more difficult to give away free over a sustained period. Software, however–once created–may be given away pretty much at will.

One example of this is a company I once knew that was developing an easy and effective method of transferring large files online, overcoming shortfalls with email and FTP transfers. They had a revenue model figured out which seemed to be quite lucrative. The innovators were among the earlier companies recognizing and addressing this problem and soon had a product ready for market.

However, at about the time the product was ready, the entrepreneurs saw to their horror that several large companies had also seen this problem and had developed solutions to it that they were willing to give away for free to the users of the large company's other products. Although the innovators had developed a robust and elegant solution to the problem, the fact that large companies were willing to give away similar products ended up being their death knell.

A similar example is the Netscape Navigator Web browser, which had nearly a 90% market share in the mid-1990s before Microsoft developed its Internet Explorer (IE) Web browser and deployed its first version of IE in 1995. Although Netscape did not charge consumers for the use of its technology at the time IE was introduced to the market, its income was based on the number of "eyeballs" using its Navigator browser.

Microsoft bundled its IE product with its Windows operating system–essentially giving IE away for free–and giving much easier access to IE than to Netscape or any other competitive browser. The result was the death or near-death of all competing browsers, with IE gaining a 90+% market share by the year 2000.

The fact that Netscape was basically a one-product company, with only Navigator and its later iteration Communicator to rely on for revenue, contributed greatly to its weak competitive position relative to Microsoft.

Approximately ten years later competition started to heat up in the browser arena once again, however.

COMPETITIVE ANALYSIS

It is of course very important in marketing to thoroughly understand your competition. Your competition includes *every method* that people are currently using to address the problem or issue that your new technology solves or addresses.

<u>Inside Scoop:</u> Take the time to research and record *every method* that people may use to address the problem that your technology solves.

Many new-technology developers are highly dismissive of the competition, almost to the point that it seems that the "new-technology-development gene" and the "dismissive-of-competition gene" are linked! However, existing companies can adapt to your presence in the market and may be able to quash an upstart through marketing, promotions, price discounts, etc. on their products, even if their products are inferior. (Sometimes especially if their products are inferior.)

Pitfall: Dismissing the competition

In researching your competition, you want to determine on what basis they compete in the market: quality level; price level; value; large product selection; convenience; high performance; heavy advertising; advanced technology; category domination; stellar brand, etc. Often companies compete using a combination of these elements.

In assessing how well your technology will be able to compete in the market it is important to realize that it is generally difficult to get consumers to change their behavior. If your technology requires your customers to change their behavior, they may stay with the existing products because of the comfort of doing so, even if this choice otherwise makes no sense.

In assessing the market and your competition, you want to determine whether you will truly have *first mover advantage*. This is an advantage that many innovators have in the market simply due to the fact that they were first. First mover advantage is not a "natural right" enshrined in the constitution! It is a *potential* advantage that may be brilliantly exploited or may be mindlessly scattered like diamonds into the mud of the market. Many failed entrepreneurs were first, performing little but beguilement, thus lighting the way for a more able competitor to barge in and bury them. Such was the case with social networking pioneer Friendster, at one time the most popular social networking site. Along came Facebook with a more elegant solution. With breathtaking speed the masses un-friended Friendster.

FORECASTING BEST CUSTOMERS

It is absolutely critical that you determine who will be your best customers at various stages in your development. For instance, your initial best customers may be those known as *early adopters*, who are often those who are more adventurous or those more interested in new technology, those with more disposable income, leaders, etc. Later, your best customers may shift to other demographic or psychographic groups.

You may be able to get an idea of who your best customers will be by studying who are the best customers of your competitors.

If you do not think that this is all that important then consider the following:

You have certainly heard of the 80/20 Rule. When applied to the concept of best customers, this rule would state that 80% of your business will come from 20% of your customers. The 80/20 Rule does not apply to the movie business however. In that industry, 90% of movie-theatre tickets are purchased by just 10% of all movie-ticket buyers; it is a 90/10 rule!

Now, imagine if you are planning to enter the movie business and you:

1) Do not realize that this is true
2) Do not know who that 10% is
3) Do not know what is important to that 10%

I bet that when you imagined that, it looked like quite a nightmare!

GETTING HELP

I hope you believe my message that marketing research is critically important and requires a great deal of time and effort to properly accomplish.

If you do not feel that you can accomplish the necessary marketing research as described above, you should seriously consider hiring someone to do this for you. Professional marketing firms will conduct marketing research, though usually at a substantial cost.

If you do decide to hire a market research firm, be sure to get references, look at their previous work, and check them out thoroughly. There are many people and firms that overcharge for shoddy work in this field. Give them the list of questions from earlier in this chapter that must be answered in marketing research and tell them that they must answer each.

The importance of thorough market and marketing research cannot be overemphasized. You should thoroughly understand the marketing for your technology or hire someone who does.

If you don't have enough time, money, or expertise to develop your product and do the marketing research, you should seriously question whether you have enough time, money, or expertise to pursue your dream.

Inside Scoop: Poor marketing research can make all other investments into your project evaporate!

CHAPTER 7:

MARKETING

THE "HOW" OF MARKETING

The previous chapter on marketing research focused on the "what" of marketing–what markets to attack, what prospects to approach, what your competitors are doing, etc. This chapter on marketing focuses on the "how" of marketing–applied to information learned in the marketing research.

The big "how" of marketing is this: How can you communicate a message to a prospective buyer that causes him to take the action that you want him to take? Notice that I said: "How can you *communicate* a message to a prospective buyer"; I did not say "How can you *deliver* a message…" As you read this chapter you will discover in this distinction a crucial importance.

Sales vs. Marketing–A Critical Distinction

Sales and marketing are not the same. Sales can be considered a subset of the overall marketing effort. You need to approach each as intertwined but separate efforts. Marketing is more nuanced; sales is more direct. A great marketing effort "prepares the ground" for a subsequent great sales effort. If you educate the market and get people to want your product or service, they will be far more likely to respond when your salesperson calls on them.

The Rules of New-product Marketing

In this discussion of marketing strategy and marketing, I will focus on the most effective marketing strategies–the ones most likely to produce success for you as you proceed with commercializing a new technology. It is not my intent to totally discount all other strategies or approaches to marketing. I will talk about the "rules," but with the understanding that there is an exception to every rule.

The "rules" I will discuss are the ones particular to an individual or a small-to-mid-sized business (SMB) introducing a new technology to market on a limited budget. Some of these product launch strategies and "rules" would not apply, for instance, to Apple Inc., which has already built a very enviable brand image, a well-developed product line, and has boatloads of money.

Customers: Missing in Inaction

The first concept you must understand (obvious as it is) is this: A prospective buyer will not take action on your message unless they receive it and believe it. The fact that you attempted delivery means nothing. Did they receive it? Did they believe it? This is what matters. Otherwise your customers are missing… missing in inaction.

Here is an illustration of this reality:

Let's say that I go out and rent a house. After three months, the landlord calls me and says he is evicting me because I have not paid the rent. I tell him: "Well, I've been sending you a check every month." The landlord says "Oh, OK. I haven't received a check from you, but as long as you have been sending out checks, you are free to stay in the house." *Not!* The landlord will say: "I don't care, I haven't received them. I have a nice cardboard box that you could live in for free, though."

In the same way that attempting to deliver a check to the landlord means nothing if he has not received it, your attempt to deliver an advertising message to a prospect means nothing if he has not received it. Your prospect could have thrown your mail in the garbage without reading it, been on vacation when you ran your ad in the newspaper, or gotten up to get a snack when you ran your ad on TV, etc.

Now, let's say that when the landlord calls me about the rent, I tell him: "What's the problem? I know you have received the IOUs I have sent you every month." Do you think the landlord will tell me: "Oh, OK, everything is peachy then. Stay in the house. I'll just recycle my big cardboard box."? *No!* The landlord will say "Yeah, I have been getting them, but I don't believe your worthless IOUs."

Likewise, even if a prospect receives your message stating that you have the best product, in the best quality, and at the best price, he is unlikely to believe it just because you said so. Who has ever delivered him an advertising message that says anything but that? You are just another of the hundreds of "blah, blah, blah" messages that assault him every day.

In order for your marketing message to be effective, the prospect must *receive it* and *believe it.* Only then do you have a snowball's chance that he will take action on it.

1) Receive

2) Believe

3) Take action!

These are the steps through which you must pull your prospect if you are to be successful in your marketing efforts. Thousands of books have been written on how to accomplish this goal. Hundreds of universities worldwide offer PhD programs in marketing. Top marketers at *Fortune* 500 companies make gargantuan salaries for their expertise. Obviously, those three little steps are not so simple and not so easy!

Of equal importance in your marketing communications is the relevance of your message. Imagine if I had replied to my landlord: "Well I have been paying my credit card bill in full every month." This message may be received and believed by the landlord, but it is not relevant to his problem. The issue of determining what is truly relevant is a major stumbling block for many marketers.

MASSIVE MARKETING STRATEGY

The goal of your marketing strategy can be summed up in one word: SELL.

I take that back; it takes three words to sum up your goal: SELL, <u>SELL</u>, **SELL!!!**

Robust sales has a funny way of making most other problems go away. *Lack* of sales, on the other hand... well, we don't want to think about that, now do we!

So, now that you know your goal, let's dig deeply into the strategy to achieve sales and how you achieve that goal.

Strategy is very important in everything you do. If you do not operate with a strategy, you are just firing away randomly, hoping to get lucky and hit something. You must develop an overall strategy on how you will grow your business through effective marketing.

There are actually many similarities between the importance of strategy in the conduct of effective military campaigns and strategy in the conduct of effective marketing campaigns. It has been my experience that many entrepreneurs understand the importance of strategy in military campaigns, but they somehow do not understand the parallels with marketing. Great strategy is just as important in marketing as it is in war. Both the American Revolution and the Vietnam War prove that having the best tools of the trade (soldiers, training, weapons, etc.) is not all that it takes to win. The same is true in marketing.

This fact can work to your advantage if you are in the position that you lack the funds to acquire the best marketing tools… focus on your strategy instead, and you can still win!

Actually, it is somewhat instructive to think of marketing as the same as war–the only difference being that you do not shoot your opponent.

<u>Inside Scoop:</u> In war your opponent's army is your enemy; in marketing, your prospective customer is your enemy.

Yes, you read that right–in marketing, your enemy is the prospective customer! He is out there wanting to ignore your advertisements, dismiss your claims, and hang onto his money.

You want him to pay attention; he wants to ignore you. You want him to believe you; he wants to call you a liar. You want him to spend his money; he wants to hang onto it. Now tell me that I am wrong when I say that you should think of him as the "enemy."

In developing a dynamic marketing strategy, as in developing a great war strategy, you must:

- Survey the "battlefield"
- Develop solid intelligence
- Evaluate your strengths and weaknesses
- Plan your strategy
- Build alliances
- Bolster your resources
- Deploy your resources strategically
- Exploit your enemy's weaknesses
- Avoid your enemy's strengths
- Anticipate your opponent's every move
- Analyze your wins and defeats
- Prepare backup plans

Again, your prospective customers are your primary opponent–they want to ignore your advertising message, disbelieve your claims, and keep their wallets closed. You must wage a concerted "attack" on them in order to get them to do what you want them to do–things that they are by nature disinclined to do!

WHY WON'T THEY BUY?

As pointed out above, it is in general difficult to get a prospective customer to purchase *any* product–let alone a new technology–due to general traits of human nature. However, you must analyze your target customers at a deeper level than these general traits. You must determine and address the actual reasons why your target prospects may not purchase your product. These reasons would be barriers to the adoption of your product or service.

For instance, if you are developing a technology in a market in which there are very strong brands, brand loyalty could be a barrier to adoption. If your product will be higher-priced than competitive products–even if your product is better in some way–this higher price could be a barrier. If you are for some reason locked out of certain channels of distribution–such as big-box retailers–this could be a barrier.

Be sure to thoroughly analyze and address such issues in your marketing plans.

TOOLS OF MARKETING

"Marketing" means taking something to the market. This is very broad and all-encompassing. Some people mistake the relatively narrow field of advertising for marketing, but advertising is just one of the tools used in the marketing effort.

Marketing is *difficult and complex*. Like anything difficult and complex, there are many specialized tools available to carry out marketing processes and myriad things to consider in your marketing efforts. To help you understand the scope of marketing, I have listed below some (but not all) of the tools and considerations applicable to your marketing efforts. Some of these marketing tools "bleed over" into other areas such as business model and strategic planning, but the lines between these areas are often quite fuzzy.

As you will see the list is shockingly–almost disturbingly–long. This isn't to intimidate, but to impress; not to impress you with my marketing knowledge but to impress you with marketing's breadth and depth. I have not made much effort to group these tools logically–this is an attempt to emphasize their diversity. Fortunately, you will need to deploy only a few very carefully chosen tools as you bring your product to market. Trying use too many at once would constitute a lack of focus, and if you do not yet know how much I deplore a lack of focus you soon will!

I realize that the list below may be overwhelming, especially if you try to absorb it all the first time you read it, but I do want to provide you with a fairly complete reference to use when you are developing your marketing strategies and campaigns.

90 Powerful Marketing Tools and Considerations

1) Company name selection
2) Pricing
3) Logos
4) Product names
5) Packaging
6) Brochures
7) Direct mail
8) Television
9) Radio
10) Billboards
11) Google AdWords

12) Google AdSense
13) Customer testimonials
14) Celebrity endorsements
15) Scientific studies

(Whew... long list... time for a breather)

16) User groups/online user forums
17) Fan clubs
18) Warranties
19) Free shipping
20) Return policies
21) Employee training
22) Loyalty/rewards programs
23) Customer purchase behavior analysis
24) Merchandising
25) Copy writing
26) Tie-ins with other products
27) Coupons
28) Telemarketing
29) Catalogs
30) Websites

(Time for another breather)

31) Product-line offering
32) Internal sales staff
33) Independent sales reps
34) Distribution channel selection
35) Distributors
36) Retailers
37) In-store promotions
38) Product sampling
39) Sales incentives
40) Sales contests
41) Trade shows
42) Print shops
43) Layout software (PageMaker, etc.)
44) Social media
45) Personal networking

(Another breather here)

46) Blogs
47) Mailing/emailing/phone list providers
48) Electronic newsletters
49) Email marketing services (Constant Contact, etc.)
50) Mobile devices
51) Mobile apps
52) Widgets
53) Experiential marketing

54) News/product releases
55) Journal/magazine articles
56) Buyers' guides
57) Support of worthy causes
58) Product design
59) Terms of sale
60) Informational/technical seminars

(Focus… focus…)

61) Speaking engagements
62) Government relations
63) Public relations
64) Customer service
65) Customer surveys
66) Customer referrals
67) Toll-free phone numbers (especially memorable ones)
68) URLs (especially memorable ones)
69) Marketing plan
70) Demographics
71) Psychographics
72) CRM software
73) Sales analytics
74) Knowledge of consumer behavior
75) Choice of ad agencies

(OK, only 15 more to go!)

76) Sky-writing ☺
77) Strategic acquisitions of rivals/partners
78) Market trends analysis
79) Advertising specialty items
80) Product bundling
81) Product tying
82) Leasing
83) Rent-to-own
84) Premium/first class offerings
85) Beta testing
86) Sneak previews
87) Vendors (Yes, even your vendors are tools to be used in your marketing.)
88) Time
89) Money
90) Creativity
    …and more!

(Made it!!!)

Although only some of them are, it is important to think of the above items as physical tools. When you embark on the marketing process, you must think of yourself as being in a room full of these tools, just as if you were in an auto mechanic's shop full of wrenches, lifts, wheel balancers, and computer analyzers.

Do you know what you are doing? You could put me in an auto repair shop and give me all of the necessary tools, but if someone drives a Mercedes in and complains of weird clunking noises in the transmission and engine stalling during acceleration, I won't have a clue how to fix the problem using all of the fancy instruments I have at my disposal.

Pitfall: Trying to market when you do not understand the tools of marketing.

Your "Job #1" in marketing is to learn about marketing tools and how to effectively and efficiently deploy them like a maestro conducting them in Beethoven's 5th Symphony. What are their nuances and how do they all perform together? How can you get the most bang for your buck? You will learn a lot in this book, but you must read other books and also sit down and speak with others with marketing experience and expertise. Develop mentors as you create and execute your marketing plan.

PREPARING A MARKETING PLAN

It is imperative that you develop a marketing plan. Full detail on how to write a marketing plan is beyond the scope of this general overview book on technology commercialization, but many books are available on the subject. (This just may be the subject of my next book, which I hope you will read if so.)

Pitfall: "Winging it"

Inside Scoop: If you just "wing it" you will not succeed in the manner that you desire!

You must approach the marketing of your technology in exactly the same methodical way that you approach the development of your technology. You need to be creative in both product development and marketing, yes. But that is not all. When developing a product, you cannot just take a bunch of parts, throw them in a box, shake them up, and dump out a beautiful new invention. In the same way, *you cannot just take an assortment of marketing tools, fumble them around for awhile, and walk away with hot-shot sales of your new product.* With your marketing, the same as with your product development, you have to have a plan. You have to design it. You have to know what you are doing.

EXECUTING A MARKETING PLAN

After you develop a marketing plan, you must execute that plan. The biggest and most important part of this execution consists of a sales process that is very hard work!

"Tough Love": Marketing and sales are very hard work and can get extremely discouraging at times. If you are not up for this, then *get out of the game while you still can.*

Think about that last statement. We know that there are various levels of skill and ability among football players. We know that not every skillful player is adept at every position. It takes a team of skilled, tough players playing under a masterful coach to consistently win in the big leagues. When you attempt to commercialize new technologies, you are definitely playing in the "big leagues." I have yet to see anyone attempt to commercialize a new technology solely within a local market. The national and global markets are the big leagues, *for sure*!

Now, you may say: "I saw a lady on a talk show the other day that started out with $1,000 and made cookies in her kitchen. She just winged it and now she's a multi-millionaire." In fact, I know that this has happened, and more than once—but this scenario will not happen to you.

How can I be so sure?

Think about it this way: I will bet you $10,000 that if you go out right now and purchase a lottery ticket, you will *not* win the grand prize. If you do not win the grand prize, you owe me $10,000. Are you willing to take me up on that bet? Of course not! Yet, we both know that people win lottery grand prizes all the time, and we see them on talk shows. The same is true with successful unplanned marketing—we both know that it happens, but it will not happen to you.

Pitfall: Putting your entire fate, future, and fortune in the hands of raw luck alone by assuming that it will happen to you

WINNING ATTITUDE

I know a person who, over a period of a few years, made a number of half-hearted attempts to develop new businesses. He talked to me many times about his business ideas and attempts and I tried to help him with advice as he struggled to generate revenue.

I tried persuasion, cajoling, and just about anything else I could think of to get him to acknowledge the need to create strong networks of influential people, develop a marketing plan and execute a sales process if he expected to generate more than a few customers here and there. Despite my many conversations with him about the absolute necessity of doing so, he never did it. One day, after about a year of working on a certain project he decided to shelve it and move on to something else (for about the third time since I had known him).

When he made the decision to shelve the latest project he sent me an email stating: "I'm going to move on to [project #4] but I'm going to keep [project #3] on the back burner. I'm hoping that one day the doors will just swing wide open."

Well, something finally sort of snapped in me and I shot back this reply: "The doors will <u>never</u> swing wide open. You will have to <u>blast</u> them open!!! This is a very important concept."

As of two years later the doors had neither swung open nor been blasted open and it pained me greatly to see him lose his house to foreclosure because he lacked the income to pay the mortgage.

Pitfall: Waiting for the doors to swing wide open

Now for a bit of the good news, let's take a look at a man who did it right. This man was Jim Winner, who in the 1980s developed and marketed "The Club," a vehicle antitheft device. The device is basically a thick metal rod with hook-like projections that allow the rod to be attached and locked onto a steering wheel so that even if the car is hot-wired, it cannot be driven because one end of the rod projects beyond the wheel to the extent that the wheel cannot be turned within the confines of the car.

Mr. Winner did not invent this concept; it had already been around for decades but with no commercial success. Yet, Mr. Winner achieved the kind of prosperity with his new product that almost everyone else only dreams about. How was he able to accomplish this with virtually the same product with which others had failed? Well, I can tell you this: The details of how he achieved success are moot, but the philosophy that he used is momentous.

I learned about Mr. Winner when he unfortunately passed away in 2010. In an obituary, the *Wall Street Journal* paid him a tribute that began with these six words: "Jim Winner was a consummate salesman..." The obituary gave some details of his life and business success, then ended by recalling words that Winner had said during an interview for a 1993 *WSJ* article: "The product is not my cause. I like to sell."

If you cannot adopt this attitude, then go home while you still have a home to go to.

Many entrepreneurs I have met will bob, weave, back-peddle, make excuses, obfuscate, and even do back-flips rather than develop and execute a vigorous sales process. Not one of those people achieved the success they expected. Not one!

Inside Scoop: **The entrepreneurs I know that took a sales attitude and executed a vigorous sales process have succeeded.** *Every one of them!*

DEVELOPING SALES COLLATERAL

Once your advertising or other marketing efforts pay off and your sales person gets to meet or speak with a prospective customer, you will need to support him or her with *sales collateral*. This refers to materials that are used to assist in selling your products. Below is a list of common sales collateral items, some of which can be found in the previous list of marketing tools:

- Brochures
- Business cards
- Price sheets
- Catalogs
- Websites
- Custom letterhead
- Custom business envelopes
- Custom presentation binders
- Product data sheets
- PowerPoint presentations
- Telephone sales scripts

Advertising specialties such as pens, coffee cups, mouse pads, golf balls, etc. with imprinted company name or logo may also be considered sales collateral.

It is wise to have a uniform look and feel to all of your collateral, with consistent messaging as well. Be sure to include proper notice of trademarks and copyrights at least once on each piece.

UNIQUE PRODUCT SYNDROME

Very few entrepreneurs take the approach of Jim Winner: Finding an existing technology and treating it right. The vast majority of entrepreneurs have conceived something better, faster, or cheaper. The entrepreneur patents that uniqueness to prevent competition. "Here I am–all alone in the market. From here, it's all just downhill coasting."

Pitfall: Unique product syndrome

(I know what you're thinking: "Why'd you have to throw a pitfall in here? That downhill-coasting was sounding so good!")

When I consider the amount of emphasis put on unique product attributes and patents in the world of technology commercialization, it is not surprising to me that most inventor-entrepreneurs view the fact that they have a gee-whiz new technology, unique in the market, with "no competition" as a huge advantage for their business.

In fact, this situation is often *the biggest obstacle that they face.* I feel the need to repeat that: This is often *the biggest obstacle that they face.*

There are two reasons for this:

1) First and foremost–simply because the inventor views it as an advantage. This causes fatal neglect of the hard work of marketing. An inventor-entrepreneur should think about how he would build a business based on a commodity product that has *very strong* competition. This will help focus that person on marketing.

   Think about this: If you were going to break into and dominate the market of selling corn, how would you do that? Since your corn is the same as everyone else's corn, you would have to actually *out-compete* your competition!

2) Secondly, it is an obstacle because many consumers are skeptical of new-product claims and/or they may not understand a new technology's advantages. It takes time and money to educate these consumers. Many entrepreneurs blow their meager initial marketing funds trying to educate a big market on the advantages of their new technology, but the market just doesn't accept the message. In marketing new technologies, sometimes "the second mouse gets the cheese." Such was the case–as we saw above–with social-networking service Friendster after the debut of Facebook.

Another, more "cloak-and-dagger" illustration of this "second mouse" concept is TiVo Inc., which in the late 1990s developed and marketed a new technology allowing users to record TV programming for playback at a later time. The company was initially highly successful and a one-time stock market darling. However, by the mid 2000s the company struggled as satellite and cable companies began horning into its market by selling their own digital video recorders (DVRs).

The satellite and cable companies had a far better marketing channel to consumers than did TiVo, by virtue of the satellite and cable companies' pre-existing "installed base" of tens of millions of satellite and cable subscribers. Cable companies, however, were initially very reluctant to embrace DVRs due to the fact that they allow viewers to skip over commercial advertising. At the time of the late 1990s, cable companies dominated the non-broadcast TV market and satellite TV was a relative upstart with its new smaller-diameter dishes.

TiVo got off to a strong start because, as the "new kids on the block" looking for a competitive edge over cable operators, satellite TV companies embraced the TiVo technology and successfully used TiVo devices as an enticement to win over subscribers from cable. Then in the early 2000s, satellite operator DIRECTV Group Inc. licensed TiVo technology and incorporated it into its own DVR that DIRECTV offered to its customers.

Once the cable operators saw that they were losing customers to satellite operators offering DVRs, they too jumped on the DVR bandwagon, but using their own technology, not TiVo's.

Unfortunately for TiVo, even DIRECTV later began offering a DVR without TiVo technology. This occurred after News Corp. acquired a controlling interest in DIRECTV. Why did it occur then? Probably because News Corp. also owns controlling interest in NDS Ltd., a competitor to TiVo!

In referring to the TiVo experience, Tom Wolzien, an analyst at Sanford C. Bernstein & Co. was quoted in 2005 as saying: "The world is littered with innovative companies that wound up innovating for somebody else."

Imagine No Patents
I sometimes wonder if it would be better for small entrepreneurs if there were no patent system. Then the entrepreneurs would know that they have to rely on building a nimble, competitive business in order to succeed. If they were not willing to do that, they would not make the attempt to commercialize their technology. The U.S. Patent and Trademark Office has done studies that show that only 2% of persons that receive a patent ever make a profit from it. Think about the fact that only 2% of people who receive a patent ever make money on their invention and why this is.

More About Unique Product Syndrome
A little more for you about Reason #1 above as to why the Unique Product Syndrome is an obstacle to inventors (that reason being that the inventor views uniqueness in the market as an advantage): I once advised a company that was developing a handheld car-washing device for use by consumers in washing their car in their driveway or garage. The device was to attach to the end of a hose. Now, there were already quite a number of devices that attach to the end of a hose that were marketed for this purpose, and my "students" were well aware of these. However, they believed that their product had a number of performance advantages and they dwelt upon these while explaining to me their marketing plans.

These entrepreneurs did not have much money to devote toward marketing and had no previous experience marketing consumer products. Therefore they were looking to me to provide advice and guidance in these efforts. They could not, however, get beyond the brilliance of their technology innovations. After trying for a long time with no success to get them to understand Unique Product Syndrome, I finally became exasperated and decided to get a little more creative in my explanation.

I threw them somewhat for a loop when I asked them if they had ever seen a large sponge being sold for the purpose of washing a car. Of course they had—in perhaps every store that sells auto supplies—it's a ubiquitous generic product. "Now," I said, "how many of these sponges do you think are sold each year?" Of course, their guess was "many millions," because the sponges don't last that long, there are hundreds of millions of vehicles in the world, and many vehicle owners have at least one.

"I want you to go out and take the car-wash-sponge market by storm," I told them as a way of illustrating a point. "You would be plenty rich if you cornered 75%, 50%, or probably even 25% of that market. Not only that," I threw in, "but I want you to offer the exact same product that your competitors do. I even want you to purchase the sponges from the same manufacturer with the exact same specs that your competitors have." "Can't we make it better?" they protested. "Absolutely not," I replied. "Do we really have to buy from the same manufacturer?" they queried. "I don't really care," I finally said, "just so it has the exact same specs and is the exact same product." "But can't we add…" they started in again.

"No product advantages!" I raised my voice. "Drop the product advantages!!!"

Now I would like you to tell me: Do you think that if these innovators could devise a way to take the car-wash-sponge market by storm under the tough conditions that I laid out for them, that they could also devise a way to sell a boatload of their gee-whiz new technology? Of course they could.

Their problem was that their product advantages *kept getting in the way of their marketing!* Don't let this happen to you.

> Pitfall: I've seen it until I'm sick of it: almost all "newbie" inventors let their product advantages *get in the way of their marketing.*

Read that again: almost all "newbie" inventors let their product advantages **get in the way of their marketing.**

Here is the key to success:

1) Develop a strategy and campaign that can succeed in marketing a generic product.
2) Execute that level of campaign on a technology that *has* unique advantages.
3) $ecure an accountant to $helter your income.

Here's fun little story that illustrates the right way to treat your new technology:

When my son was about ten years old he liked to put an ocean of ketchup on almost everything that he ate. Nearly every time I asked him what he wanted for lunch or dinner, he would come up with something like: hot dogs; French fries; hamburgers, or chicken nuggets. It was always these or something else upon which he could squeeze the tasty delight of rich red glop-glop-glop from the ketchup bottle.

Now, I have always liked to tease my kids and I have to admit that I take every opportunity to do so. One time, when it was getting around lunchtime, I said to my son: "I already know what you want for lunch today. I don't even have to ask." He said "Oh yeah? What?" "A ketchup substrate," I replied with a laugh. And you know what? He admitted that I was right.

It didn't matter what the food was, as long as it had ketchup on it.

In the same way, it does not matter what your technology is or what it does... it is simply a "marketing substrate" upon which you apply the "ketchup" of a solid marketing effort. That "ketchup" makes every product so appealing that customers cannot resist it.

> **Inside Scoop:** *What the world really wants is the ketchup, not the substrate.*

(Remember in the Introduction when I told you I would reveal the "Secret Sauce," and that it is actually a sauce?)

MARKETING FOR CORPORATION VS. A STARTUP

> **Pitfall:** **Assuming that just because you have experience in marketing for a major corporation, you can market for a new-technology startup**

A person with experience in marketing products for a well-established company should not assume that the same strategies, vehicles, and activities will work in marketing new technologies from a new company. Marketing for a new company is completely different than marketing for a well-established company. A major reason for this is that a well-established brand or reputation goes a long way toward getting attention for advertising messages or easing entry into distribution channels, etc.

Another reason is that in major corporations, there are many marketing personnel and often each is expert in one field of marketing rather than a jack of all trades. In a startup, the marketing department often consists of just three people: You, Yourself, and Thee.

Thou shall not have thine former advantages when thee go out on thy own. Maketh thee sure that thee take this into account in ye olde marketing plans by hoisting all thine sails. (Translation: You won't have these advantages when you go out on your own. Be sure to take this into account in your marketing plans by kicking on your afterburners.)

RECRUITING AND MANAGING INDEPENDENT SALES REPS

A very common method of sales and marketing used by companies commercializing new products is to hire an independent firm to sell the product. Typically in this arrangement the independent firm is primarily responsible for sales and the manufacturer is primarily responsible for marketing, including marketing collateral.

Independent sales representatives and *manufacturer's representatives* are two names for the same type of entity. These will market products for manufacturers or software developers– although with software, they are often referred to as *value-added resellers* (VARs). These "reps" could be either individuals or firms with several employees. Typically, a rep will cover only a certain region of the country. One or more of these reps may agree to sell your product for a straight commission of around six to ten percent of gross sales for manufactured goods or 20 – 30% for software.

Note that independent reps do not take delivery of your product nor do they stock it–in the same way that a real estate agent does not take possession of a house. Businesses often refer to "hiring" an independent rep or rep firm, but this is not hiring in the sense of putting them on the payroll, and no salary is paid to them by the manufacturer. The manufacturer is known as the *principal* in this relationship with the rep.

You must negotiate and sign a contract that details the terms of your business relationship with the rep. You may find sample contracts by searching the term "sales representative contract," etc. online. One useful sample is available free at the following address: http://smallbusiness.findlaw. com/business-forms-contracts/business-forms-contracts-a-to-z/form1-38.html. The rep is expected to continue servicing the sales accounts after the initial sale and you are expected to continue paying the commission on future sales. It is sometimes possible to exclude certain customer types (i. e. online sales, "big box" stores) or existing customers, etc. from this arrangement when setting up the contract with the rep.

Pitfall: Assuming that an independent rep will sell significant amounts of your new product

For various reasons, new companies that offer new technologies to the market very rarely have success with independent reps. It is wise not to count on them as a significant source of sales, despite what they may tell you. Because of this fact, be very careful about making an agreement with a rep that leaves you little flexibility to find a new rep or make other changes if they are not successful.

In the rep's defense, however, it is sometimes the fault of the entrepreneur if the rep is unsuccessful in selling the entrepreneur's new technology. If you do retain a rep firm, make sure that you know how to properly deal with, support, and incent them.

To understand the reason that entrepreneurs have such low success with rep firms, you must "put yourself in their shoes." It is expensive for the rep to go around and visit their sales accounts showing products etc. Often, the rep has a limited amount of time to spend with the buyers they visit. If the rep is successful in his business, he already has several lines of products from other manufacturers that provide his "bread and butter." He must be sure that these lines are properly serviced. Remember that these other manufacturers are introducing new products as well. You are competing for the rep's time and attention with their existing manufacturer accounts.

Alternatively, let's say that you find a rep that does not already represent several strong product lines. In this case you will not be in a competitive situation with other manufacturers, which initially sounds pretty good. However, that rep may very well lack the money to go visit accounts due to the lack of a strong existing product line. You can see that in either case a startup firm with a new technology is at a disadvantage when attempting to utilize independent sales reps.

Inside Scoop: It is up to you, the entrepreneur–not the rep–to create a fruitful relationship if you hire a rep firm!

Although entrepreneurs rarely have success with manufacturer's representatives, there is typically little to lose in contracting with them, as long as your contract has escape clauses. At the least, reps can provide great insight into the market. A good resource for finding a rep is the Manufacturer's Agent National Association, http://www.manaonline.org.

Pitfall: Assuming a subordinate position to your rep

I have seen a number of startups that signed up a rep firm early-on and thought they had hit the big time. "We're lucky to have them," the entrepreneur thought, regardless of how the situation developed going forward, "I hope I don't do something to tick them off." This is a very unhealthy attitude to have concerning an entity that has very little incentive to really work hard for you, but that is tying up a geographic region of the country.

If you do retain a rep firm, you must work with them to develop a sales plan for them. To do this, ask them:

- How many accounts exist in their territory for each major account type–such as mom & pop stores, big box chains, distributors, etc.–that you expect them to call on.
- How many of each account type they call on in a month and in how many of those visits they expect to show your product(s)
- Is there a seasonal variation to any of these activities
- How many of those demonstrations they expect to convert to a sale for each account type
- What they expect the average initial and follow-on order sizes to be for each account type
- What is their projected sales volume by quarter?

Then consider what they tell you and if you determine it to be reasonable, put it in writing. If not, propose a more aggressive plan and be sure that you can justify your reasoning for it.

After you have jointly developed the plan you must monitor the rep firm's compliance with it. Request monthly or quarterly reports from them detailing to whom they have demonstrated your products and then verify this information. Reps are essentially your contract employees–make sure they are performing. Again, whatever you do, do *not* adopt an attitude that you are grateful simply to have the rep agree to carry your product and therefore you are reluctant to push the rep to perform! I have seen this attitude among many entrepreneurs and it never works out well for the entrepreneur.

To verify the information in the rep's reports, request the contact information of the persons to whom he has shown your product. Tell the rep that you need this information in order to follow up with the prospect and directly thank the prospect for their interest. Then actually follow up with the account. In addition to verifying the information provided by the rep, this will let the prospect know that he is important to you.

Inside Scoop: If your rep will not give you this contact information, you need a different rep!

I cannot stress that last statement strongly enough. Do not waste your valuable time with a rep who will not provide this contact information. Do not accept any excuse whatsoever from the rep on this point! One of the most common attributes of a rep who is failing to sell is a cavalcade of excuses coupled with attempts to withhold information and shift blame. Be sure that you are doing your own job correctly and then hold your ground against excuses from the rep.

Lastly regarding manufacturer's reps, there is the issue of salesmen's samples. Typically the rep will need product samples to show to prospective customers. The rep may ask you to provide these samples at no cost, but be aware that manufacturers often require the independent reps to purchase the samples. If you do provide samples free of charge, be sure to get an agreement in writing that they will be returned at your request–although do not have too high of hopes that they will actually be returned.

MARKETING VS. DISTRIBUTION

It is very important to understand the concept of distribution as compared to marketing. In preparing to market a consumer product, do not plan how you are going to push your product out onto store shelves–this is a distribution plan. Instead, plan how you are going to get consumers to demand that stores put your product onto shelves–this is a marketing plan.

Pitfall: "Push" marketing

The route that a product takes between the place of its manufacture and the end user is called the *distribution chain*. This chain can include: your warehouse; trucking companies; wholesalers; distributors; store warehouses; retail outlets; catalog companies, and package delivery companies such as UPS.

I have found that most people who develop a new product are quite naturally highly product-focused, and many of these people also become highly distribution-chain focused once the product has been developed. Perhaps this is because both product development and distribution entail dealing with physical entities. For consumer products especially, the process of filling up the distribution chain is usually confused with marketing. Great effort goes into securing distributors, retail stores, catalogs, Websites, etc. while consumer-level marketing is pursued sluggishly if at all.

Inside Scoop: Remember this or die: Distribution and marketing are two vastly different endeavors. Getting your product *into* a store is not the goal of marketing.
The goal is to get your product *out of* the store in a consumer's shopping bag.

Think of the distribution chain as exactly that: A chain. You cannot push hard enough on the distribution chain to move your product through it. Your product must be pulled through the distribution chain. You need to create "suction" in the marketplace–the consumer purchase that causes the store to call its distributor and purchase more product, causing the distributor to call you and purchase more product, causing you to go to the bank and make a deposit!

Some retailers will not carry a new product until they get customers coming in asking for it. When I first attempted to market my own new consumer product these retailers would really tick me off when my sales manager ran into them. How narrow minded and lazy can they be? Can't they see the potential of this great new technology?

Inside Scoop: I have since learned that these are the retailers who really know what they are doing.

It is up to *you* to drive the consumer purchase. The retailer has far too many other things on his mind to do this for you and therefore he will not properly do it.

Do *not* celebrate when you get that important first order from the major retailer that you worked so hard to get. Do party wildly when you receive from that retailer your first *re-order*.

<u>Inside Scoop:</u> **Be re-order focused!**

CUSTOMERS VS. CONSUMERS

An entity that you think of as your customer may not be your technology's end-user or consumer. For instance: You sell to a distributor or wholesaler, who sells to a retailer, who sells to the person or business that will use the product. All can be considered your customer, but only the last is the consumer. This is an important distinction. Selling to the distributor, wholesaler, or retailer (the distribution channel) requires *trade marketing* and selling to the end-user requires *consumer marketing*. You must be well-versed in each of these and have separate strategies for each as the two are entirely different.

<u>Understanding Trade Customers</u>
Most people are familiar with trade-level customers such as wholesalers, distributors, and retailers and these entities require no further explanation here. There is another less-familiar type of entity in many distribution channels. This entity is a *buying group*.

The purpose of a buying group is to give group purchasing power to the members of the group. Buying groups exist for product lines that are sold through retail–such as sporting goods or hardware–and for product lines that are sold to businesses, such as hospital supplies. For instance, a group of small independent sporting goods stores may form a buying group to obtain group purchasing power from vendors. A group of hospitals may form a buying group to obtain group purchasing power from their vendors.

In the case of retailers, the buying groups are typically set up so that the member retailers may better compete against the "big box" stores.

Buying groups select certain items to put in their catalog of products that they make available for their members to purchase.

Most buying groups will have periodic vendor shows. For instance, a manufacturer or vendor wishing to have its products "picked up" by a retailer buying group will set up a table or booth at the show and the store owners or buyers for the stores will review the products. Personnel from the buying group will make a decision whether to offer the product in the buying group's catalog based partly on feedback from the individual store owners or buyers.

Buying groups will require that you sell to their members at a price lower than you sell to similar entities that are unaffiliated with the buying group–that is the whole purpose of the group. Typically, they require a 5% discount. The individual entities may order directly from you and you may ship directly to the store or hospital, etc., as the case may be.

<u>Tips on Trade Marketing</u>
The tools of trade marketing have much in common with the tools of consumer marketing, but may be used in different ways. A couple of tools that are unique to trade marketing are trade shows and trade magazines.

I will repeat a point from the previous section because it is so important to your success: Distributors and retailers simply serve as pass-through agents for your product. They are not very concerned with properly marketing your product to their customers, no matter what they may tell you to the contrary. This is especially true in the case of retailers.

Pitfall: Believing a retailer who tells you that on their own volition they will properly market your product to their customers–*they won't*

Do not try to be the exception to the rule on this one. Again, consumer marketing is your responsibility and yours alone.

One of the areas in which this rule manifests itself is point-of-purchase materials for retail stores. These materials could include signs, counter displays, display cases, shelf-talkers, brochures, etc. Do not expect that the stores will properly deploy such materials that you simply ship to the store. *They won't!* If you go to the store and set the counter display right there on the counter, do not expect that it will stay there for long. It probably won't. You need to really bird-dog these things.

If you decide that you want to create a counter display, come up with something functional that is less likely to get pushed aside. A good example of this is those penny trays that you see with an ad on them near the cash register. Maybe your display could incorporate something like this.

Here is a real-life example of the above points: I once advised a startup company from the eastern U.S. that signed up one of America's largest grocery chains to a trial of its product (a non-grocery item) in 125 stores on the West Coast. The chain's corporate marketing department offered to create the display racks, signage, etc. required for in-store promotion at their initial expense and bill my client for these items later. The total cost for the racks and the product to fill them was $750,000. Upon hearing of this arrangement I congratulated the CEO of the company I was advising and told him that he needed to hire someone on the West Coast to monitor deployment of the inventory and marketing materials in the stores. Lacking funds, the CEO did not do so.

After about four months the corporate officials called the CEO and stated that they were cancelling the trial due to poor results and that the CEO's company needed to pay for the displays. I very strongly urged the CEO to get on a plane and go check on deployment in the stores of the product, displays, and marketing materials, knowing full well what he would find.

What he found was a 25% compliance rate with the proper deployment of the displays, marketing materials, and inventory. Documenting this failure on the part of the chain with photos and other evidence, he was able to get $700,000 in charges related to the trial cancelled!

Direct/Indirect Consumer Marketing
Not only can marketing be divided into the two general sectors of trade and consumer marketing, but consumer marketing can be further divided into direct and indirect consumer marketing. Direct marketing entails selling directly to consumers, whereas indirect marketing places a retailer between you and the consumer. Again, different strategies are required for direct and indirect consumer marketing.

Many new technologies are launched with a strategy of starting out by marketing directly to consumers to build awareness and demand–while at the same time capturing full retail price–

then switching to marketing through retailers once the "cream" has been skimmed off the top of the market. Of course, the later sales to retailers are at the much lower wholesale price. This is often done with products launched through infomercials. Retailers reach a different or often broader market than do infomercials.

The opposite strategy normally does not work. You do not see companies launch a new product in retailers and then later create infomercials to sell the product directly to consumers in competition with their retailers.

Direct marketing is an entire art and science in and of itself, and again, a full discussion is beyond the scope of this book. The Direct Marketing Association: http://www.the-dma.org/ is a great resource for further education on this subject.

CREATING CONSUMER DEMAND

So far in this book we have looked at whom your customers are, whom your consumers are and the fact that you must get consumers to demand that stores put your product onto store shelves if you use that distribution channel. I have pounded home the message about the need to create consumer demand, and rightfully so. I have probably created a demand among you–my consumers–that I tell you how to go about doing that.

Well, I'm glad you asked!

The good news is that there are myriad examples of triumphal technology introductions to use as your guide. We will review a few of them further below. These fascinating tales recount some of the most amazing daredevil feats in marketing history! (I told you this is where it would start getting fun.)

The bad news is that a complete discussion of how to create consumer demand is–like many other topics–beyond the scope of this book. However, realize that marketing a consumer technology on a national level is a very complex endeavor that takes years of actual experience to understand. You can spend a lot of money trying to learn as you go. My observation is that people who spend money and "learn as they go" usually never get there.

Pitfall: Trying to "learn as you go."

It is possible for a product to just "catch on" and practically sell itself, but this is quite unlikely. The phenomenon is more likely to occur with highly visible products such as Rollerblade in-line skates (in the 1980s) or Razor mini scooters (in the 1990s) because these products have mass public visibility when users ride them up and down the streets. More importantly, the product benefits are fun and readily obvious.

Of course, there was also a lot of initial creative marketing behind these two products. To learn more–as well as get a break from hearing *me* drone on and on–you may want to read the very intriguing history of inline skates at: http://www.fundinguniverse.com/company-histories/Rollerblade-Inc-Company-History.html

One could argue that the Internet and the ability of products to "go viral" online can provide the same advantage as the public visibility of inline skates or mini scooters. However, one critical difference is the immense clutter of the Internet vs. a neighborhood street. When a person is skating or scootering down a street or sidewalk, he or she is pretty hard to miss.

Inside Scoop: *Avoid a common mistake; assume that you will need to* create *consumer demand.*

For now, that is the message I want you to absorb regarding creating consumer demand.

LEFT BRAINS AND RIGHT BRAINS

We have all heard that our brains are segmented into two halves: The left brain processes rational thoughts and the right brain processes emotional thoughts. This is very fortunate for marketers, because it means that they only need to market to one half of their prospective customer's brain, not the entire thing!

That fact really opens up an awesome market because it means that you can sell to anyone with half a brain. ☺ Well–as long as that person has the proper half. Of course, the unfortunate thing for us is that marketers have to use their entire brain in marketing to their customer's half-brain.

Pitfall: Marketing to the wrong half of the brain

As mentioned earlier in this book, in marketing a product or service it is more important to cause people to *want* it rather than to convince them that they need it. For this it is best to appeal to consumers on an emotional level rather than on a rational level. Many studies on consumer behavior have shown that most consumers make buying decisions emotionally, not rationally. (Thus my "half-a-brain" wisecrack.)

Inside Scoop: Create a burning desire.

Double Scoop: Desire is an *emotion,* **not an analysis.**

What is Bottled-Up Inside?

How can you put this deep wisdom into practice? Well, for instance, instead of simply listing your product features, focus on your skillful presentation of how those features will benefit the consumer emotionally. Engage as many of your prospect's senses as possible in this effort, though not necessarily all at once. How will your product "ride in on a white horse and save the day" regarding an emotional issue for your customer that is urgent but unfulfilled? Don't fool yourself; everybody has these longings.

Many of these concerns, desires, fervors, and emotional triggers are listed below. By the term *emotional trigger* I mean an emotional aspect of a person's life strong enough that its fulfillment will cause a person to take an action he may not otherwise take. The differences between some of the items in the list are nuanced, but important. I have added blank lines to break up this very long list.

74 Concerns, Desires, Mental States, & Emotional Triggers
1) Prestige
2) Comfort
3) More free time
4) Longevity

5) Health
6) Love
7) Passion
8) Worry
9) Worry-free
10) Carefree

11) Sexiness
12) Hope
13) Playfulness
14) Certainty/Clarity
15) Change
16) Beyond the ordinary
17) Pride
18) Respect
19) Power
20) Honesty/Trust
21) Envy

22) Achievement
23) Anger/Outrage
24) Prejudice
25) Reduced frustration
26) Career advancement
27) Family-related issues
28) Safety/Security
29) Avoiding physical pain
30) Avoiding fears, failure, bad outcome
31) Saving money

32) Making money
33) Independence
34) Freedom
35) Us vs. the "big guys"
36) Rooting for the underdog
37) Feeling pampered, cared for
38) Feeling admired
39) Feeling first-class/A cut above
40) Feeling privileged/Getting privileged access
41) Feeling blocked or locked-out
42) Feeling like rights have been trampled on

43) Feeling burdened
44) Feeling athletic
45) Feeling adventurous
46) Feeling feminine
47) Feeling masculine

48) Feeling youthful
49) Feeling like a trend-setter
50) Feeling in control
51) Feeling smart, intelligent, wise
52) Feeling like you made the right choice

53) Being a leader
54) Caring for others/Compassion/Altruism
55) Being with the "in crowd"
56) Competitiveness
57) Risk-taking/Thrill-seeking
58) Association with a reputable brand or a certain brand image
59) Happiness/Humor
60) Following a leader
61) Easiness/Hassle-free
62) Beauty
63) Longing for olden times, old-fashioned ways or things

64) Reminiscences/Fond memories
65) Respect for heritage/Tradition
66) Hand-made/Home-made
67) Naturalness/Back-to-nature
68) Camaraderie/Friendship
69) Slow/Laid-back
70) New/Modern/High-tech
71) Fast & furious
72) Membership
73) Environmental consciousness
74) Sensory gratification

Now consider that list and add to it–especially regarding your own client base. How does your product serve as a tool to fulfill deep, fundamental desires?

Regarding your market, your brilliant realization and grand call to action is this:

**Inside Scoop: Inside, your customer is an emotional white-board.
Get in there and draw pictures in wondrous bright colors.**

Colorful Selling

The process of getting in there and drawing pictures in brilliant colors I refer to as *colorful selling*. Think of a time when you heard someone described as a "colorful character." What connotation does this bring up? Yahoo Answers describes the term *colorful character* as: "Someone with a big personality. Someone full of life, well rounded, interesting, usually happy go lucky. It is a positive way to describe someone who stands out & is different."

Your marketing needs to be like this!

A classic example of colorful selling is a magazine ad written for the U.S. School of Music by ad-man John Caples. Decades ago the U. S. School of Music sold piano-playing instructional materials to the public. In his ad copy Caples could have focused on how the materials were based on thoroughly researched instructional methods and were well organized, etc., but he was far too wise for that.

Instead, he began his ad with the boastful line: "*They All Laughed When I Sat Down at the Piano. But When I Started to Play!*–" He went on with a first-person narrative of an ebullient customer who amazed his skeptical friends when he sat down at a party and let the symphonic sounds of a virtuoso flow from his fingers. Needless to say, the reader was being prodded into: "I want to be the envy of my friends and amaze them too. Sign me up!"

The issue is not the technicality of playing the piano; it is the emotional benefit that this skill imparts. The product is just a tool to make customers the envy of their friends and to make customers swell with pride. Of course the reason that this is a classic example is because of the ad's extraordinary effectiveness in generating sales. You can read the ad at http://www.power writing.com/caples.html. Do not proceed farther in this book without doing so. For a person like me who has written a fair amount of ad copy, this creation is so masterful that it can send shivers up my spine. (Yeah, I know–that's rather weird.)

I can assure you that Caples did not simply whip this charmer out of his typewriter in an hour. Thesaurus in hand, he must have spent days agonizing over each word, sentence, and paragraph–as well as the precise relative positioning of each–in order to pull the reader through the exact cascade of thoughts and emotions required to create a burning desire.

In a more recent example of the power of emotional selling, television shopping channel HSN in the late 2000s changed the way it presented merchandise, enabling it to successfully sell high-fashion and high-profit items. According to the *WSJ*, the network: "adopted a softer selling style pitched to more-upscale consumers. Rather than using high-pressure tactics, it emphasized making the item seem desirable–in an entertaining way–by showing how a garment drapes on a model, for instance."

Whose Fault is it, Anyway?
I have found through my own experience of marketing items ranging from cloud-based Web services to $25,000 original oil paintings that if someone really *wants* something badly enough, they will usually find a way to pay for it. They will refrain from some other purchase, not pay the credit card bill in full that month, or otherwise shift their finances if necessary to allow a purchase of something for which they have a burning desire. Of course there are certain limits to this, in that not everyone can make accommodations to purchase a $25,000 oil painting.

Pitfall: Assuming that poor sales is not your fault

Inside Scoop: If qualified prospects are not buying your product, it is because YOU have not made them WANT it enough.

*There is no other reason, **period**!*

Your goal is to find out what emotional benefit your potential customers really want and then convince them that your product can provide this to them–this is marketing in a nutshell.

<u>Emotional Extras</u>
Here are a few leftover tidbits on the subject:

Unfortunately, dishonest marketers can and have throughout history taken advantage of this technique, relying on very strong emotionally driven marketing to sell boatloads of shoddy or even nonexistent products or services. You, of course, must ensure that you can deliver on the promise.

It is important to realize that utilizing product endorsements from experts or famous individuals and using testimonials from satisfied customers are forms of emotional selling, as is showing photos of people in your ads. In fact these are some of the most powerful forms of emotional selling.

I you look around, you will see many ads that focus on product attributes rather than emotional benefits. This may lead you to doubt what I have said here, if so many advertisers are not following this concept. However, decide for yourself: Go back and re-read the Caples ad for the U.S. School of Music. Which would create a burning desire if you were in the market for piano instruction: that ad or a tedious recitation of the technical aspects of the course?

In contemplating the emotional aspects of selling, you may think to yourself: "Self, I am trying to sell a hardware item to a bunch of hard-nosed, geeky engineers. My technology has no emotional benefit for them." To this I would say: "Oh, yeah? Didn't I list 'career advancement' as one of the emotional benefits sought by people?" Many engineers are people too. (I've had the term "engineer" in my job title before, so I can say that.)

AVANT-GARDE MARKETING

Those who develop new technologies are by definition technology innovators. However, a person who wants to be successful in new technology commercialization will think of him/herself simply as an innovator. This broadened outlook on innovation should then be applied to the marketing process–this is how you will make your money.

Over the years I have had many clients who came in and said that they have an innovative product, but their business is failing because they need better marketing. Not one client has ever come in saying that they have innovative marketing, but their business is failing because they need a better product. The former happens all the time; the latter has never happened. Your goal is to combine the best of both worlds:

If you have innovative products <u>and</u> innovative marketing, you can be a juggernaut.

To help spur your creative juices on this topic, several examples of America's top marketing innovators from the past 150 years are listed below. It is important to note that some of these "innovators" did not actually create the marketing concept, but rather they energetically implemented it at an early stage with great success, often to existing products.

<u>Market Magicians of the Past 150 Years</u>
<u>Isaac M. Singer</u>: Developed franchising in the 1850s into a mainstay of marketing, primarily by creating a practical, cooperative contract between the Singer Co. and its franchisees for what had previously been an ad-hoc, unstructured business model. As a manufacturer, Singer was also an early adopter of and popularized the installment purchase plan offering, allowing easy periodic payments for purchases of relatively "big-ticket" items such as sewing machines. Customers could put a dollar down, take the sewing machine home, then pay a dollar a week.

116

With its franchise and installment-plan marketing initiatives, Singer became the largest sewing-machine company in the world.

In an ironic example of the power of marketing vs. the power of patenting, Singer in 1854 was found to have infringed on the patent of Elias Howe and ended up making Howe quite wealthy through royalty payments. Howe had previously been unable to sell his own machines. It is reported that in 1845 Howe held a product demonstration and his invention out-sewed five seamstresses, but he could not sell even one machine as a result of the exhibition.

Aaron Montgomery Ward: Pioneered mail order sales in 1872. Ward founded Montgomery Ward Inc., which became–for a long time–the world's number-one mail order business and one of the largest of all retailers in the U.S. Ward is also credited with introducing in 1875 the revolutionary policy of: "satisfaction guaranteed or your money back," realizing that this was necessary in order to get rural residents to trust a far-off vendor to send them good-quality merchandise through the U.S. mail.

Sperry & Hutchison Company: Introduced rewards programs to the market in 1896 with its S & H Green Stamps. The company set up programs with retailers such as grocery stores and gas stations in which customers received stamps based on their purchases. Stamps could then be redeemed for merchandise from the S & H catalog. In the 1960s this catalog was the largest publication in the U.S. and there were three times as many S & H stamps issued as there was U.S. postage stamps. This innovation led eventually to the ubiquitous airline frequent-flier and credit card bonus-point reward programs of today.

Thomas Edison: Realized that he had to develop an electricity generation and transmission infrastructure if he was to sell his electric light bulbs; and then did so.

King C. Gillette: Reported to have in the 1920s created the "razor-and-blades" business/marketing model, in which a single razor-blade holder is sold at a low profit margin so that the company may later sell many razor blades at a much higher profit margin. One researcher states that Gillette did not adopt this model until his 1904 patent was about to expire in 1921 and he anticipated competition, but that once he did adopt it, his profits jumped.

Note that the researcher states that due to an innovative marketing strategy, Gillette's profits *jumped* after his patent expired. (See http://www.law.uchicago.edu/files/file/532-rcp-razors.pdf.)

General Motors Inc.: Created brand segmentation for various consumer tastes and income levels, primarily under the leadership of Alfred P. Sloan in the 1920s and 1930s. GM also out-competed Henry Ford by creating a subsidiary and offering loans through GMAC starting in 1919. Customers could now make: "easy monthly payments." (Where else have you heard that marketing concept?) This not only juiced product sales, it created an additional and highly lucrative revenue stream for GM: Interest payments.

Although Henry Ford holds a well-deserved place in American history as a business luminary and pioneer in manufacturing processes–revolutionizing production with his implementation of the assembly line–he was personally opposed to the two market innovations embraced by GM and adopted them only late and reluctantly. For example, Ford said in his 1909 memoir, *My Life and Work*: "Any customer can have a car painted any colour that he wants so long as it is black." In stark contrast, GM's creative marketing drove it zooming past Ford as the largest automaker by the late 1920s.

Ford also said in his memoir–only two sentences after the above quote–"The selling people could not of course see the advantages that a single model would bring about in production." There is no question that as a short-term plan this paid off handsomely for Ford, as he was able to build and sell nearly 3.5 million of the Model T, a low-priced "motor car for the great multitude." This approach also changed the world by allowing "everyman" to enjoy the freedom brought about by an automobile. But that strategy applied over the long term did not keep up with the rapidly evolving market and once Ford fell to second place it has never regained in the auto business its former pinnacle position.

Earl Tupper: Developed Tupperware products in the 1940s using the new polyethylene plastic and then marketed them though in-home parties. Tupper did not "invent" in-home-party retailing, but saw the value of the concept and drove it from relative obscurity to a worldwide mainstay of marketing, becoming a multi-millionaire in the process.

USA Today: Began by marketing its newspapers to business travelers in hotels rather than just to residents of a city and also initiated color photos on the front page of newspapers, realizing the alluring power of color vs. black & white. The entire newspaper industry followed suit with color photos, eventually leading to color photos inside the papers as well. At the time that USA Today was rapidly gaining ground in the 1980s it shook the entire newspaper industry top-to-bottom. It is today the nation's largest-selling newspaper.

Miller Brewing Co.: Market-changing introduction of a "Lite" product which ricocheted across all sectors of the food industry. Miller used macho athletes to endorse the low-calorie beer as being "less filling" to avoid a diet-product image and to encourage higher consumption. The name "Lite" also accomplished this goal. It would be hard to come up with another marketing initiative that has had as great of an impact on the massive food and beverage industry.

Xavier Roberts: Invented in 1976 what would eventually become Cabbage Patch Kids. In addition, Roberts developed the marketing masterstroke of requiring customers to "adopt" his dolls and provided adoption papers to commemorate the occasion. This brilliant and innovative marketing produced perhaps America's first actual toy frenzy. The dolls were one of the original "must-have" Christmas gifts for children and for a time in the 1980s prompted fights among mothers scrambling for scarce merchandise.

HSN Inc.: Introduced the first television shopping channel, originating as a radio show in 1977 and then transitioning through a stage as a local-access cable channel.

American Express Inc.: Established the first national cause-related marketing campaign with its support of Statue of Liberty restoration in the 1980s. For every transaction on an AmEx card, the company pledged a donation to the restoration effort.

MBNA Inc.: Created affinity credit card programs that tie in with membership organizations by donating to the organization based on members' card use, thus rising from a small regional bank in Maryland to become the largest issuer of credit cards in the world, beating the likes of Citibank, Chase, and Bank of America at this obscenely lucrative game.

Nike, Inc.: Logo placement (Don't need to say much on that one, do I?)

Ron Popeil: Pioneered direct-TV product sales and TV infomercials.

<u>Adobe Systems Inc.</u>: Gave away Acrobat Reader viewer software to spur sales of its Acrobat document development software and therefore became the "industry standard" for such development software.

<u>Charles Schwab Inc.</u>: Popularized online stock trading in the mid-1990s, becoming by May 1997 the largest online brokerage with over 700,000 active accounts. This new marketing channel also fueled the company's growth to one of the top five brokerages in the U.S.

<u>Steve Jobs</u>: Inspired by Steve Jobs, Apple's numerous marketing innovations completely devastate its competitors. For example, the hundreds of thousands of iPhone apps have created an immense hurdle for later competitors. In early 2011 Apple's app store passed a milestone with the 10-billionth app download. The iPhone has re-defined what it means to be a cell phone and has crushed everyone else. For instance, Nokia Corp. had long been the dominant player in the U. S. market for the older-technology standard cell phones, but as of October 2010, Apple had 25% of the U. S. smart phone market vs. Nokia's 3%.

According to the *Wall Street Journal*: "Apple [has] created an ecosystem of eager consumers, software developers and media around their products that has helped boost phone and app sales. Nokia notably lacks similar enthusiasm around Symbian." (Symbian is Nokia's smart phone operating system.) "Having ceded much of the high end of the smartphone market to Apple, Inc., slower-footed rivals such as Research In Motion Ltd., (Blackberry) Nokia Corp. and Motorola Inc. are jostling for what remains up for grabs. Nokia's business is melting like an ice cube."

Not only have Apple's cell phone competitors attempted to copy Apple's success with apps, but other industries have tried to replicate Apple's app-led market power as well. Lexmark International Inc.–maker of printers for the home market–has launched a project to develop apps for its printers. According to the *WSJ*: "Lexmark's app store comes as many companies try to adopt a business model honed by Apple Inc. with its iPhone and iPad devices. Ford Motor Co., Google Inc., and Intel Corp. are among the companies that have invited developers to write programs to be used in conjunction with their products... in an effort to keep their customers using their [offerings] in a market full of similar products."

Additionally, Apple has maintained its stranglehold on the digital-music-download business by tightly tying its software and iTunes store to its popular iPod music player. Other companies offering digital music downloads, such as Amazon.com, have not been able to crack this innovative marketing firewall. Coming to the market in 2007–four years after Apple–Amazon initially attempted to gain share by under-pricing Apple and by not having copy protections on its downloads. However, in late 2010, recording-industry executives estimated that iTunes maintained a 90% market share. As digital downloads represented 50% of all music sales in 2011, the math shows that in a few short years Apple cornered about 45% of the entire U.S. music market–a market in which it was not even a player at the start of 2001.

Apple's marketing success in digital music has been so extreme that it has created fear in related industries. Movie studios are looking at Netflix, Inc.–which has moved into the digital movie download business–and worry that Netflix could end up dominating that business in the same way Apple's iTunes store dominates music. One movie-industry executive is quoted as saying: "I think 'concerned' is a gross understatement."

Now *that's* the power of innovative marketing!

Zynga Inc.: Popularized social-networking games such as FarmVille employing the marketing concept of allowing basic game play for free, but requiring the purchase of "virtual goods" such as a tractor for a small fee, or *microtransaction*. As well, the games are developed to take advantage of the social-network platform on which they run. Players are encouraged to seek advice from their friends and to send virtual-goods gifts to friends, causing the game to spread virally. FarmVille was released in June 2009 and by June 2010 had reportedly surpassed 85 million users.

McDonald's Ventures LLC (Redbox): Developed a new channel to the market for DVDs that contributed to the bankruptcy of previous market-leader Blockbuster Inc., which had a "brick-and-mortar" marketing channel. Amazingly, the Redbox DVD vending-machine kiosk was conceived by McDonald's as it was conducting market research into ways to drive more traffic to its stores. McDonald's then partnered with Coinstar Inc. to roll the concept out to a broad market because Coinstar already had a similar marketing channel established in retail stores with its coin-redemption kiosks. Since purchased by Coinstar Inc., Redbox and its ubiquitous kiosks offered a level of convenience unmatched by Blockbuster, which has introduced its own kiosks in response to the competition.

Netflix, Inc.: The Company participated with Redbox in the demise of Blockbuster Inc. (as of 2010 operating under bankruptcy) by offering another new channel for DVDs: Ordering via the Internet and direct-shipping to homes. However, Netflix was astute enough to foresee that streaming video would soon put a killer choke-hold on its lucrative distribution channel.

In a rational response, the company has begun a streaming video service. But much more brilliantly, Netflix has launched that service into hyper-drive by creating arrangements with TV and Blu-ray player manufacturers to place a "Netflix button" on TV and Blu-ray-player remote controls so that Netflix's service is highly visible and incredibly simple to use. As of 2011, Netflix had signed agreements with Panasonic Inc., Samsung Electronics Co. Ltd., Sharp Corp., Sony Corp., and Toshiba Corp. to place the Netflix button on their remote controls. Imagine being a Netflix competitor trying to compete with that marketing innovation! There is no patent, trademark, copyright or especially trade secret involved here–only that poor, forlorn stepchild so cruelly scorned by most new-technology developers: **marketing innovation**.

A few lesser-known but equally impressive examples of marketing innovators are:

Wall Drug in Wall, South Dakota: "Saturation" signage created a tourist attraction. A small drug store on the main Interstate highway leading to Yellowstone National Park created a tourist attraction "from thin air" simply by putting up many intriguing signs, beginning more than 100 miles from the store location. The first signs offered free ice water to summer travelers in the pre-air-conditioned 1930s. Read the story at: http://www.walldrug.com/t-history.aspx

Realtree Camouflage: The Realtree Company's comprehensive marketing campaign deposed the previous industry leader. Trebark camouflage, the original innovator of more-realistic camouflage patterns for sportsmen, was usurped by the newcomer Realtree that focused much more heavily on effective and innovative marketing. Trebark has nearly "vanished" as a result of being out-marketed!

I have personal insight into this situation in that I knew Jim Crumley, developer of Trebark, and also Bill Jordan, developer of Realtree. I remember Jim as personable and laid-back, like a perfect southern gentleman. Bill Jordan had a different demeanor; personable but much more driven and energetic. This, I feel, is the reason for the opposite outcomes.

(Innovator unknown): Clamshell packaging revolutionized product display. Those clear plastic packages that are nearly impossible to open have allowed a revolution in in-store product display compared to "pre-clamshell" days.

DIG THAT MOAT!

Your new technology, the money that you and others have put into it, and the business that you have built are all very valuable. Any time people see something valuable there will be those among them who will want to copy or steal it. Related to this, a fairly common metaphor in the field of technology commercialization is that of a moat. You need to "dig a moat" around your "castle" to prevent competitors from pillaging your prized possessions.

Most entrepreneurs think only of protecting their IP as the means of digging their moat, but that is often a very ineffective method for a small company to keep competitors at bay. The most effective moats are based on how the company markets its products or how it does business. These moats can serve as a very strong "inner ring of defense" in case anyone gets past the weaker ring of IP protection.

Below is a listing of several well-known companies that have completely dominated their markets and have maintained an unassailable position through market-based or business-based moats. You may look at these corporate giants and wonder how this could apply to a little guy like you, but think about this: How do you think these companies came to be corporate giants?

<u>15 Ways Today's Biggest Winners Keep Losers Gasping for Air</u>
1) <u>Company</u>: Wal-mart Stores, Inc.

<u>Moat</u>: Cost advantages

In my opinion, Wal-mart crushed its competition because the company realized that it was not really a retailer, but merely the last link in the distribution chain. There is no question that Wal-Mart crushed its competition because it focused very hard on building efficiencies into its supply chain and into its distribution system. This allowed Wal-Mart to brutally under-price everyone else in the market, driving to bankruptcy many long-established retailers with their bloated, anemic systems and procedures. Note that Wal-Mart did not get a patent on "efficiency." Many of Wal-Mart's competitors have tried to copy it, and after several decades, some are catching up. But Wal-Mart's moat is now wide as an ocean and will remain so until Wal-Mart too succumbs–as every company ultimately does–to "corporate management" and old age.

2) <u>Companies/Products</u>: Research in Motion Ltd./BlackBerry; Sony Corp./PlayStation III

<u>Moat</u>: High cost of switching

Once corporations adopted BlackBerry smart phones it was difficult to switch to a competitor. This was due security issues, capital cost, and the employees' comfort in using the BlackBerry system. Consumers adopted the iPhone much faster than did corporations.

In a similar way, once a consumer purchases a Sony PlayStation III video console it would be very difficult to sell that consumer a game cartridge for a Microsoft X Box 360 due to the cost of the proprietary game consoles required to play the games of each company. Once Sony or Microsoft gets someone to purchase their console, they have locked up a customer for a long time.

3) Company: Facebook Inc.

   Moat: Building large networks

   I am not really sure how Facebook was able to rocket from relative obscurity to the behemoth of social networking in such a short time, but one thing is for sure: Once they had climbed to the top of that mountain, their position became virtually unassailable. After you have your friends and other contacts all set up and using Facebook, it will be extremely difficult for a competitor to convince you to switch yourself and your entire network of friends over to another social networking site.

4) Companies: Microsoft Corp. and Google Inc.

   Moats: Tied-up critical strategic partners/Product bundling/Product tying

   Both Microsoft and Google were yanked from obscurity by much-larger strategic partners and their stories are quite amazing. In addition, once Microsoft itself became powerful it is widely considered to have muscled into new markets through product bundling and tying.

   Microsoft-Tying up Strategic Partners

   In the case of Microsoft, Bill Gates in 1981 secured from IBM the rights to provide the operating system, (MS-DOS/PC-DOS), for IBM personal computers. Gates did not develop this OS but instead purchased from Seattle Computer Products Co. At the time, IBM was the world's largest computer company and it embarked on rapid growth as it launched its line of PCs, hauling Microsoft along with it as the sole source of the critical OS. IBM did not need two operating systems, so anyone coming along later offering to sell an OS for IBM PCs would be frozen out, and indeed they were. Further, IBM allowed other computer companies to utilize aspects of its PC framework, causing PCs and *PC clones* (made by companies other than IBM) to dominate the market and crush–for a time–Apple's MacIntosh computer. IBM caused Microsoft to grow to–for a long time–the most valuable technology company in the world.

   Microsoft was handed a virtual monopoly in operating systems, the "backbone" of the world of personal computer software applications. However, over the long term, a monopoly is a very bad thing for the company holding the monopoly and this came back to bite them. This monopoly removed the need to truly innovate in the fast-changing world of high technology. As of 2010, Microsoft has ceded its lofty position to Apple, Google, and Facebook. Analysts see Microsoft as a laggard in new markets such as tablets like the iPad. Microsoft's stock price is rotting while Apple's shines. (Not much of a pun, but it was intended)

   Intel Corp. had from the early stages been a part of this arrangement between Microsoft and IBM, providing the X86 processors running PC-DOS/MS-DOS on PCs and PC clones. After PC clones came to dominate IBM-branded PCs the duopoly between Microsoft Windows OS and Intel was so dominant and tight that it came to be called: "Wintel." Also a victim of its own monopoly (actually a duopoly), Intel by the late 2000s has not been able to capitalize on newer markets requiring different chip designs–particularly those that consume less power–for the smartphone and tablet markets, which is where technology is heading for the future.

   The Wintel alliance started to unravel as a result of its sluggishness in penetrating new markets and in the late 2000s the two companies began to compete in each other's formerly exclusive domains.

Microsoft- Product Bundling/Product Tying

After Microsoft developed a virtual monopoly in operating systems and office software applications (Windows/Office), it is alleged to have used this virtual monopoly to penetrate and dominate other product categories, in particular: Web browsers. Microsoft bundled its Internet Explorer (IE) into the Windows OS, so that virtually all computers came pre-loaded with IE and were set up with very easy access to use it. This arrangement essentially killed off competitive browsers in the late 1990s and Microsoft was accused of illegal product tying. In the U.S. this was not proved in a long court battle, but in March 2010 the European Commission required Microsoft to offer a choice of browsers as part of the installation and upgrade processes. Within nine months, IE tumbled out of first place among browsers in the European market.

Google- Tying up strategic partners

In the case of Google, the company partnered with Yahoo Inc. in 2000 to begin providing search results for Yahoo. Yahoo set up this arrangement because Google had developed a much better search technology than had Yahoo, which at the time was the most popular search engine on the Web and much larger than the upstart Google. Due to the partnership, when a person used Yahoo to conduct a search, they saw that the results were provided by Google—thus giving Google wide exposure directly to its target market.

I do not know why the relationship ended, but I certainly know who lost out. After its upbringing Google launched from the nest as if by an ejector seat and began raptor-ripping great chunks from the market in a matricidal frenzy, soaring far ahead of its "mother" in search traffic, stock price, and revenue.

5) Company: Maryland Bank, National Association (MBNA)

Moat: Affiliation with member-based organizations

MBNA originated the concept of marketing credit cards through member-based organizations such as alumni associations and environmental groups. MBNA signed these groups to multi-year contracts, thus banishing its competitors to the hinterlands among these groups. MBNA had no patent on this strategy, but by its power the bank vaulted from obscurity to become for a time in the U.S the largest issuer of credit cards.

6) Company: Google Inc.

Moat: Nimbleness in the market

Google keeps a very close eye on what the market wants and how it can serve its customers in more ways than just providing search results. It constantly experiments, releasing beta versions of new products, and buys up innovative companies to bring them into the fold. By 2011, Google offered over 70 different online services for businesses and consumers and released a Chrome operating system that allows users to access and store all of their computing needs through the cloud. The Chrome operating system is intended eliminate the need of consumers and businesses to spend hundreds of dollars on Microsoft's Windows OS and Office Suite. In a Darwinian process, Google shuts down services that do not achieve success in the market.

7) Company: The Coca Cola Company

Moat: Effective branding

The Coca Cola Company of course has a trademark on the name Coca Cola. However, it is not this trademark that is valuable to the company; rather it is the brand reputation that the company has built around that trademark. I could start a soft drink company named Sunset Cola and protect it with a trademark, but what profit would that provide? None! I need to build a reputation for the brand in the marketplace that causes the trademark to have value and therefore provide profits to my business. If I were to actually start Sunset Cola, what would be the biggest hurdle I would face in trying to compete with Coca Cola? Of course it would be trying to assail their well-entrenched, stellar brand reputation.

8) Company: Apple Inc.

Moats: Relentless product innovation & user friendliness

Anyone with their eyes open can see that Apple's relentless product innovation has caused it to dominate its markets. Competitors simply cannot keep up. Not only does Apple innovate, but they hit the wants and needs of the consumer market dead-on nearly every time. Throughout its history, Apple products have been all about user-friendliness. Apple's Macintosh computer utilized a mouse and graphical user interface (GUI) while Microsoft-based PC users were still dealing with green-text command-prompt screens and the up, down, enter, delete buttons rather than the Mac's simple mouse-overs and clicks.

Apple did not invent the mouse or the GUI, but simply saw their value and adopted them at an early stage before others were really onto it. Apple did not introduce smart-phones to the market, but the tile-based user interface of the iPhone caused iPhone to take the market by storm. Apple did not invent the concept of downloading digital music but it created iTunes as a legal means for the public to do so at a time when all other popular means were illegal. iTunes quickly rocketed to the largest music retailer in the world, where it remains to this day. This position is not protected by a patent!

Apple has fully demonstrated that the best way to protect an invention is to build a successful business around it. Apple did receive a patent on its tiles-based interface for its iPhone, but all of its other marketing masterstrokes are what have devastated its competitors and keep them gasping for air. Apple shows beyond a doubt that if you have innovative products and innovative marketing, *you can be a juggernaut!*

9) Company: TIAA-CREF Corp.

Moat: Deep penetration within a market segment

The company name stands for Teachers Insurance and Annuity Association- College Retirement Equities Fund. Note that the name says nothing about selling insurance to accountants, truck drivers, hotel clerks, restaurateurs, steelworkers, farmers, mayors, or any other of the myriad groups that are in the market for insurance products. This is called *focus*! The company grew monstrous by focusing diligently on a narrow market that was large enough to grow monstrous in and ignored everyone else. If truck drivers want insurance, they are welcome to go elsewhere for it! This focus on a target market allowed TIAA-CREF to say to its target audience: "We are specialists that understand your needs better than any of the other generalists out that there that will sell their products to anyone who walks in their door."

If I am in the market for something as important to me as insurance and retirement products, I surely will purchase from someone that I believe understands my wants and needs better than anyone else and has created products customized for me.

It is interesting to note that TIAA-CREF is not only a marketing innovator, but a product innovator as well, having "invented" the variable annuity, now a mainstay of virtually all large life insurance companies.

10) <u>Company</u>: Amazon.com, Inc.

<u>Moat</u>: Pre-paid purchase plans

In 2005 Amazon.com introduced a new service offering called Amazon Prime that caused a word to pop into my head when I first learned of it—sort of like that psychological word-association exercise.

The word was: "Beautiful!"

The offering was pre-paid shipping. (I know… you wonder what I was smoking at the time. How could I get that excited about pre-paid shipping?)

So, why is this "beautiful?" Because it strikes at the very heart of competition among online retailers: the shipping charge. With its Prime program Amazon charges $79 for:

    a. a full year of free shipping on many orders that otherwise would incur a shipping charge
    b. reduced pricing on overnight shipping.

Now you and I both know that anyone paying $79 up front will ensure that they get maximum value for this investment; they will shop Amazon diligently instead of Amazon's competition for the *next full year*.

As a humorous little side note for you I have to tell you this: As I was researching online for this book to find the pricing of the Amazon Prime program—which I had forgotten—I came across a blog by Dave Taylor (*The Business Blog at Intuitive.com*) that gave an analysis of Amazon Prime when it was announced in 2005. In his analysis, Taylor began by saying: "This is a beautiful example of what a company can do…" So I guess I am not the only one who was smokin' something!

11) <u>Company</u>: Costco Inc.

<u>Moat</u>: membership

The membership fee that Costco and similar retailers charge acts in the same manner as Amazon Prime and is really another form of a pre-paid purchase plan.

12) <u>Company</u>: New York Times Co.

<u>Moat</u>: Subscriptions

Ditto for periodicals like newspapers and magazines with their subscription-based business model.

13) <u>Company/Product</u>: Apple Inc./iPhone

<u>Moat</u>: Ancillary products

The example of the apps for the iPhone recited earlier in this chapter illustrates that ancillary products can form a moat that holds competitors at bay.

14) <u>Company</u>: UnderArmour, Inc.

<u>Moat</u>: "Coolest" or "hippest" product persona

UnderArmour did the impossible. The upstart athletic apparel company smashed head-on into market-monster Nike, Inc. As a result, Nike now has a very big chink in its armor (pun intended) and is giving up ground in key markets. UnderArmour hit the market with shiny tight T-shirts that were made of moisture-wicking synthetics rather than cotton, which holds onto sweat and tends to stretch and fit loosely. Synthetic moisture-wicking apparel was not new at the time, but UnderArmour introduced it to a new market and in a new way.

Rather than focusing entirely on the performance of the apparel, the company's advertising featured dramatically lit muscular athletes wearing shiny skin-tight UnderArmour apparel that showed off the athletes' attractive physique. This created a very cool, very hip image that caused the viewer to think, sometimes actively and sometimes subliminally: "I want to be like that! This product will fulfill my fantasy of being a big macho athlete."

The ads had *impact*. And that impact created an *emotion*. That emotion created a *burning desire*. That burning desire created a *purchase*!

I have a funny little story to tell you about the impact of these ads. I am a hunter, and one day I was in Dick's Sporting Goods with my hunting buddy and we walked past a display of expensive new UnderArmour-branded camouflage hunting apparel. I was just about to comment sarcastically that I can't believe that anyone would pay that much just because of slick marketing when my friend belted out: "I want that. That's what I am asking for for Christmas."

As a result of emotional selling of a hip image, UnderArmour logos are showing up on team jerseys that were once Nike's exclusive domain and the company has muscled into Nike's turf of footwear, outerwear, sports bags, and more. I think that after a quarter-century of absolute domination by one company, consumers are ready for a change.

15) <u>Company/Product</u>: Energy Brands Inc./Vitaminwater

<u>Moat</u>: Attractive packaging

Later in this chapter I present the example of Energy Brands–also doing business as Glaceau–and its Vitaminwater product as an example of innovative packaging. You will read about how the enormous appeal of this packaging has created an immense barrier to others coming along with their otherwise-similar products.

CHOOSING AN ALLURING NAME AND LOGO

<u>Name</u>
The name of your company and its product(s) are very important. They say a lot to potential customers about your business and its products. You should carefully consider to whom you will be marketing and what type of message to which they would be most responsive. If your company or product were a person, what would be its personality? Try to convey this personality through your name.

It is also important to consider whether you plan to expand your product base in the future. In this case, it may be good to avoid a company name that is tied too tightly to your initial product. Cue up UnderArmour with its restrictive name, although I believe that its massive marketing push has gotten over this handicap.

Of course it is important to thoroughly check trademarks, both federal and state, before choosing your company or product names. You must also check business registrations in your state–typically through the Department of State–as not all business names will have been registered as a trademark.

Logo
Think about all of the logos you see everywhere. Why are logos plastered all over everything? Because a picture is worth a thousand words! Many companies have adopted a logo that simply conveys a feeling and contains no words, as does the Nike swoosh. Other sporting goods companies such as Reebok International Ltd. and UnderArmour have followed suit and emphasized their logo instead of their name. Such a strategy is known as *brand minimalism.*

In early 2011 Starbucks Corp. re-designed its logo, removing the circular "Starbucks Coffee" wording surrounding the mermaid image. The resulting logo became simply the mermaid set in a round green background, a change driven by the company's plans to expand its product line into non-coffee items.

Starbucks' move was quite gutsy, considering that just several months prior–in October 2010– Gap Inc. unveiled a new logo and pulled it from the market just a week later after failing to fend off withering consumer criticism of the new design.

Crowdsourcing
One major disadvantage of being an entrepreneur is that you do not have access to the many co-workers that you could interact with if you were at a large firm. This problem may manifest itself when you try to develop creative logos.

Like many other issues facing small businesses, the Internet can solve this problem, in this case through *crowdsourcing.* Websites that facilitate crowdsourcing allow you to post a description of what you want in a logo and then set it free in cyberspace for hundreds or thousands of minds to deliberate. You choose a winning design and pay the winning designer. There are quite a number of logo crowdsourcing Websites which you can find through a search engine.

GENERATING FREE PUBLICITY

Many newspapers, magazines and Websites will review new products. This is a very effective way to get free advertising. Local newspapers may do a write-up on your new business in addition to reviewing your product. Similar opportunities may exist with local radio or television stations in certain cities. Contact the appropriate editor and ask about opportunities.

The lead time for magazine articles can be up to six months or so. Be sure to submit your product well in advance of when you want the article to run, especially if your product sales are seasonal.

Corporate communication to the media is typically done via a news release, also known as a press release. A news release regarding the introduction of a new product is typically called a *new-product release* or a *product release* and that is how it should be titled.

You should provide the media with a professional-quality new product release and good quality digital images of your product. This reduces the workload for media personnel, as they can simply reproduce all or part of your review and photos. Note that they often do edit the release, so be sure that you are succinct and put the "good stuff" at the top, saving less important details for the latter portion of the release, which should be one to two pages double-spaced; preferably one page.

Pitfall: Including hyperbole and hype in your new-product release

If you fall into this pit, your new-product release stands a very good chance of being tossed in with you.

Media do not always run product releases for free. Particularly in magazines dealing with technology, there may be an advertising requirement or other fees involved, sometimes thousands of dollars. Other media, such as many magazines targeted to sportsmen, however, do not charge to run a release.

A new-product release is written similarly to a press release and a good description of how to write press releases is available at: http://www.wikihow.com/Write-a-Press-Release. Fee-based services related to press releases and release distribution are available at http://www.sightquest. com/business/example-of-press-release-2808.htm.

In addition to printing short product releases, many media will run full-length articles regarding a new product–sometimes free, sometimes for fee. Typically the article will detail the writer's use of the product. The writer may be on staff or freelance. You should find out who the writers are in your industry and get to know them. One easy way to find out who they are, of course, is to call the media or to review media looking for writers' names.

Another way to find writers that may write about your product is *Bacon's Media Directories* from Cision at: http://us.cision.com/products_services/bacons_media_directories_2011.asp, which lists over 250,000 reporters, editors, and columnists by subject area of interest in print, broadcast, and Internet media. There is a fee for this information.

There is usually no need to provide a product sample for a short product review, although it is usually necessary to do so if you want a feature-length article. You can request that the product be returned.

There are a number of distribution services that will get your product release out to the proper media. One free service is PR Log at http://www.prlog.org/. There are also fee-based services such as PR Web at http://www.prweb.com, PR.com at http://www.pr.com, and PR Newswire at http://www.prnewswire.com/.

Additionally, you should sign up as an expert on a subject area on the Help a Reporter Out Website at: http://www.helpareporter.com/. The service describes itself as follows: "Founded in 2008 by serial entrepreneur Peter Shankman, Help A Reporter Out (HARO) is one of the fastest-growing social media services in North America.

"Every day, HARO brings nearly 30,000 reporters and bloggers, over 100,000 news sources and thousands of small businesses together to tell their stories, promote their brands and sell their products and services.

"Since its inception, HARO has published more than 75,000 journalist queries, has facilitated nearly 7,500,000 media pitches, and has marketed and promoted close to 1,500 brands to the media, small businesses and consumers.

"HARO is entirely free to sources and reporters, and unlike a majority of social media services, is independently owned and funded and has been profitable since day one. In addition, HARO serves as a vital social networking resource for sources, reporters and advertisers who use the service at www.helpareporter.com."

SECURING ENDORSEMENTS AND TESTIMONIALS

Product endorsements by celebrities or authoritative people can be a very effective method of establishing a brand name and reputation for a new product. This approach should be considered if at all possible. As with anything, there are potential pitfalls, but the advantages usually outweigh the risks. One obvious risk is that your celebrity later receives bad publicity for something they are alleged to have done. You would normally have to get quite creative in order to make an arrangement in which the endorsement of a national celebrity is affordable. However, you can start out with local or regional celebrities such as coaches and local TV personalities.

An endorsement or seal of approval from a respected organization can have a dramatic impact on sales. Proctor & Gamble introduced its Crest toothpaste to the market in 1955, then in 1960 won the American Dental Association's Seal of Acceptance due to Crest's sodium fluoride additive, which was shown to reduce cavities among Crest users. After affixing the seal to the Crest package and advertising the endorsement, P&G saw its Crest sales boom, with a threefold increase in just two years.

Testimonials from satisfied customers are another highly effective means of convincing prospective customers that they should purchase your product. If you do want to use a testimonial, be sure to get a written release to do so from the individual or group. Marketing studies have shown that testimonials from satisfied customers are among the most highly effective marketing tools. Including a photo and the name of the satisfied customer will boost effectiveness even higher.

HELPFUL CLUBS AND ORGANIZATIONS

There may be clubs, organizations, professional societies, trade associations, unions, etc. whose members may be your target customers. For example: garden clubs; gourmet cooking clubs; investing clubs; fishing clubs; AAA; the American Medical Association; American Dental Association; AARP; carpenters unions, etc. The list is practically endless. Do your best to find these organizations and determine how to capitalize on the opportunity that they present. Just as was mentioned in the chapter on market research, the best way to determine how to capitalize on the opportunity is to ask this question to the organization.

Such clubs and organizations are extremely important for entrepreneurs without much money to spend on marketing. Think about it: Your target customers–otherwise dispersed throughout the general population of 300 million in the U.S. alone–have concentrated themselves into an available group of typically several tens or hundreds of thousands. Here they become much-easier pickings.

DOGGED DETERMINATION

If at first you don't succeed, try, try again. This adage is very important in entrepreneurship and also in marketing your new technology.

If thorough research has shown that you have a product that is manufacturable, economical, usable, desirable, otherwise viable in the market, and you have set up a sound business to support it, then don't let anything stop you! Once you have determined all of the above then the only thing left is **persistence**. This can mean *years* of persistence and coming at the problem in many different ways.

For instance if you have identified a great marketing venue and try it once or twice with limited results, you should take a thorough look at *why* it did not work, and then develop a plan for addressing the issues that stood in your way. Don't just fall down when you hit a defender–get back up, find another hole, and keep running for the goal line.

Inside Scoop: One of the worst things you can do in marketing is to drift aimlessly from one venue to another without ever stopping, driving a stake in the ground, and fighting it out.

One of the primary reasons that entrepreneurs find themselves drifting aimlessly from one marketing effort to another is that they are in a very tight cash situation and they cannot wait for their advertising efforts to begin paying off. They run a few ads and when that does not produce immediate revenue they go off and try something else in a desperate scramble for sales.

The vaccine for this malady, as I will discuss further below, is to refrain from getting yourself into such a tight cash situation in the first place.

THE POWER OF THE PACKAGE

Packaging is often given little thought by those new to the process of commercializing new products, but is an integral part of your product and its marketing. If you get everything else right but get the packaging wrong it can be like dragging an anchor in the market. On the contrary, exciting, creative, and innovative packaging can be like strapping a booster rocket onto your product. I will show you further below some fun and interesting examples of this critical concept in action.

Market research has confirmed the importance of package design in consumers' purchasing decisions. For instance, in an online survey conducted in January 2011, Consumer Edge Research found that 49% of the 2,000 respondents choose Coca Cola Company's Simply brand orange juice partially due to its nice packaging.

Inside Scoop: Your product must be carried to market inside of a rocket, not a buggy.

Various distribution channels may require various packaging types or concepts. Be sure that you understand the types of packaging that will be expected for your product in the various channels. For instance, some smaller stores may want a small high-value product to be displayed in a glass case or behind a counter, whereas large chains may want it to be displayed in a clamshell package with a security tag and hanging on a peg.

You need to be just as innovative in your packaging as in your product development and marketing. Large companies understand this.

22 Sales-Boosting Packaging Ideas
There are many examples of products that were reinvigorated by a simple re-packaging. For example: Dannon yogurt repackaged in containers with animal themes as Danimals to appeal to children. Another example is Yoplait GoGurt, which is yogurt packaged in flexible plastic tubes with a tear-top for "on the go" spoonless eating.

Interesting concepts, but do they work? Yes they do! The yogurt market doubled from 2000 - 2010 and this was attributed in late 2010 by General Mills, Inc.–maker of Yoplait and GoGurt in the U.S.–to being largely due to package innovations such as yogurt in a tube.

An extreme example of package power is when in 1969 Hanesbrands Inc. introduced pantyhose packaged in colorful plastic egg-shaped containers and called them L'eggs. Although the hosiery was the same as nearly all others on the shelf, L'eggs took the market by storm and for many years was the largest-selling brand of pantyhose. People were actually buying the package more so than the product inside it. This is said to be one of the most successful "new product" launches in history, although it was not really a new product launch at all–the pantyhose were not that unique–it was primarily just a "new packaging launch."

Other examples of the product-packaging-marketing link are: fruit drinks in aseptic cartons with an attached straw; "1/3 More Free" bottles of shampoo; individually wrapped slices of cheese, and coffee in foil-laminated bags. Some packaging innovations are designed to improve ease of product use, such as: plastic jugs for cat litter instead of paper sacks; squeeze bottles; pump bottles; spray bottles; "upside-down" ketchup bottles, "refrigerator pack" 12-pack dispenser-packs for Coke cans, and pull-top cans for Campbell's soup.

Speaking of cans: I am not sure if it is done deliberately or not, but I have noticed that some canned goods are packaged in cans in which the bottom is slightly smaller in diameter than the top, thus allowing the cans to be stacked well on the grocery shelf and of course also in the consumer's pantry. If I have the choice, I will buy a brand that is packaged in such a can in preference over a brand that is not. I guess that is the "neat-freak" in me coming through. I wonder if canned-goods companies think of the need for order and neatness when evaluating their customer's needs. It is not a primary decision point in my case, but it does have an influence.

Consider how soft drink companies have created myriad "products" simply through repackaging the same substance in different ways: 6-packs; 12-packs; 24-oz. bottles; 6-packs of ½-liter bottles; 2-liter bottles, soda fountains, etc.

These days, when someone enters a fast-food restaurant, they expect to see "value meals" and children's meals on the menu. But it was not always that way. McDonald's years ago "repackaged" its a la carte offerings into Extra Value Meals with great success that was copied by all of its competitors. In the case of the Happy Meal, there was an actual package involved. Bob Bernstein, owner of an advertising agency used by McDonald's, realized that kids liked to read cereal boxes while eating breakfast. He simply took this concept to lunchtime and designed a colorful box with games and cartoons to contain a hamburger and fries. Bernstein received a bronze replica of a Happy Meal on the tenth anniversary of its launch in recognition of his immense contribution to corporate profits.

Clamshell packaging has revolutionized product display and retail sales. (A *clamshell* is a semi-rigid clear plastic package–front and back–typically sealed around the edges.) A clamshell package is perceived as higher quality than a *blister package*, in which the backing is paperboard.

Another example of the power of packaging is the story of J. Darius Bikoff. Mr. Bikoff is credited with the invention of the "sports bottle" with the pop-up-nozzle top. This package is not only functional, but it creates for packages an aura of athleticism and fitness that becomes associated with products packaged in this type of container. Now the product becomes not just bottled water, but also a statement about the person using the product. (Hmm… water at $1.79 a bottle–how's that for a packaging miracle?)

After he developed the pop-up nozzle, Mr. Bikoff went on to found Energy Brands Inc., which markets Glaceau' Vitaminwater, a bottled water containing flavorings and vitamins. Glaceau' pioneered the concept of adding electrolytes, vitamins, and flavorings to bottled water and eventually became one of the leading brands in the natural foods category of bottled waters, bigger than Evian and Perrier, the previous bottled water market leaders.

Constantly innovating, Mr. Bikoff challenged his supplier to come up with a packaging concept that reflected the company's image and position in the market. The result was a metalized polypropylene label for Vitaminwater that gives the product a high tech look and feel.

Now, according to Glaceau corporate attorneys, more than half of the legal team's time is spent protecting Glacéau's most important asset: Vitaminwater's distinctive, trademarked packaging. Other companies sell a similar product, but Vitaminwater's packaging has played a definitive role the product's massive category domination, with sales upwards of $1 billion annually. Its labels are very eye-catching, with a sleek, minimalist design and bright bands of pink, purple, red, or yellow, along with the brand name running vertically in simple font.

It's amazing what creative packaging can do for plain ol' H2O!

What? Still not convinced about the power of packaging–I mean convinced enough to actually do something about it? Here is another interesting example of how packaging can affect products: For many years, ice cream was sold by supermarkets in rectangular paperboard cartons. Then, premium ice cream became available in round cartons. A number of years later, market research was done on consumer perceptions regarding rectangular and round ice cream cartons. The researchers found that in taste tests, 80% of consumers stated that ice cream packaged in round cartons was higher quality than ice cream packaged in rectangular cartons, *even when it was the same ice cream*!

A product's packaging says a lot to the consumer about the product itself. Packaging is extremely important, must be carefully considered, and the innovation process must be fully applied.

Pitfall: Using your head only by nodding it "yes"

Create New Products by Re-packaging Old Ones
A shining example of effective re-packaging is Activision Blizzard Inc.'s video game Guitar Hero, which re-packaged old rock songs into a video game in 2005 and over the next five years generated more than $3 billion in revenue. In this game the player pretends to play the guitar along with a virtual rock band shown on a video screen. Millions of units of the game have been sold, providing a nice new revenue stream for the rights-holders of the songs.

It is interesting to note that the rights holders did not re-package their own material; someone else did it for them. The band Aerosmith is said to have experienced a 40% boost in sales of their music in the months after the release of *Guitar Hero: Aerosmith* in 2008.

Alas, Guitar Hero's lightning riff did not last long; Activision announced that it plans to discontinue the game in 2011. At least one industry analyst stated that this shows the wisdom in selling a product that generates recurring revenue, rather than a product that creates a one-time sale as does Guitar Hero.

Boost Sales by Bundling

In the above illustration of the McDonald's Extra Value Meal, the combination of a hamburger, fries, and drink is an example of *product bundling*. If the process is carried out with services it is *service bundling*. Creation of six-packs of soda was a form of product bundling, although in this case each item in the bundle was the same. Bundling can be a very effective form of marketing as of course can be seen by the success of Extra Value Meals and six packs.

Tying—a Hidden Path to Profits

A marketing concept closely related to bundling is that of *tying*, in which the purchase of one product is made to be dependent upon the purchase of a different product. I will discuss *tying* here in the packaging section of this book as a form of "virtual packaging." Although entrepreneurs typically think little about it, if done properly, tying can be an effective means to boost profits.

Certain forms of tying may be considered anticompetitive and illegal. For instance: Tying the purchase of a popular product to the purchase of an unpopular product. If I were to say to a store that they had to purchase 100 units of my slow-selling item in order to be able to receive any of my hot-selling item, that could be considered illegal tying, especially if there was no natural relationship in which the two would need to be purchased together.

Tying related products as a means of marketing can be exceedingly effective. For example, as was discussed earlier, Microsoft in the late 1990s was alleged to have annihilated Netscape Navigator and other competitive browsers by tying its Internet Explorer Web browser to the purchase of its Windows operating system, the latter of which had a virtual monopoly in the personal computer market. In 1998 the U.S. brought suit against Microsoft for illegal tying in this arrangement. After a long trial and appeals process, Microsoft was not required to de-bundle its IE from Windows, although the European Commission in 2010 did require Microsoft to provide better access to competitive browsers.

Talking Packages

Your product's packaging can also provide a unique opportunity to communicate directly with actual customers and get their feedback regarding how and why they use your product, how they view its quality, why and where they purchased it, etc. Such information is especially important for innovative products. This can be accomplished by enclosing a warranty registration card that includes a questionnaire, printing a toll-free phone number on the package, or printing an email address, etc.

When a customer makes contact with you, you can query them about what features and benefits are especially important to them, what improvements they would like to see, what their lifestyle is, etc. Be careful, however, in accepting suggestions for product improvements. In this case you must understand the risks and legal issues involved. These are discussed later in the chapter on manufacturing in the licensing section, but in the present case you would be on the "other side of the fence" from the situations in that chapter. Be sure to seek competent legal advice.

A major international food company recently found that only 20% of calls made to the toll-free number printed on its packages represented consumers calling in with complaints. Many of the remainder was customers that had such a strong affinity for the product that they called in suggestions and otherwise provided valuable insights about product use, etc.

Packages That Jump Off the Shelf

Just kidding! Unfortunately, there are no packages that jump off the shelf and into a shopping cart. (Maybe you could invent that… but you could not patent it because I just now disclosed the idea). ☺ However, you must develop the next best thing to a package that automatically jumps into a cart: A package so appealing that consumers despite their best efforts cannot resist it.

In this regard you must focus with <u>absolute intensity</u> on creating that one highly critical motion that you must get the consumer to make. The one that sets up every other element of your grand plan. The one that the consumer is so incredibly loathe to make:

The arm extension!

If you cannot get a person to reach to the shelf or to the peg, you are dead in the water. An attractive, innovative package that clearly states the benefits is the one and only way to generate the arm extension. Save the lesser details for the back of the package; the second-most critical motion you must get a consumer to make is the "package flip."

Focus in the front on the most significant one, two, or three benefits; you only have a second or two to get the consumer to make that wisest of choices: arm exercise! The ugly alternative is leg exercise, and you know what that means.

Especially try to find a way to get your package to stand out from the crowd of similar items it must slum around with on the shelf.

<u>Inside Scoop:</u> It is very helpful to go to stores and study package innovation. I mean exactly that: Go to stores and spend hours studying packaging innovation. Take a cue from what others have done and put your creative mind to work!

Donning Trade Dress

When dealing with packaging, it is important to understand the concept of *trade dress*. Trade dress is a distinctive, non-functional design aspect, typically of packaging, but sometimes of product, that signifies to the consumer the source of the goods. This distinctiveness can be either inherent or acquired.

Trade dress is a form of intellectual property and is protectable under trademark laws. An instructive example of a trade dress case that went all the way to the U.S. Supreme Court in 2000 is found at http://www.law.cornell.edu/supct/html/99-150.ZS.html.

The key in the above definition is: "that signifies the source of the goods." Trade dress is similar to trademarks in this regard. A good illustration of trade dress would be the design of a Coke can, with its red background and two swirled white stripes. For instance, it would not be permissible to market a soft drink in a red can with several straight white stripes, as this would constitute confusion by deception. This was actually attempted by a soft drink company in the 1970s and it was ruled impermissible.

In another illustration of trade dress: Glaceau may not be able to stop competitors from selling brightly colored flavored water containing vitamins, but has been very successful in preventing them from selling products that imitate too closely Vitaminwater's distinctive two-toned labels with a horizontal color band and its bell-shaped bottle.

It is important to understand concepts of trade dress, because if you infringe on the trade dress of another, you are liable to civil legal action by that party. Also, if you can develop your own trade dress, this will assist you in protecting your place in the market when competitors come along.

As I mentioned, a design element of the product itself may constitute trade dress. So how is protection of product design through the trademark system different than protection of product design through the patent system via a design patent? It is primarily this: If you have a unique product design, but a consumer would not be able to look at that design and know that it came from your company as opposed to some other company, the design does not constitute trade dress. You would need to consider a design patent if you wanted to protect that design from imitation.

Securing Bar Codes

Well, we have taken a look at most of the fun, sexy aspects of packaging, but we have to take care of the more mundane business as well, and that is the subject of bar codes for your product, typically applied to the package.

Bar codes were set up by the Uniform Code Council (UCC) and today are administered in the U.S. by the nonprofit GS1 US. The system was initiated in the 1970s by U.S. grocery chains as the *Uniform Product Code (UPC code)* and has since spread to a great many other products worldwide as the *European Article Number (EAN)*. The EAN is basically the UPC with an extra digit added to allow application to far more products so that it may be used globally. Although the name EAN originally denoted "European," the system is now universal around the globe including the U.S.

Various consultants are available to assist you with obtaining bar codes for your products. Be sure to shop around if you decide to hire one, however, as pricing and services can vary greatly among them.

CRITICAL LESSONS IN BRANDING

Branding is a very complex and ethereal subject. Very simplistically, a brand is a name and/or associated image that identifies the source of goods or services, and as such, may be trademarked. *Branding*, however, is the difficult process of building value into that name or image. Branding is the process of creating the feeling in the mind of the market that the brand owner wants to be conjured up when the market sees or hears of the brand.

$150 Billion Can't Be Wrong

The American public has been whipped into submission by brand messaging. We want desperately to buy brands. U.S. advertising spending in 2008 exceeded $150 billion, much of it blasting the brand message through the brains of the populace. The carpet-bombing cannot be avoided. Swoosh has become our nation symbol, worn by unashamed football players so they can buy, perhaps, an additional Ferrari.

Successful brand managers at major corporations make huge salaries, and for good reason. A Google search on the term "branding seminar" yields 1,510,000 results, also for good reason.

Inside Scoop: *When you take your technology to market, you will experience branding in one of two ways: Either by watching in amazement at how your effective branding keeps your competitors face-down in the mud or by staring in horror at how your competitor's effective branding keeps your target customers buying inferior products.*

Nothing but Brand

The best example that I can think of to illustrate the concept of branding is bottled water. A close second is premium vodka. Water is of course, *water* and vodka is simply pure alcohol mixed with water. The Bureau of Alcohol, Tobacco, Firearms and Explosives–which sets the rules for the U.S.–defines vodka as without distinctive character, aroma, taste or color. Yet look at the myriad brands that have been developed around these commodity products, each brand attempting to impart various emotional aspects to their offerings.

The advertising campaign devised for Absolut vodka was recognized by *Advertising Age* magazine as one of the top 100 advertising campaigns of the 20th Century. The success of this branding effort eventually led to many other successful efforts to create an ultra-premium segment of the "pure water & pure alcohol" market, with Grey Goose, Chopin, and Armadale among them.

Once this lucrative trick was accomplished by vodka marketers, the rest of the spirits industry rose from decades in the grave of staid product promotion and took notice. Now you will find premium and ultra-premium bourbon, rum, tequila, and any other spirit genied-up in creative new packaging.

For a fun little "side trip," you may want to read an interesting article from *Slate* at: http://www.slate.com/id/2106004/ in which the author conducts a taste test of premium vodkas.

Create Your Brand Image

Branding can perhaps best be described as the way that you make your market feel about your product or service. A brand paints a picture in your customer's mind. This is referred to as your *brand image*. It is very structural, underlies your entire business, and it flavors everything you do. It is who you are. Learn about it!

Here is the world's shortest course on brand image:

Chevrolet – Ferrari

Enough said?

COMPETITION: WHERE DOES IT LURK?

As mentioned previously, many people are brand loyal. We have seen that this fact is very important in competition. Let's take a look at another important factor.

An unconventional and stark way to view competition is this: *There is always competition for a dollar!* You are in competition with the mortgage company, the grocery store, the cellular phone company, the travel agent, the bank savings account, and every restaurant in town. You must get your customer to choose you instead of all of the other companies out there vying for the customer's dollar. This is the choice that your customer is making.

As an example of the above, consider a man who has several hobbies, among them golf and fly-fishing. This gentleman sees several ads for a new fly-fishing rod and finally takes the action the manufacturer so lusts by going to the sporting goods store to buy it. On the way back to the fishing department he passes a nice display of fancy new driver golf clubs with the latest space-age technology and with one end the size of a basketball (which is where driver size is "heading", I think). Now he remembers the horrible drives he had in his last few rounds of golf and the ceaseless ribbing he took from his buddies.

His wife will "kill" him if he comes home with both a new fly rod and a new driver, each costing around $250. Very importantly, he realizes that fly-fishing is generally a solitary sport, but he golfs with at least three of his buddies. He will be able to show off a new driver and his improved performance, but with a new fly-fishing rod, not so. Before he makes it back to the rear of the store he picks up the driver and heads for the checkout. I can assure you that the person who introduced the fly-fishing rod to the market did not consider golf club manufacturers to be competition, but indeed they are.

Inside Scoop: *Never* think that you have no competition!

PRICING FOR PROFITS

Pricing, like most other aspects of technology commercialization, is quite complex. There are many factors to consider in pricing and many pricing strategies. I will provide a brief overview here. However, there are many references available on this subject and it would be useful to study a few if you are not familiar with this subject.

Importance of Average Selling Price

One key pricing issue that is often overlooked: In setting your price, be sure to consider the average selling price of your technology, not just the list price that you set. There may be discounts from list price that are normally given in your industry or channel of distribution. The *average selling price* is the average price that you actually receive after all of these discounts. The more common discounts include:

- In-house salesperson's commissions
- Manufacturer's representative commissions
- A 2% discount for payment of invoices within 10 days
- A 20 –25% discount for stocking distributors
- Discounts to buying groups, etc.
- Special sale price promotions
- Slotting fees
- A 2% co-op advertising allowance

A couple of definitions are in order here: 1) A *slotting fee* is a fee that a manufacturer pays to a retailer to secure shelf space. This is very common in the grocery business, but not so in other retail segments. 2) Manufacturers will often offer retailers a rebate of 2% of the amount of prior-year purchases to be used by the retailer to advertise the manufacturer's products in the store's sale circulars, etc. This is called a *2% co-operative (co-op) advertising allowance.*

Developing a Pricing Strategy

Inside Scoop: *Be sure to set your list price high enough that you can pay the commissions, fees, support, and give the discounts required, yet still secure the revenue you need. This is why you see products on the shelf marked with a suggested retail price of, for instance, $19.95, but the store is selling the item for $16.95; the manufacturer has set the list price high enough that everyone in the distribution channel can offer a "discount."*

Common pricing strategies include:

1) Determine your cost of production and mark it up by a certain percentage.
2) Determine what the competition charges and price accordingly
3) Determine what the market will bear and price accordingly
4) Set a price and persuade people to pay it

FYI: I really, really like strategy number four. The first three sound very boring!

Of course option number four is not that simple. You must ensure that your price provides you with a viable business. Also, you obviously must be able to actually persuade people to pay the price that you ask.

In general, though, if you have a product that will be sold to a wholesaler or distributor, then to a retailer, and finally to a consumer, you should set your suggested retail price at least four times your cost of production (or your cost of acquisition if you are purchasing the product from a contract manufacturer). Shopping channels such as HSN or QVC will typically want to sell items at four times the amount they pay for them. The same rule of thumb applies if you direct-sell through your own TV commercials–a 4X markup.

Common Pricing Structures
A typical pricing structure for hard goods that may be sold through a distributor or to a member of a buying group is given below. In this scenario you would be the "manufacturer" even though you may contract out the manufacturing. In this example I have for clarity not included master distributors, which may participate in certain distribution channels:

Manufacturer's suggested retail price (MSRP)=	$10.00
Cost of manufacture or acquisition=	$2.50
Mfr's selling price to a retailer=	$5.00
Mfr's selling price to a stocking distributor=	$3.75
Stocking distributor's selling price to a retailer=	$5.00
Mfr's selling price to a buying-group member=	$4.75
Retailer's selling price to consumers=	$8.33
Mfr's selling price if sold directly to consumers=	$10.00

In the above structure, the manufacturer has *gross margins* (selling price divided by cost of goods) of: 50% on sales directly to retailers that do not belong to a buying group; 33% on sales to distributors, and 45% on sales to members of buying groups. The stocking distributor in turn has a 25% gross margin on sales to retailers. The retailer has a 40% gross margin on sales to consumers unless the retailer is a member of a buying group, in which case his margin is 43%.

Note that the product is often not actually sold by retailers for $10.00; that is just the MSRP set by the manufacturer so that he can give the expected "discounts" to the players involved in the distribution chain.

The chart above illustrates pricing structure in a way intended to assist you in understanding it, but it is not presented in the terms that are commonly used in business. Pricing in such scenarios is given as discount percentages. Using common business terminology, the above pricing structure in the trade channel would be given as follows:

MSRP =	$10.00
Less 50% to retailer =	$5.00
Less 25% to stocking distributor =	$3.75 (% off standard $5.00 retailer price)
Less 5% to buying group =	$4.75 (% off standard $5.00 retailer price)

Note that in the above example, the "less 50% to retailer" means a 50% discount from the MSRP. However, the other discounts are referenced to the selling price to an independent retailer, which is considered to be your highest standard wholesale price.

Remember that all of the other discounts such as salesmen's commissions, slotting fees, 2% co-op advertising allowance, etc. may reduce the manufacturer's actual receipts as well.

Particulars of Profit Margins
In general, profit margins are lower for hard goods than for soft goods such as clothing. Whereas many retailers are satisfied with a 40% gross margin on hard goods, they often can get 50% or more for soft goods, fashion items, etc. The same trend is true for computer hardware vs. software, but normally much more strongly so. Also, it is often easier to defend your price against price competition if you sell a service than if you sell a product.

For these reasons, savvy investors will typically prefer to invest in companies selling computer software or soft goods rather than those selling computer hardware or other hard goods.

Product Returns
I often get questions from entrepreneurs about what happens to product that their distributor, retailer, etc. is unable to sell. Can the distributor or retailer return the unsold product for a refund? Such return of unsold inventory is not standard business practice and you should avoid it. The only product category that I am aware of that is commonly sold on a returnable basis is periodicals such as magazines. Periodicals cannot be left indefinitely on store shelves. Other than periodicals, it is up to the retailer to mark down slow-moving inventory to get it to sell.

Protecting Price Lists
Most companies that sell to businesses (B to B or B2B) are highly protective of their price lists and their pricing structures throughout the distribution channel. You may want to consider this strategy as well. You generally do not want your competitors knowing your pricing structure.

One way to facilitate this is to refrain from putting pricing information on your marketing brochures. Maintain a separate price list, or separate price lists, that you can give out only to those to whom you want to provide the information. For printed materials this also makes sense because you can adjust your pricing without having to print new marketing brochures, which are typically expensive to produce. A price sheet can be printed on much less expensive paper, in black ink.

You generally must offer the same price to similar buyers, not favoring one buyer over the other without good reason.

Minimum Resale Price/Minimum Advertised Price
The practice of setting a minimum price at which a distributor or retailer may sell your product is known as *resale price maintenance* or maintaining a *minimum resale price.*

For decades manufacturers were prohibited by law from setting minimum resale prices, but in 2007 the U.S. Supreme Court overruled previous rulings that had established this policy and it is now legal in most instances. A related concept is *minimum advertised price* (MAP), which is a minimum price at which a manufacturer decrees that its product may be advertised by retailers. It is now also legal for a manufacturer to set a MAP.

Dangers of Competing on Price
In the business world it is normally considered unwise to compete on price alone. This is especially true if you are a small startup. A large corporation can undercut your price and compensate for the loss with revenues from other products that they sell. You will have to make your own judgment as to the likelihood of this happening to you and how you would respond if it does. Maybe your costs are so low that you could drop your price to match the large company. There are examples of companies that have successfully competed primarily on price, such as Wal-Mart. There are other examples of companies that were stomped into oblivion because they tried to compete on price alone, such as—well—you've never heard of them because they were stomped into oblivion!

Pitfall: Assuming that your costs will be lower than the "big bloated corporations"

If you think that your costs will be lower than the big bloated corporations, you had better be very sure of this, because it is quite unlikely. Large corporations have very efficient manufacturing facilities and supply chains. They purchase in large volumes that give them discounts. Many of them are *vertically integrated*, which means that they own a large portion of their supply chain. An example of vertical integration is Henry Ford, who built his own steel mills when he had difficulty getting supply from existing steel companies. Ford did not have to pay a profit margin to somebody else in order to receive the steel for his primary product. That reduces cost!

YOUR MOST CRITICAL MARKET

Well, now that you know a bit about pricing, your next challenge will be in determining to whom to charge that appealing price.

Pitfall: "Help me! I can't focus on a target market."

A terrifying yet near-universal mistake among first-time entrepreneurs is a profound and inexplicable inability to identify and focus on an initial target market. This is one of the most pervasive blemishes among the otherwise-dazzling clients I have served and it has driven me to distraction for many years!

Inside Scoop: It really does not matter to whom you intend to sell after you are large and well-established; this is moot if you die before you get there.

A tightly focused marketing effort to a tightly focused market on your first day; first week; first month, and first year in business will allow you to get established and start generating positive cash flow. You can then worry about customers in years two through infinity. (I am *not* suggesting that you create a product for which there is an insufficient total available market.)

A lack of initial focus on a tight market niche is often fatal in a most excruciating way, or at a minimum, it causes you to keep begging investors for more and more money to sustain your business until you start generating positive cash flow. Eventually your investors will wise up and stop "throwing good money after bad." Then things for you will get really tough.

The easy answer that everyone ignores is to start with a well-defined niche that is small enough for you to "chew," as in: "Don't bite off more than you can chew." It takes an onslaught of marketing, with some real "horsepower" behind it, to get any one prospective customer to make a purchase. Most startup entrepreneurs simply cannot afford to sustain this onslaught toward a large group. And contrary to what many believe, a Website does not magically negate this fact.

Inside Scoop: Here is the secret to launching a new technology:

1) Pick a niche to which you can effectively market.
2) Devise a creative strategy to gain the attention of that niche.
3) Execute a campaign that ensures the message is received and believed.
4) Check to see if it's working.
5) Adjust as necessary.

Here are a couple of fun little hypothetical situations that illustrate this point:

The Hamburger-stand Example
Suppose that I start a business and my business plan consists entirely of the following:

1) Establish a hamburger stand near you.
2) Sell you a hamburger.
3) Close down.

Suppose I have $10,000 in marketing funds with which to accomplish my goal of selling you a hamburger. Assuming that you are in the market for hamburgers, do you think that I could accomplish my goal in my first three months of business with $10,000 to spend, great marketing materials, and years of relevant marketing expertise? Of course I could!

Now, assume that my business plan says to sell every hamburger-eater in the world a hamburger in my first three months of business, with $10,000 to spend on marketing. What are the chances of accomplishing that goal? Nada! Why is this?

Here is another illustration of this very crucial point:

The Cavemen Illustration
Suppose that there are two cavemen hunters standing in a woods looking out into a field. In the field are various animals: numerous rabbits, a group of moose, and several mammoths. The goal of the cavemen is to secure as much meat as they can for their tribe. The only weapons

141

they have at their disposal are golfball-sized stones. Which prey do you suggest that they attack in order to achieve their goal?

Now, suppose that there are two modern hunters staring out into a field. In the field are various animals: numerous rabbits, a group of moose, and several elephants. (Yeah, I'm aware of where moose and elephants actually live.) ☺ The goal of the hunters is to secure as much meat for their party as they can. The weapons they have at their disposal are large-bore elephant guns. Which prey do you suggest that they attack in order to achieve their goal?

Now, in each situation what was the determining factor in your suggestion regarding the prey that the hunters should attack? Of course, the prey depends on the weapons that the hunters have at their disposal!

In this example the hunters represent entrepreneurs, the stones or rifles represent their financial resources, and the animals represent the customers that the entrepreneurs must secure.

Think about it... when you first start out, you can usually buy only very limited marketing "weaponry." You have golfball-sized stones. Therefore you must attack "prey" upon which that weaponry can be effective. This means a truly small and focused niche market–rabbits. As tempting as it is to go after the moose or mammoths, your efforts will never succeed–short of a miracle–if you just dumbly throw small stones at moose and mammoths.

Pitfall: Instead of attacking the rabbits with the stones, virtually all of the entrepreneurs that I have ever met decide to directly attack the mammoths with the stones.
This does not work!

In developing your marketing plan, you need to think about what marketing effort would be necessary to get just one individual within a target market to purchase your new product. It is very safe to assume that no individual will respond to your first, second, third, or even sixth marketing contact. For instance, it may take seeing your ad several times, followed by an email, followed by a visit to your Website, followed by hearing you as a presenter at a conference, followed by a phone call from you, followed by a personal visit. (BTW, you cannot just guess at this process. You must talk to someone who truly knows the answer by virtue of having gone through it him or herself.)

In any case, the amount effort will always be *substantial*. Now, think about how many people on whom you have the money to deploy that amount of marketing. The size of that market is very small, analogous to a rabbit. Think about a concept I call "marketing horsepower." Do you have the "marketing horsepower" to deliver the above type of marketing effort to, for example, all small business owners in the U. S.?

If you are throwing stones, you must hunt rabbits, not mammoths!

A "rabbit" could be a large corporation or a few large corporations, but it is not an entire industry group of corporations. A "rabbit" could be a subset of expectant mothers, but it is not all expectant mothers in the U.S. A "rabbit" could be small businesses, but not all small businesses in the U.S.–not even all small accounting firms in the U.S.–this is still too big. But perhaps your "rabbit" is all small accounting firms in your metropolitan area, your section of the state, or perhaps your state, depending on the population sizes.

142

The point is to look around at what marketing "weaponry" you have and then attack the appropriate "prey." If you want to go after the big game, you must first secure the big weaponry. This is a major reason that many Silicon Valley tech startups go after $10 – 20 million in investments very early in their life cycle. They intend to go directly after the mammoth markets and they know that in order to do so, they must secure the proper weaponry.

Now, just for fun, let me throw a big kink into what I said above: If you are astute, you will have discovered a glaring flaw in my cavemen example. Can you tell me what it is?

[Please hum the *Jeopardy!* "waiting" tune here.]

Here's a hint: It is in the "cavemen" section of the example, not the "modern hunter" section.

Got the answer? No?

Here's another hint: I deliberately used the word "dumbly" when referring to throwing stones at moose and mammoths.

Give up?

OK, here it is:

[Please do not read further until you are done with the *Jeopardy!* tune]

Elsewhere in this book I talk about the three basic marketing weapons that you have at your disposal. These are:

The Three Basic Weapons of Marketing
   1) Money
   2) Time
   3) Creativity

The flaw in the cavemen example is that in it I have ignored time and creativity. I did this for simplicity, but also to help illustrate the point that follows.

First, let's examine the issue of time. Unfortunately, this weapon is not always in your marketing arsenal. Many entrepreneurs get themselves into situations where they do not have the luxury to take advantage of time as a weapon. They have loans to pay, investors' or their own unrealistic expectations to fulfill, etc., which cause the dire need to generate large amounts of revenue very quickly.

In the cavemen example, an analogous situation would be that the cavemen and the tribe relying on them for sustenance are all starving–a hair's breadth from death's door. These hunters do not have the luxury of taking the time to use their brains and get creative in capturing their prey; they must hurl their small stones and collect the proceeds immediately.

If the cavemen and their tribe are instead well fed, with a stockpile of dried meat already stashed away, the hunters have time to effectively use their stones to capture the meaty moose or mammoths instead of the scrawny little rabbits by using their most devastating weapon of all: THEIR BRAIN!

The cavemen could devise a sling to throw the stones with great force; they could use the stones to weight the perimeter of a big net, which would help them hurl it over a large animal; they could use the small stones to chip bigger rocks–fashioning the rocks into digging implements–and then use those implements to dig a pit trap; they could use the small stones to chip flint and affix it to the ends of spears, they could... well, you get the point (no pun intended).

OK... it was intended.

The common element with each of the above solutions for using golfball-sized stones to take down large prey is that they all require time to:

1) Survey the situation

2) Create the idea

3) Implement the solution

They also require planning and coordination of efforts. These things sound a lot like what makes us human, don't they? In your marketing, you need take advantage of the "gifts God gave you" instead of dumbly throwing your stones at the mammoths.

Your brain is your most devastating weapon–Use it!

You can attack the larger markets with meager resources, but only if you get extremely creative, spend $1 to get $10 worth of "bang," and have the time to wait for these efforts to pay off.

First, however, you must prepare yourself to be able to take advantage of these "gifts God gave you" by not getting yourself into a situation in which you are financially a hair's breadth from death's door.

The cavemen illustrate the use of and the differences between the three basic marketing weapons of:
1) Money
2) Time
3) Creativity

FIRST MARKET/FIRST BLOOD

In order to apply what you have learned regarding targeted marketing, you must think about who would be your very first customer generated through a true marketing effort. A sale made directly by you does not count, unless that is your marketing plan going forward. You also need to define exactly how you would secure that very first customer through an arms-length marketing effort. Then, think about how many similar people you could persuade to purchase through that marketing effort, considering the tools at your disposal and the likely response rates.

Does the scenario make sense? Are the numbers there? Is that the right niche? Is it the right niche for launch, but so small that you will almost immediately need to move up to a larger one? (Nothing wrong with that as long as you realize it beforehand.) Once you start to think about these things you can start developing a marketing *PLAN*.

FOCUS ON A DISTRIBUTION CHANNEL

Note that a tight focus on a channel of distribution or a method of marketing may be an acceptable substitute for a focus on a targeted group of customers; for instance: Effective use of the Internet or dynamic direct-mail campaigns.

I have a client that for its first two years in business was struggling to sell more than around $50,000 per year in innovative lighting products that could be purchased by either commercial or consumer customers. The owners talked about selling to consumers via the Internet and had a rudimentary Website, but no effective use of it. On the commercial side, they attempted to sell to municipalities, hospitals, casinos, universities, public schools, and "corporations," (i.e. everyone). Despite my repeated admonishments that this strategy (Actually: Lack thereof) would not lead to success, and that a focus was required, for two years nothing changed.

Then the son of one of the owners graduated from college and came aboard. He was given the task of optimizing the Internet sales, which he learned about and then focused on and at which he was highly successful. After 18 months of intensive focus and *effective* use of the Website, the company was selling products to a range of customers over the Internet at a rate of $1.8 million per year! Yes, you read that right: the application of a focus in their marketing efforts allowed them to go from $50,000 per year to $1.8 million per year in only 18 months. In this case the focus was on a means of marketing rather than a customer group.

After the fact, I asked the owner what was the reason for their success and the owner stated: "We focused our marketing efforts."

It is interesting to note that after about a year of effective use of the Internet to sell to a broad range of customers, the client began to discern that a certain group of customers purchased more product than other groups. The client then began to focus its marketing efforts on this group. In this case, the group of customers on which they should focus their marketing efforts identified themselves!

PRODUCT-LINE DEVELOPMENT

As mentioned earlier in this chapter, the proper selection of the products that you are offering to the market is a very important consideration in marketing. This starts with the fact that it is nearly impossible to sustain a large high-growth company on only one product. Large companies and many smaller ones are very reluctant to open up a new vendor account for a vendor with only one product to sell them.

Therefore if you develop–for instance–a new product that attaches to the end of a hose and that is to be used by consumers to wash their cars in their driveways, you must think of yourself as entering the automobile cleaning accessories market or perhaps some market even larger. Plan immediately for your follow-on products.

STAYIN' ALIVE

Although I absolutely detest that 1970s disco hit by the Bee Gees, and using the title here caused an unpleasant tune to get stuck in my head (yours too?) it is the most appropriate title for what I am about to tell you.

After reading this chapter you may get the idea that I am proposing that marketing is the only thing critical to new technology commercialization. Nothing could be further from the truth. Let's take a closer look at the various criteria for success, though.

If you think about it, a business is the same as a life in that both require certain inputs in order to survive. They cannot just continue along under conditions of total neglect. So let's take a look at what it takes to make each survive. Below are listings of five major inputs necessary to maintain a life and to maintain a business. The lists are not exhaustive, especially for business.

LIFE ESSENTIALS
Water
Food
Sleep
Air
Shelter

BUSINESS ESSENTIALS
Product
People
Market research/Marketing
Quality
Customer Service

First, let's take a look at what it takes to maintain a life. If you were to ask me whether any of the inputs listed can be neglected I would say: "Absolutely not." Each is definitely essential to maintain life. The same is true of the list for business.

However, in the list for life, one item stands far above the others in its importance. Which one is it?

It's <u>AIR!</u>

If you have no air, can you die of lack of sleep? If you are not breathing, can you perish from thirst or starvation? How about lack of shelter? All of the inputs are essential, but there is one that will "get you" before all of the others, isn't there.

<u>Inside Scoop:</u> In business, marketing is air.

If you cannot sell your product, it does not matter whether you have good customer service, because you will have no customers to service. Ditto for product quality–you cannot have a reputation in the market for a quality product if not enough people have experienced that quality to cause the market to understand this.

Regarding your precious technology: If you have done poor market research, you may well have developed the wrong product for the market. You don't even really need a product at all. Many businesses have successfully sold "vapor ware" or taken advance orders for technologies and then did not deliver them.

These are the theoretical reasons why proper market research and marketing is of the greatest importance to your business. But here is the practical reason: I see it happen with my clients every day! The ones that struggle do so because of lethargic marketing or because they built their business on a crumbling foundation of poor market research.

BASICS OF SELLING TO THE GOVERNMENT

The U.S. federal government is the largest purchaser of goods and services in the world. It may be beneficial to consider government markets: federal, state, and local, including school districts and public university systems.

The term *government procurement* refers to the government's purchases of goods and services. Highly complicated, government procurement will not be covered in full detail here and I again of course refer you to qualified consultants if you plan to pursue this avenue. A couple of important points to consider are that there is a great deal of "red tape" involved and the federal government generally will not do business with a startup entity with less than a two-year commercial track record.

Remember that even though you are dealing with a huge impersonal federal agency, it is people that make the decisions and it is very helpful to learn who is involved in the decision-making and influencing processes and to develop a warm personal rapport with them. This includes both the procurement officer who makes the actual decision from whom to purchase and the person at the agency that decided previously that the agency needed the item or service in the first place. These are usually two different individuals or departments.

Federal contracts are often awarded through a bidding process and at times it is the low-price bidder that wins. There are exceptions to both the bidding and low-price scenarios, however. For purchases under $100,000 and particularly for purchases under $10,000, competitive bidding may not be required. Purchases under $2,500 do not require competitive bidding and may be made via credit card, so be sure that you can accept credit cards if this scenario applies to you.

If you sell to the federal government you will be subject to the *Federal Acquisition Regulations (FAR)*, which are very complicated. Your procurement officer should be able to assist you with understanding these regulations. Information is available online at: https://www.acquisition.gov/Far/. Companies selling to the Department of Defense are subject to the Defense Federal Acquisition Regulations (DFAR), and information regarding them is available at: http://www.acq.osd.mil/dpap/dars/dfarspgi/current/index.html.

DUNS AND CAGE NUMBERS

The federal government tracks entities that conduct business with it though two codes: the Dun & Bradstreet Universal Numbering System *(DUNS) Number*, which is a number assigned by the private business Dun & Bradstreet, and the Commercial and Government Entity *(CAGE) Code*, which is assigned by the federal government. The DUNS number can be secured on the Dun & Bradstreet Website at: http://smallbusiness.dnb.com/ and the CAGE code can be secured by registering with the federal government though the Central Contractor Registration (CCR) site at: https://www.uscontractorregistration.com/index.php?option=com_chronocontact&Itemid=69. Note that it may take several days after registration to receive your CAGE number.

Government Set-Asides for Women, Minorities, Etc.
Federal law sets a goal that 23% of all federal contract awards should go to small businesses. There are also goals for small businesses owned and actually controlled (don't try to cheat on this!) by women, minorities, service-disabled veterans, and small businesses located in *Historically Underutilized Business (HUB) Zones*. A HUB Zone is a region that has been declared economically depressed. You can find if you are located in a HUB Zone at: http://map.sba.gov/hubzone/init.asp. The Department of Veterans Affairs sets a goal for 7% of all of its contracts to go to veteran-owned small businesses. Note that in the case of the VA there is no requirement for a service-related disability.

One of the mechanisms by which the federal government facilitates the award of contracts to businesses owned and controlled by socially or economically disadvantaged individuals is the

8(a) Business Development Program administered by the Small Business Administration. More information can be found at: http://www.sba.gov/content/8a-business-development.

Finding Procurement Opportunities

The federal government posts all contract solicitations and awards that are in excess of $25,000 at http://www.fedbizopps.gov. You can use this site to find which agencies purchase items or services such as yours. Be aware that many agencies purchase items that many people would not expect; this is especially true of the Department of Defense.

The *Federal Procurement Data System* lists summary information for federal purchases below the $25,000 threshold. It is available at: https://www.fpds.gov/fpdsng_cms/.

It is useful to contact the procurement offices of each federal agency to which you are considering selling. The SBA Website lists federal procurement offices and has much more information regarding federal procurement at: http://www.sba.gov/category/navigation-structure/contracting/contracting-opportunities.

The *GSA Schedule* is a listing of businesses that the General Services Administration has cleared as eligible to conduct business with the federal government. If you are listed on the GSA Schedule, the agency with which you are attempting to conduct business does not have to do its own investigation on your eligibility; it can simply refer to the GSA Schedule. This will greatly facilitate your ability to do business with federal agencies. More information is available at: http://www.gsa.gov/portal/content/104447

Free Help From PTACs

The U.S. Defense Logistics Agency operates Procurement Technical Assistance Centers (PTACs) in locations across the country. These entities provide low or no-cost services to assist small businesses in selling to federal, state, and local government entities. If you are unfamiliar with so doing, it is highly recommended that you contact the PTAC that covers your region of the country.

A PTAC can assist you with registering as a women, minority, or service-disabled-veteran owned business, for example. The federal and some state and local governments set targets for purchasing a certain amount of goods and services from these types of businesses. More information is available at: http://www.dla.mil/db/procurem.htm.

Benefitting From Government Subcontracts

The federal government requires large *prime contractors* to sub-contract a certain amount of their large contracts–typically ten percent–to small businesses, particularly those owned and controlled by women, minorities, and service-disabled veterans. Many large prime contractors have departments specifically set up to facilitate subcontracting to these small businesses. A common name for such department is the Office of Small and Disadvantaged Business Utilization. Be sure to contact these companies to see if there are any opportunities available for you.

SELLING TO LARGE CORPORATIONS

Basics of Strategic Selling

For many entrepreneurs, making a sale to a *Fortune* 500 company is the Holy Grail. Almost always this will involve *strategic selling*, which is a sales process that involves contacting, understanding the needs of, and developing a rapport with a number of decision makers and influencers and typically has a long sales cycle. The entire process of strategic selling is beyond the scope of this book, but there are many fine sales publications that you can refer to for guidance.

One major point regarding strategic selling is the concept that there are both buyers and influencers in the purchasing decision. The buyer makes the actual decision, but may be taking advice from or seeking the opinions of others. Be sure to understand the dynamics of such purchasing decisions.

It is often advisable to start off by selling to smaller companies and then work your way up the food chain before you approach major corporations. One of the reasons that it is advisable to start off selling to smaller companies is the extremely long time that it can take for a major corporation to come to a purchasing decision. For instance, it takes six months to a year to get into a Wal-Mart store on a national level. Smaller companies are usually more nimble and selling to them allows you to sustain your business while you are attempting to sell to the big boys.

Large corporations do not like to purchase from companies offering only one product. They also do not like to account for a large percentage (more than 25 –30%) of your total sales, knowing that if they stop buying this has a good chance of putting you under.

As with any entity, remember that you are dealing with people, even though it may seem like a large faceless corporation. Take the time and interest to build a rapport with the buyers and decision makers.

Caution: You May Get Badly Burned
Large corporations are the big dogs and many of them act the part. In particular, they can be very slow to pay their bills, knowing that extremely small businesses have little leverage over them. When cash gets tight–and it can even for the largest companies–they have to prioritize payments to their vendors and the large important vendors get the cash before the pipsqueaks.

Also, large corporations will often fine vendors that do not comply with the corporation's rules of how to do business with them. For instance, an infraction regarding how or where you label your shipping cartons could incur a fine of thousands of dollars.

You will also often have to invest in getting set up for *electronic data interchange (EDI)*, which is a system by which you communicate orders and inventory levels with the corporation.

Supplier Diversity Programs
Many large corporations have supplier diversity programs and attempt to funnel a certain amount of their business to small or disadvantages businesses, often following the same criteria as does the federal government.

How to Capitalize on Local Assets
Instead of trying to go directly to corporate headquarters with your sales pitch, try approaching local branch offices, stores, regional or district offices, etc. Often these are much more approachable. They also may have the local region at heart and want to see a local vendor gain a big contract with the big corporation.

Here is a personal story to illustrate the effectiveness of working with local branches: I at one time worked for an international membership-based non-profit organization and had responsibility for marketing, including cause-related marketing. In a cause-related marketing arrangement a corporation may, for instance, donate a certain percentage of each sale of a certain item to a good cause.

I had identified Sears Roebuck & Co. as a great prospect for a certain program that I wanted to develop and I made many attempts to speak with the national brand manager for the product line in which I was interested. Phone calls, letters, emails, and everything else went into a deep black hole for several months. Finally I got the brainstorm to approach the manager of the local Sears store to seek advice and assistance. It turns out that the manager was a member of my organization and was glad to help. He wrote a nice cover letter to go with my letter to the brand manager and my marketing materials, and at my request he even sent everything to the brand manager in an official Sears-return-addressed envelope.

Think about it: If you were the Sears brand manager and you were receiving 3,000 unsolicited proposals per year, which envelopes would you open?

Guess what? Within a week my phone rang and on the other end of the line was the Sears brand manager calling from corporate headquarters in Hoffman Estates, Illinois.

The story does not have a completely happy ending, in that I was not able to secure the deal. But what I did get was a careful and thorough consideration of my proposal and I had a number of discussions with the brand manager over a period of several days. It turns out that I had been beaten to the punch by a couple of months by a larger and more prominent non-profit organization.

HELPFUL TRADE ASSOCIATIONS AND PUBLICATIONS

There are a number of marketing trade associations and publications dedicated to marketing and various marketing specialties. These can be extremely useful in learning about marketing and in picking up great marketing ideas and strategies. Following is a partial list:

- American Marketing Association: http://www.marketingpower.com/
- Direct Marketing Association: http://www.the-dma.org/index.php
- Direct Response Marketing Alliance: http://www.responsemagazine.com/the-direct-response-marketing-alliance-drma
- Business Marketing Association: http://www.marketing.org/i4a/pages/index.cfm?pageid=1
- Promotion Marketing Association: http://www.pmalink.org/
- Mobile Marketing Association: http://mmaglobal.com/main
- eMarketing Association: http://www.emarketingassociation.com/
- Web Marketing Association: http://www.webmarketingassociation.org/
- Word-of-Mouth Marketing Association: (includes social media marketing) http://womma.org/main/
- Marketing Research Association: http://www.mra-net.org/
- Advertising Age Magazine: http://adage.com/
- Marketing Today Magazine: http://www.marketingtoday.com/
- Marketing Experiments Journal (online marketing only) If you have a Website, you really *must* use this resource, available at: http://www.marketingexperiments.com .
- International Events Group (IEG)/*IEG Sponsorship Report* at: http://www.sponsorship.com

INVENTION PROMOTION SCAMS

It is worth reiterating that you must be extremely careful before sending your hard-earned money to the invention promotion firms advertising online or on television. The USPTO and the Federal Trade Commission (FTC) both warn on their Websites against this.

There are many predators waiting to prey on naïve inventors with high emotional attachment to their technology and dreaming the Great American Dream. Remember what I told you about emotions and buying–you are on the other end of the equation here!

In general, you can tell if you are being scammed by whether or not the firm asks for up-front payment in order to help find customers for your product. Legitimate firms will either purchase your product and then sell it or ask for payment only if they actually sell your product, not just for "attempting" to market it.

These firms will often try to sell you overpriced services of dubious quality, some of which services you can obtain at higher quality and for free from various economic development agencies, etc.

PROFITABLE ONLINE MARKETING

Because entire books can be (and have been) written on just various subsets of this topic, I will not try to cover it fully here. However, I will give a few pointers.

What is Your Internet Strategy?
First, you must decide whether you want to be found online or whether your Website will simply serve as an online brochure with limited functionality. In the latter case you will be depending on offline means to drive traffic to your Website. A Website that is simply an online brochure is relatively cheap and you could reasonably have your nephew build it for free. You could also use one of the many inexpensive Website templates available at low cost via the Internet.

If, however, you intend to market primarily through online means such as *search engine marketing (SEM)*, this is a different story entirely–you must use a professional who knows what they are doing regarding *search engine optimization (SEO)* to create your site and manage it continually. This is very expensive or else it will take a lot of time and effort on your part.

Valuable References
I very highly recommend the book *Google AdWords for Dummies* if you intend to do any online marketing. The author Howie Jacobson is in my opinion a marketing genius and his book bursts like a plump ripe peach with juicy tidbits of Internet-marketing masterstrokes. I will even provide the link to Amazon so you have no excuse to not purchase this gem: http://www.amazon.com/Google-AdWords-Dummies-Howie-Jacobson/dp/0470455772

You should also take some time out of each day to read the tech and gadget blogs for research purposes and more importantly, for developing a rapport with the bloggers for marketing purposes.

Several popular blogs are: *Slashdot; Daringfireball; Boing Boing; Scribd; Gizmodo; Ubergizmo; Crave/CNET; All Things Digital,* Wired.com/*Gadgetlab* and AOL's *Engadget* and *Tech Crunch*.

Do You Need an Online Sales Force?

Pitfall: *"My business is online; I don't need a sales force."*

Well, it is not necessarily true that you do not need a sales force if you have an online business. Earlier I related the story of how Google found that large businesses can and do utilize their AdWords technology, which brings in the large majority of Google's $24 billion annual revenue, but small businesses largely do not use AdWords. Google realized that they must have human interaction to assist the smaller businesses in understanding and using the technology. As of 2010, Google has started hiring a sales force to do this, seeing the immense revenue potential from the small-business market.

Of course, the downside is that this will increase Google's costs and thus perhaps its net margins. I say "perhaps," because AdWords search terms are sold on an auction basis; the selling price of search terms among local businesses is largely unknown at this time since a robust market for them has yet to develop.

And then there is Groupon Inc., achieving $1 billion in revenue faster than any other company–faster even than market-rocket Google. As fate would have it, Google offered to purchase Groupon in December 2010 for a reported $6 billion. Just three short years earlier, online-coupon issuer Groupon was just a dream in Andrew Mason's head; in December 2008 it had only 400 subscribers. A later over-hyped IPO does not negate these facts.

How did it happen, this massive market explosion? Well, for one thing, Groupon has an army of salespeople burning up the phone lines and working online soliciting businesses in cities it has targeted. Groupon started in Chicago and is expanding across the country city-by-city.

Does this sound like initial-target-market focus or what? Of course it does–and that brings up an intriguing point. Groupon's business model is that it offers up a highly discounted local-business coupon deal, and then a certain number of consumers–perhaps a couple hundred–must commit to purchase the deal before it "tips" and becomes actually available for purchase. This business model forced Groupon to stick with marketing a deal until it succeeded in signing up a significant number of customers; the company could not just try to move on and chase the next rainbow–the latter being a very common ailment among entrepreneurs.

Interestingly, Groupon grew out of the failure of an earlier business started by Mr. Mason.

Speaking of failure of businesses started by Mr. Mason: It will be very interesting to watch, going forward, whether Groupon can maintain its dominant market position. If so, it will definitely be based on its business acumen, not its intellectual property. Its business model has rapidly been copied by hundreds of imitators large and small. This includes all manner of local media such as newspapers, radio, Websites, etc., some of whom actually offered somewhat similar deals prior to Groupon's burst upon the scene.

Testing to "Juice" Your Sales
Perhaps the greatest benefit of the Internet for savvy marketers is the fact that marketing materials, messages, promotions, etc. can be changed rapidly and for little expense. Back in the day, once you printed 10,000 brochures for $12,000 you were stuck with what you had until you got rid of them. No longer.

Now the Internet provides great opportunities to experiment to see what works–make use of this amazingly powerful tool!

A/B Split Testing

One of the very powerful methods of utilizing your ability to test on your Website is *A/B split testing*. In this test method, different site visitors are shown one of two different messages, promotional offers, etc. or they are routed through to the checkout in different manners. The test could be set up, for instance, so that every other visitor experiences alternately test A then test B; hence the name. By tracking results and tweaking, you can generate very large increases in your Website's success rate through A/B split testing.

WHAT ABOUT WARRANTIES?

As mentioned above, warranty policies can be thought of as a marketing tool, although they definitely have different and additional long-term implications compared to most marketing tools. Be sure that you will be able to handle warranty claims.

A couple of other notes are in order here. First, remember that a warranty will be a legal contract, so be sure that you know what you are doing in making warranty statements. Second, it is fortunate for startups that existing companies publish their warranties for all to see. When I started my first consumer-product company I did not have the money to pay an attorney to create a warranty statement for me, so what I did was to look at the warranty statements of several competitive products and use them as my guide to create my own.

FINAL NOTE ON MARKETING

It is relatively easy to *sell* a few of your product to people whom you know, with whom you have developed a rapport, or to whom you have given a personal demonstration of your technology's advantages. However, *marketing* your technology is all about determining how to sell mass quantities of it to people who do not know you, your brand name, or your technology's advantages.

OH WAIT... ONE MORE NOTE ON MARKETING:

*Use your **BRAIN**, not your WALLET!*

CHAPTER 8:
PRODUCT DEVELOPMENT

OK, now that you understand the role and limitations of patents, how to build a business, and the importance of marketing research and marketing, you can safely spend money on product development.

EASIER SAID THAN DONE

It is much easier to contemplate a product than it is to actually produce it economically in commercial quantities. One of the best ways to ensure that your product can be produced economically in commercial quantities is to *keep it simple*. Simplicity not only lowers cost, but it increases ease of use... what's not to love about that?

Even large companies retool their existing products for simplicity. For instance, in early 2011 Neal Mohan, Google Vice President for Product Management, said Google has 1,000 engineers around the world working to remove complexity and challenges from the Internet display ad market, an attempt to get more advertisers to spend more money online.

In one sense, developing a manufacturable product is more difficult than selling the product. For instance: If you can convince someone that you can make a perpetual motion machine, you can take an order for it. Heck, you may even get them to pre-pay you for it. However, when it comes time to deliver the machine, you will have a problem.

PRODUCT DEVELOPMENT PLAN

By now, you should be able to predict what I am going to say is the first step in developing a manufacturable product. Of course... it is our ol' pal: Planning!

If you want someone to invest in your business who knows what they are doing, you must show them a credible product development plan that includes anticipated timelines, necessary resources, and projected costs and outcomes. (I can't do anything about the fool who will part with his money without this plan). You need it for your own guidance and sanity as well. Remember that you are a major investor in your own business, even if that investment consists mainly of time and *opportunity cost* (e. g. the loss of the opportunity to earn money in a paying job)

In short, you need to be able to tell someone exactly what you are going to spend their (or your own) money on and what they (or you) will get in return.

The operative word in the term product development plan is the word PLAN. A plan sounds like this: "First I will ___, then I will ___. Next I will ___. To complete step one I will need $___ in materials and the following tools: ____. I will require the services of ___ people with ___ expertise for a period of ___ which will cost $___. I anticipate the completion of step one to yield

___ within ___ months. The product of step one will be used for ___. Based on the results of ___ I will proceed with step two, anticipated to occur by ___."

The above is greatly oversimplified, but you get the point.

For example: If you will be developing prototypes in your garage or basement for the first six months and then expect to have to move into a leased building, say so. If you expect to have to purchase $500 worth of materials for your first crude mock-up, which will take two months to build, say so. If you will have to pay someone $1,000 to develop a 3D computer model from which build your first rapid prototype, say so. If you expect to spend $10,000 on materials and machining to build your first functional prototype, say so.

If you will be developing software, you must decide whether you can do it yourself or if you will need to hire assistance. If you need to hire someone–when will they come aboard; what programming skills and experience will they need; how much will you have to pay them, and how hard will they be to find? What is your backup if they leave or don't work out? Skilled software engineers are often in short supply.

You should include a timeline in your plan, but like all timelines, it will be obsolete before the ink is dry. Even so, the process of developing a timeline makes you stop and think about these things instead of just "winging it" without a plan, which virtually never works according to plan. (Pun might have been intended; I'm not sure.)

If you are already partially through your product development phase, then start your plan with a discussion of how you reached this point and how much money that cost. At the end of the plan, be sure to discuss near-term future products that you anticipate developing and your best estimates of how that development will proceed.

COMMERCIALIZATION PLAN

Your product development plan is an integral part of your larger commercialization plan and in turn, your still-larger business plan. The best way to describe for you a commercialization plan is to describe the commercialization process I went through when working in R & D and product development for a *Fortune* 500 company.

I had been brought into the most important research & development/commercialization project of the division of the company I was employed by after the company had been working on it without much success for eight years. In order to produce the desired end-product, I had to develop new adhesives, new coatings, new coating processes, as well as find a way to produce products based on these new items, on new and existing manufacturing equipment.

I began in the first couple of months by reviewing the efforts and results of the previous team, conducting a very comprehensive review of the current state-of-the-art technology and also getting myself up-to-speed on what our competitors were doing.

I then formulated a plan for simultaneous product development of the adhesive and coating processes, as the two were tightly inter-dependent.

Following this I spent several months conducting laboratory bench-top experiments to refine formulations and processes.

The corporation had a pilot-scale production facility at its R & D campus. (The term *pilot-scale* refers to a stage of production intermediate between laboratory work and full commercial production. It is an approximation of the commercial production environment.) After developing a new adhesive that worked in the laboratory, for instance, I would go across the R & D campus and try it out on the pilot equipment.

It was not at all uncommon to find that the results on the pilot equipment were not the same as in the lab, and if so, I would have to "go back to the drawing board," conduct more bench-top work, and go back to the pilot equipment until I got the desired result for the stage I was investigating.

Following the success in-house, I would schedule time on the somewhat-larger pilot facilities at a trade organization's research facility. Again, it was sometimes back to the drawing board after the trial.

Once I got the process to work at the trade organization I scheduled a one- or two-days-long trial at one of my company's manufacturing facilities. Here again, I initially found that although I had made great progress vs. my predecessors, it was not yet good enough.

So the whole process began over with bench-top work, but from a much-higher plane as a starting point.

It was then back to the in-house and trade-organization pilot facilities; then back to my company's manufacturing plant. Once I achieved the desired success at one manufacturing facility (after about three trials) I had to follow up by proving-out the process at several others, since my company planned production at several dozen plants around the country and even internationally.

During the later stages of the above development of the adhesive formulation and the production process, I was concurrently developing a new coating process that would treat a portion of the raw material used for the end product. Unfortunately, my company was not yet in the coating business and had no pilot or commercial-scale coating equipment.

My team (by then there was more of a team involved) therefore had to find another company willing to rent out its manufacturing equipment for purposes of our commercial-scale coating trials. We were fortunately able to do so and conducted several such trials over a period of about a year until the process was perfected. After the first few trials, it was "back to the bench-top," however.

Finally, as we were able to produce good-quality finished product during commercial-scale trials that met the myriad design parameters and test specifications, the company brought in a team of manufacturing engineers to design a production coating facility. The coating process was a central part of the product and the company wanted to keep it in-house rather than contract it out to another manufacturer.

Also as the results looked more and more promising, the company brought in its product development personnel, who had strong contacts with the customers. These personnel were utilized more directly in the later stages of development, although they always had input. The company also involved its purchasing and accounting departments to develop the cost and pricing profiles of the product. Of course the company also involved its marketing personnel to develop the marketing plan and its execution.

After the product was demonstrated to be commercially viable, the next steps, which I was not involved in, were actual production followed by marketing.

The entire commercialization process took three years from the time I became involved and in the process the company filed for three patents based on my research work.

This is how the process worked at a *Fortune* 500 company, but it is the same for an independent inventor. I know this because I have gone through a similar process as an independent inventor.

RESEARCH ASSISTANCE FROM FEDERAL LABORATORIES

Federal Laboratory Research Partnerships
Through partnerships with federal research laboratories, entrepreneurs may set up joint research projects or access technologies developed by the labs. For instance, through their Office of Technology Transfer each federal lab offers for use by the private sector various technologies that the labs have developed. You may contact that office at the laboratory of interest. There are many thousands of patented inventions just waiting to be utilized by someone in the private sector and maybe there is one that could be utilized in your product or technology.

Office of Scientific and Technical Information (OSTI)
You can learn about current federal research projects at http://www.osti.gov/fedrnd/

Federal Laboratory Consortium (FLC)
The best portal to access technologies across the spectrum of laboratories is through the Federal Laboratory Consortium for Technology Transfer's Website at: http://www.federallabs.org/ locator/

Department of Defense Laboratory Partnerships
A useful site for information about how to access Department of Defense research and research capabilities is: http://www.dodtechmatch.com/DOD/index.aspx

Center for Technology Commercialization
The Center for Technology Commercialization (CTC) at: http://www.ctc.org/ describes itself as follows: "Focusing on state and local public safety communities and those government agencies and suppliers who support them, CTC, Inc.—a private non-profit 501(c)3 company—provides quality advice and assistance as it relates to public safety and homeland security activities."

National Technology Transfer Center
The National Technology Transfer Center (NTTC) at: http://www.nttc.edu/ facilitates transfer of technologies from federal labs to private sector commercialization.

Cooperative Research and Development Agreements (CRADA)
Private companies can partner with federal laboratories through a Cooperative Research and Development Agreement (CRADA). The Argonne National Laboratory Website has a good description of the CRADA program on its Website at: http://www.anl.gov/techtransfer/ Information_for_Industry/CRADA/

FUNDAMENTALS OF PRODUCT DESIGN

A key component of your technology development and commercialization plans is product design. A great product starts with a great design. There are many considerations in product design, among them:

- Simplicity

- Manufacturability
- Form
- Function
- Reliability
- Quality
- Safety, and
- Regulatory compliance.

Issues related to simplicity, manufacturability, form, and function are covered generally at several points in this and other chapters. Software design considerations are well beyond the scope of this book and will not be covered. However product reliability, quality, safety, and regulatory compliance issues are given further treatment below.

Designing for Reliability

Don't you just hate it when something breaks? Especially something that you look at and wonder: "Who on Earth designed it that way? Anyone could see that it would never hold up!" This is perhaps my greatest pet peeve: Poor product design. (Please don't let me down on this one with your product.)

An entire field of engineering has developed around product reliability in recent decades, driven by the example of Japanese manufacturers. I am old enough to remember when "Made in Japan" was equated with cheap toys and other low-value products, in the same way that "Made in China" is viewed today. You are probably old enough to remember when, in the early 1990s, Korean automobiles were ranked near the bottom of quality and reliability surveys. We both know that Japanese cars, optics, electronics, and other products are absolutely the most reliable in the world. Joining their Japanese counterparts, Korean cars have climbed their way to the upper reaches of quality surveys.

You may have thought this happened by chance, but you would be wrong.

It happened, of course, because of engineers who are totally focused on *design for reliability* (DFR). DFR techniques ensure that a product performs as designed, is fit for its purpose over a long period of time, and if the product does fail, it *fails safe*, which means that it does not fail in a way that causes damage or injury. Many factors must be considered in DFR, especially the average and the extremes of the environment in which the product will operate, as well as the number of cycles the product will experience in its lifetime. Some systems experience many cycles, such as an airliner's jet engine. Others experience only one cycle, such as a booster rocket launching a satellite to orbit.

Entire books have been written on DFR processes and techniques. My goal here is simply to whet your appetite, ensuring that you consider reliability in your product design and that if necessary you seek out more information. (Remember that pet peeve of mine!)

Ensuring Quality

Quality: what an overused word! Yet so extremely important. For a writer, the word quality presents a problem: It has–in the field of quality control–no synonyms. Maybe this is why the word is so overused.

Quality can mean level of quality: Good, better, best choices in paint, for instance. Some people do not want a high-quality product. For instance: A builder buying windows, paint, carpet, roofing, etc. for a "spec home," who just wants it to look nice enough to sell at the asking price but does not care if the homeowner has to pay high future heating bills due to leaky windows or high repair bills because the builder used cheap roofing materials.

There are quite a few "cheapskates" in the world who simply want the least expensive product, knowing that it will not last as long or perform as well as a more expensive choice. Others may want, but feel they cannot afford the higher-quality product.

Your task will be to design a product that delivers the maximum quality for the price and to meet the quality expectations of the purchaser, whatever those may be. Through your marketing you should set those expectations. This gets us to the concept of *value*. Does the purchaser feel that they received a good value for their hard-earned money? Henry Ford is reported to have said that his goal was not to see how *little* he could deliver for the money, but to see how *much* he could deliver for the money.

Inside Scoop: Set your quality expectations and then meet them
for *as low* of a price as possible.

Regulatory Compliance

Remember the good old days before all of those pesky, intrusive, job-killing government regulations? Back before cars were required to have seatbelts that prevent children from being killed in 35-mph accidents, before bathroom electrical outlets were required to have ground-fault-interrupt circuits that prevent electrocution when using a hairdryer, and before lawnmowers were required to have safety shutoffs preventing tens of thousands of severed fingers and toes? Ahhhh... if we could only go back to those halcyon days–what a utopia it would be for all of the survivors.

Now, I do agree that some regulations have gone too far (the federal government has over 100,000 standards in place) and some of the required warning labels are beyond ridiculous, but there is no question that government regulations have overall prevented millions of senseless debilitating injuries and deaths. As well, they are a fact of life; we absolutely must understand how they apply to us and then comply.

Not all rules and regulations are set by governmental agencies. Some are set by trade groups, the expectations of the market, and even by common sense. For instance, Chrysler Corporation began installing driver-side airbags in its vehicles prior to governmental requirements to do so, prodding its U.S. competitors to follow suit. In the ensuing years, it has almost become an "arms race" among vehicle manufacturers to see who can offer the most airbags in a vehicle, starting with passenger-side bags in the dashboard and now incorporating side-impact bags of various sorts.

I wonder who will be the first to offer the "air suit" to be worn by all passengers and that instantaneously creates a "human Nerf ball." Such a product may prove the "law of unintended consequences," however, as I can imagine teenage boys deliberately cracking up their cars just for the thrill of bouncing around wrapped in a balloon. "Yep, back in my younger years..." ☺

Below is a summary of many of the regulatory or standards-setting entities that may affect your business. The list is not complete, as the number of standards-setting entities is enormous:

U.S. Department of Defense (DOD)

The U.S. Department of Defense may require compliance with various defense standards, known as military standards, or more commonly *military specifications* (*mil specs*). These specifications may also be used by non-military governmental entities or even by private industry. If you are unfamiliar with DOD standards or with selling to the DOD, you should hire one of the many available consultants to assist you. Note that in general, the federal government will not conduct business with a startup entity with less than a two-year commercial track record.

National Highway Traffic Safety Administration (NHTSA)

If you plan to develop a product that will attach to or modify a highway motor vehicle, your product must comply with the federal motor vehicle safety standards (FMVSS). More information is available at: http://www.nhtsa.gov/cars/rules/import/fmvss/index.html

Consumer Product Safety Commission (CPSC)

The CPSC sets rules and regulations for products manufactured, distributed, imported to, or sold in the U.S. The agency regulates hundreds of items and it would be wise to check whether your product or future products are covered. More information is available at: http://www.cpsc.gov/ businfo/regsbyproduct.html

Federal Communications Commission (FCC)

According to its website: "The FCC has rules to limit the potential for harmful interference caused to radio communications by computers and other products using digital technology. In its regulations, the FCC takes into account the fact that the different types of products using digital technology have different potentials for causing harmful interference. As a result, the FCC's regulations have the greatest impact on products that are most likely to cause harmful interference, and little impact on those that are least likely to cause interference."

The FCC regulates devices that emit electromagnetic radiation. More information may be found at http://www.fcc.gov/office-engineering-technology.

Food & Drug Administration (FDA)

Then there is the granddaddy of all U.S. government regulators: the FDA, which oversees products representing nearly 25% of the U.S. economy. Full discussion of FDA regulations is beyond the scope of this book, but if you plan to develop a device that in any way could be considered a medical device or durable medical equipment, you must understand FDA requirements at an early stage. The place to start is: http://www.fda.gov/MedicalDevices/Device RegulationandGuidance/default.htm.

The next step after that is to call the FDA and speak with them about your device and how FDA regulations will affect you. For instance, does the FDA even consider it to be a medical device? The easiest and best way to determine if yours is considered a medical device is to call the FDA's Division of Small Manufacturers, International and Consumer Assistance at 800-638-2041 or 301-796-7100.

You must be aware early-on that the FDA requires conformance to and documentation of certain parameters during the medical-device product design phase. These regulations are known as *Design Controls*. A great start in understanding design controls is to read the FDA's *Design Control Guidance for Medical Device Manufacturers* document at: http://www.fda.gov/

downloads/MedicalDevices/DeviceRegulationandGuidance/GuidanceDocuments/ucm070642
.pdf

Prior to marketing a medical device you must submit it for FDA review or else find an allowed *exemption* from review, as further described below. Such exemptions are allowed for certain very low risk devices.

When FDA review is needed prior to marketing a medical device, the FDA will either

1) "*clear*" the device after reviewing a *premarket notification*, known as a *510(k)*, or
2) "*approve*" the device after reviewing a *premarket approval (PMA)* application.

The FDA classifies medical devices into three categories of increasing risk: *Class I, Class II, and Class III.* The FDA states on its website that only the highest-risk devices, such as mechanical heart valves and implantable infusion pumps, require FDA approval before marketing, via a pre-market approval (PMA) application. To receive FDA approval to market these high-risk devices, the manufacturer must demonstrate that its devices provide a reasonable assurance of safety and effectiveness.

However, the issue of "pre-market approval" is one of semantics only. That is the technical term the FDA uses for allowing high-risk devices to be marketed. You cannot just develop a medical device and then start selling it or even testing it. You must first receive legal authority from the FDA through one of three methods:

1) Find an exemption to FDA pre-market review
2) 510(k) Pre-market notification submission
3) Pre-market approval application

Upon completion of one of the above steps, the device will be "*cleared*" or "*approved*" by the FDA. It is not "FDA registered." Note that you cannot market a device as: "FDA cleared," "FDA approved," or "FDA registered."

Of course the lower the risk that the FDA perceives, the less onerous their review process. In fact, some extremely low-risk devices are exempted from review, as indicated in method #1 above. These low-risk medical devices (e.g., certain bandages) are exempted from pre-market review when they are for the same use and of the same technology as legally marketed devices.

You can check the FDA website at http://www.accessdata.fda.gov/scripts/cdrh/cfdocs/cfpcd/ 315.cfm to see if you can find your product type listed as exempt from pre-market review (i.e., you will not have to go through either the 510(k) or the PMA process).

The FDA's *513(g) Process* can be used to request from the FDA a determination of such issues as:

- Whether a product is subject to FDA regulation.
- Whether a medical device is exempt from pre-market review.
- Whether a 510(k) is needed for a modification to a device.
- The least burdensome regulatory pathway for a device that introduces a new technology or a new intended use.

A presentation regarding the 513(g) process is available at http://www.fda.gov/MedicalDevices/ResourcesforYou/Industry/ucm127147.htm. Click on the link for the "PDF printer-friendly format." Note that the small-business fee for this process was nearly $1,500 in 2010.

Moderate-risk medical devices (e.g., dialysis equipment and many types of catheters) and those for which there is no pre-market review exemption are cleared for marketing based on an FDA determination that they are substantially equivalent to an already legally marketed device of the same type, i.e., a *predicate device*, through the 510(k) process.

A predicate device is, according to the FDA definition: "a device legally on the market as of May 28, 1976 and for which a regulation requiring a Premarket Approval (PMA) has not been published by the FDA; or which has been reclassified from Class III to Class II; or which has been found to be substantially equivalent through the 510(k) process after May 28, 1976."

You should be aware that the 510(k) process can take up to a year or more and cost into the tens or even hundreds-of-thousands of dollars, depending on many variables. The FDA allows certain accredited persons to review 510(k) submissions through the *third-party 510(k) review process*. This process is purported to be shorter than having the FDA review the submission. More information is available at http://www.fda.gov/MedicalDevices/DeviceRegulationandGuidance/HowtoMarketYourDevice/PremarketSubmissions/ThirdParyReview/default.htm, and a list of accredited entities is available at http://www.accessdata.fda.gov/scripts/cdrh/cfdocs/cfthirdparty/accredit.cfm

The full FDA pre-market approval process for high-risk devices typically takes years and can cost from one million into the many millions of dollars if clinical trials are required.

But hey, don't whine about the cost of FDA approval for medical devices…imagine being a drug developer. Studies have shown that costs of FDA approval for a new chemical entity can range up to $2 billion!

Note that Peter Pitts, a former FDA associate commissioner, has been quoted in *Small Business Success* stating: "The words FDA and *typical* can't exist together in the same sentence. The FDA approval process is different every time." (Those words *do* exist together in *his* sentence, however!) ☺

In summary, the three classes of medical devices and typical routes to legal marketing are:

- Class I
    o Exemption from review
    o 510(k) submission
- Class II
    o Usually a 510(k) submission
    o Occasionally a PMA application
- Class III
    o PMA application

Now, let's throw a curve ball in here, and this is the *Investigational Device Exemption*, or *IDE*. An IDE allows a device to be used in a clinical study in order to collect safety and effectiveness data required to support a 510(k) submission or PMA application. Clinical studies are usually conducted to support a PMA. Only a small percentage of 510(k) submissions require clinical-data support. Investigational use also includes clinical evaluation of certain modifications or new uses of legally marketed devices. All clinical evaluations of investigational devices, unless exempt, must have an approved IDE before the study is initiated.

The FDA also requires that any manufacturing facility for medical devices comply with its *Quality System (QS) Regulation/Medical Device Good Manufacturing Practices* guidelines, which are general quality-control procedures and documentation. The facility must receive an FDA inspection and be approved by the FDA prior to the start of manufacturing. You can learn more at http://www.fda.gov/MedicalDevices/DeviceRegulationandGuidance/Postmarket Requirements/QualitySystemsRegulations/default.htm

In some cases, the process of approval of the manufacturing facility cannot begin until after the FDA approval of the device. This can cause long delays in your ability to sell your product and you will require substantial cash reserves to survive until your business is profitable on its sales.

Owners or operators of places of business (called establishments or facilities) that are involved in the production and distribution of medical devices are required to register annually with the FDA. This process is known as *establishment registration*. The facility must also list with the FDA the devices which it produces at, or distributes from, the facility. You can learn about this requirement at http://www.fda.gov/MedicalDevices/DeviceRegulationandGuidance/Howto MarketYourDevice/RegistrationandListing/default.htm

Manufacturers are required to continually monitor their medical devices after they are on the market and any injuries, malfunctions, etc. must be reported to the FDA. These postmarket requirements may be found at: http://www.fda.gov/MedicalDevices/DeviceRegulationand Guidance/PostmarketRequirements/default.htm

You can *count on* Murphy's Law applying to you during the FDA process, so be sure to have a *very large* cash cushion to carry you through to profitability. There is absolutely no way I would approach the PMA process without having access to capital that would sustain my company for a minimum of three to five years, including paying for the approval processes.

A lot of the process is subjective and over the years you will probably deal with several people at the FDA–keep this in mind.

Be sure to speak with other entrepreneurs who have actually made it through the FDA process and to seek competent advice from those thoroughly familiar with FDA rules and procedures! There are a number of consulting firms that assist with the process, but be sure to thoroughly check out these firms, as not all are equally competent.

The FDA also regulates veterinary devices for animals. More information can be found on the website at http://www.fda.gov/AnimalVeterinary/ResourcesforYou/ucm047117.htm

Firms that manufacture radiation-emitting devices must register their products under the radiological health regulations, administered by the Center for Devices Radiological Health (CDRH).

Medicare/Medicaid Reimbursement for Medical Devices and Equipment

Pitfall: Ignoring Medicare/Medicaid and medical insurance when developing a medical device or durable medical equipment

If a doctor, hospital, or patient cannot get Medicare/Medicaid or insurance reimbursement for your medical device or durable medical equipment (DME), this may be a very large hindrance to your sales. The reimbursement procedures, systems, and intricacies for medical devices and durable medical equipment are very complicated. Be sure to learn about them if you are developing a medical device or DME!

If you are developing a medical device or DME, be sure that you contact the Centers for Medicare and Medicaid Services (CMS) to determine into which reimbursement class your device will be placed. A good summary of CMS medical reimbursement codes for medical devices and DME is provided at: http://www.cms.gov/MedHCPCSGenInfo/ Downloads/ LevelIICodingProcedures.pdf. A search tool for HCPCS Level II Procedure Codes by keyword is provided at: https://drchrono.com/billing/medical_codes/. Note that this is a private-sector Website and is not run by CMS.

You may also want to demonstrate that your product is eligible for the New Technology Add-on Payment (NTAP) that provides additional payment for breakthrough technologies in the Medicare hospital inpatient prospective payment system (IPPS). To obtain add-on, a company must demonstrate to CMS that product is: new, more effective than existing practice, and more costly than existing practice.

Section 412.87(b)(1) of CMS regulations provides that a new technology will be an appropriate candidate for NTAP when it represents an advance in medical technology that substantially improves, relative to technologies previously available, the diagnosis or treatment of Medicare beneficiaries (see the September 7, 2001 final rule (66 FR 46902)). Applicants must submit a formal request, including a full description of the clinical applications of the technology and the results of any clinical evaluations demonstrating that the new technology represents a substantial clinical improvement, along with data to demonstrate the technology meets the high-cost threshold.

Obtaining approval for NTAP is typically an expensive process for a small company to bear. The process also must be contemplated long in advance. For instance, the deadline to submit an application for FY 2012 New Technology Add on Payments was November 22, 2010. In addition, it is somewhat counterproductive in general to advocate that treatments using your product are more expensive than current treatments.

Also be sure also that you understand how your product will be treated for reimbursement from private insurance companies. A good Website providing a general overview of medical reimbursement codes, including those developed by the American Medical Association, is provided at: http://www.reimbursementcodes.com/

American National Standards Institute (ANSI)/International Organization for Standardization (ISO)

ANSI is the U.S. representative to ISO. ANSI does not develop standards, but serves as a clearinghouse for its member organizations, which do set standards. More information is available at: http://www.ansi.org/. ISO promulgates global industrial and commercial standards. More information can be found at: http://www.iso.org.

National Institute of Standards and Technology (NIST)

NIST serves as the coordinator of standards-related activities within the federal government. It also administers various programs to advance technology within the U.S., including programs that benefit technology companies and manufacturers. Be sure to find out if any program pertains to your business. Information is available at: http://www.nist.gov.

Trade Associations

Trade associations represent the largest category of non-governmental standards-setting entities. Many trade associations develop standards for the products produced by members of their association or for products used by the entire industry.

Scientific and Technical Societies

Some of these organizations, especially the ones serving engineering and other technical disciplines, develop technical standards.

Exports

Products to be shipped overseas must meet requirements of the countries to which they are exported. In particular, the European Union requires for all products exported to EU countries the *CE mark* certifying compliance with the various EU health, safety and environmental regulations. This is a self-certification by the manufacturer–after performing a *conformity assessment* and signing an *EC Declaration of Conformity*–that the product has been tested if necessary and complies with all applicable regulations.

Also in Europe, the *Restriction of Hazardous Substances (RoHS)* Directive covers export to the EU of electrical and electronic equipment and prohibits various hazardous heavy metals or chemicals. Compliance with EU regulations is complicated and you must seek competent guidance if you plan to export to EU countries.

Market Demands

For certain products, the market may require listing by testing labs such as Underwriters Laboratories Inc. (UL) or a "seal of approval" from entities such as the National Sanitation Foundation (NSF). Compliance with the Uniform Plumbing Code (UPC), or the National Electric Code (NEC) may also be required either by the market or by local-government building codes.

TechStreet

The Website http://www.techstreet.com/ is a great resource to find standards that may apply to your product. The company describes its services as follows: "At techstreet.com, you can search, order and download standards from the world's leading authorities, including ASTM, ASME, API, ANSI, BSI, DIN, IEC, IEEE, ISO, NFPA and many others. Users have free access to abstracts, links to referenced standards, table of contents and document previews. We also offer certification exam packs, books, reports and other items for technical professionals."

PRODUCING PROTOTYPES

If a picture is worth a thousand words, then a prototype is priceless. In order to generate serious interest in your idea from savvy individuals or businesses, you generally must develop a functioning prototype.

Low-cost Prototyping
You must employ your creativity in coming up with a way to cheaply produce a prototype. For instance, go to a home improvement "big box" store and browse the aisles looking at pieces and parts and think about how you could modify and assemble them to create something that works

or at least approximates the form function of your new product. Ever hear of duct tape and baling wire?

If appropriate, begin by making wooden or plastic models in your own workshop. Prepare drawings to the best of your ability, including dimensions and tolerances.

If you need certain materials that you do not have, search the Yellow Pages or Internet for the material of interest, call the supplier, and ask for a free sample. Suppliers will often provide free samples, as they know it could lead to future business if you succeed.

ThomasNet, http://www.thomasnet.com, available online, lists suppliers of most any material or manufacturing process that you could need. This is an indispensable resource for persons developing new products.

There may be low or no-cost prototyping or product development services affiliated with economic development agencies, universities, trade schools, etc. in your state; check with your local Small Business Development Center (SBDC) for references. You can find the SBDC which serves your area by going to the Website of the U.S. Small Business Administration (SBA) at the following address: http://www.sba.gov/aboutsba/sbaprograms/sbdc/sbdclocator/SBDC_LOCATOR.html.

Trade schools and engineering schools that have manufacturing technology programs have manufacturing equipment and may be able to prepare CAD drawings, rapid prototypes, machined prototypes, molded parts, etc. They also may conduct engineering work. I have had clients utilize such programs to very great benefit.

Be sure, however, that you thoroughly understand the intellectual property policies of any such entity you work with. Some of them claim all developments made while working on your project as their own. If possible, get from students and professors an agreement that states that all developments made while working on your project belong to you. Note that unless there is an agreement to the contrary, the IP will by law belong to the student or professor even if you are paying them.

Rapid Prototyping
Rapid prototyping refers to processes in which prototypes can be created from computer modeling data. These processes allow prototypes to be produced much more quickly and generally much less expensively than traditional machining methods.

The precision of rapid prototyping is lower than that of machining processes and the parts are often non-functioning. Rapid prototyping is best for size and shape considerations and to evaluate interplay between parts. However, the parts are generally made of a rather weak plastic or other substance and will not stand much stress.

If applicable, rapid prototyping could be very beneficial to your project. Consult ThomasNet or search the Internet for companies offering these services.

Prototyping Assistance From Small Manufacturers
After you have done your best job of creating a prototype on your own, you will eventually need to have a more professional-looking and functional prototype developed. You typically must approach small manufacturing shops to have this done, as few if any large manufacturing companies will entertain product development projects for small or startup businesses. Many of

these small manufacturers have computerized drawing (CAD) capabilities and can prepare engineering drawings for you.

These manufacturers can be invaluable in helping to engineer your product. However, in having the manufacturer assist you with engineering, you must be careful to prevent ambiguity as to who invented what. If possible, have the manufacturer sign a document up-front stating that any developments made while working on your project are your property. Neglect on your part to do so can have serious negative consequences when it comes to trying to protect your IP, unless you don't mind sharing it with the manufacturer.

Remember that if the manufacturer develops a novel patentable improvement to your product, his name must be on the patent as the inventor, not yours—unless you are co-inventors, in which case both names must be on the patent. The agreement with the manufacturer that I mentioned above must state that he will assign the ownership of the invention improvement to you. It is up to you and the manufacturer to work out monetary compensation if any.

Some manufacturers have had bad experiences working with entrepreneurs on product development. Manufacturers of course are not charities. Typically, the reason that manufacturers agree to prepare prototypes is because of the production business that this is expected to bring. It is an investment by the manufacturer that they are counting on to pay off later. If the entrepreneur drops the ball, loses interest, or runs out of money, the manufacturer cannot recoup its investment. Even if the entrepreneur has paid the manufacturer for time spent on the project, the manufacturer still loses because it could have been spending that time on a project that brings in future production work. Idle production equipment costs money.

On the other hand, you will need to be very diligent in working with small manufacturers. They can make mistakes or turn out quality that does not meet your needs. For example, you must thoroughly check the drawings they send for your review prior to production. You will usually be responsible for the results of inaccurate drawings, even if it was the manufacturer that made the drawing error.

Be very sure to request references from small manufacturers regarding other companies they have produced for and check out those references. In particular, be sure that the manufacturer is skilled in producing the types of products with the quality criteria that you will require.

One thing to remember is that you will often be last on the manufacturer's priority list because they may have important jobs to get out the door for large customers. Have a clear understanding with them up-front of your expectations and the criteria for a successful relationship. Get this in writing.

Additive Manufacturing
The 3D printing processes that have been used to create rapid prototypes using polymers and in which the produced parts were rather weak have been improved to the point where functional metal parts are possible. This process is known as *additive manufacturing* and can be applied to plastics, ceramics, and metals. Pratt & Whitney uses the process to produce blades and vanes for compressors in jet engines, so you know the parts can be quite robust. The costs are still rather high compared to traditional manufacturing, but there could be cases in which the 3D printing processes are a viable option for you. This is particularly true for certain intricate shapes that would be difficult to machine or mold.

<u>Re-engineering</u>

Throughout the prototyping process you should think about ways to improve your product either to increase functionality, decrease complexity, or reduce cost of manufacture. In my opinion, the re-engineering exercise is more important for your project than the original engineering. After all, what are the chances that the first time around–regarding all aspects of your project–you came up with the best solution? A little extra time and thought spent here could later save many headaches and bushels of money.

In some cases you may come up with a product improvement that may warrant an addition to your product line rather than an enhancement to your initial release. This is a marketing decision with many aspects to consider. One of those considerations is the marketing power of: "New, Improved!"

There of course comes a point at which the re-thinking must cease and you need to release the hounds of your brilliance upon the market. "The perfect is the enemy of the good," someone once said for good reason. (They did not wait to say that until they had a *perfect* reason!)

Market-master Apple Inc. continually rolls out improved products. If it works for them it may work for you.

SELECTING MANUFACTURING PROCESSES/MATERIALS

You may need to develop a series of several prototypes in order to refine your idea. The prototype development process can be used to identify the best materials and manufacturing processes needed to produce a viable commercial product. It is of course best to talk to knowledgeable people rather than experiment, if possible.

There is a very broad range manufacturing processes and materials available–many more than most people are aware of. Some of these may allow your product to be manufactured much less expensively or to a much higher quality than the process or materials that you are initially considering.

It is well worth the time and effort to thoroughly research the methods and materials available. Some ways to start are:

- Contact manufacturing trade organizations such as:
  - National Tooling and Machining Association
  - Precision Metalforming Association
  - Society of the Plastics Industry
  - Metal Powder Industries Federation
  - Precision Machined Parts Association
  - National Manufacturers Association
  - Forging Industry Association
- Conduct an online search for "_____ trade association" to find other relevant trade associations.
- Go to http://metals.about.com for a comprehensive review of metals and metals manufacturing processes.
- Go to http://composite.about.com/ for a comprehensive review of plastics, composites and related manufacturing processes.
- Go to http://www.mmsonline.com for a wealth of information on metalworking processes.
- Speak with instructors at manufacturing technology trade schools.

- Attend the Design & Manufacturing show in Chicago. You can find virtually every manufacturing process and material represented there and you can speak with the experts in their booths. See http://www.canontradeshows.com/expo/dmmidwest10/ for more information.
- Call relevant manufacturers and suppliers. Always be sure to ask if the person knows of anyone else you can call.
- Contact engineering societies such as the American Society of Mechanical Engineers at http://www.asme.org/, the Institute of Electrical and Electronic Engineers at http://www.ieee.org/index.html and the Society of Plastics Engineers at http://www.4spe.org/.

FEASIBILITY STUDY

It is often advisable to have a feasibility study done on your technology. This study will determine the practicability of your idea in terms of concept, design, materials, and cost.

Private companies will conduct feasibility studies, including both product development and marketability studies. Consult your local Yellow Pages, for instance under the headings of "Plastics- Research & Consulting," "Marketing Consultants," or "Market Research & Analysis." It is important to note that such companies usually provide actual value, as opposed to many of the invention promotion firms that advertise on cable and late-night TV.

A Small Business Development Center business consultant can often assist you with an informal marketing feasibility study at no charge.

COST CONSIDERATIONS

One of the main results of all of the above planning and activity regarding technology development must be to establish the costs involved in producing your product. Of course, it is absolutely essential that you estimate these costs in advance of production, as you cannot estimate the future profitability of your business without a solid cost analysis. This analysis includes both the capital costs of buildings, equipment, tooling, molds, etc. and direct product costs such as raw materials, labor, packaging, etc.

There are two basic types of costs related to the cost of production: *fixed costs* and *variable costs*. Fixed costs do not vary depending on the number of items produced, whereas variable costs do vary depending on the number of items produced.

Capital costs such as buildings, equipment, tooling, and molds generally do not vary with production volume. (Of course, that is until you outgrow a building or need to produce additional molds, which is not considered in this analysis.) These are among your fixed costs.

Costs such as raw materials, labor, packaging, and shipping *do* vary as production volume varies, since your total cost of these items when you produce 10,000 units is obviously greater than your total cost to produce 5,000 units. These are among your variable costs.

Your costs of materials will often further vary depending on the quantities that you purchase. For instance, if you purchase 1,000 bolts on one purchase order you may pay ten cents each, but if you purchase 10,000 bolts on one purchase order you may get a price break and only pay nine cents each. Here is a money-saving tip: Your vendor may allow you to submit a purchase order for 10,000 bolts and give you the pricing at that level, yet allow you to schedule smaller release shipments over time and bill you as the bolts are shipped. It is always advisable to check into this as it can save you a considerable amount of money.

You will need to research all of these costs and then create a spreadsheet that shows your fixed and variable costs at the various production volumes that you anticipate over the first three to five years. It is also very useful to prepare a *breakeven analysis* to determine the *breakeven point* that shows how many units of your product you will need to sell in order to cover both your fixed and variable costs. In order to determine your breakeven point, however, you will need to have determined your average selling price. Pricing of your product is discussed in the chapter on marketing. The cost/selling price determination does have a bit of a chicken/egg element to it.

The cost of producing your product is generally referred to as your *cost of goods sold (CGS)* or *cost of goods (COG)*.

TOOLING REQUIREMENTS

Certain types of tooling are extremely expensive. This is true, for instance, of plastic injection molds, which can cost many tens of thousands of dollars each. I have seen cases in which the cost of the tooling sunk an entrepreneur's dreams for an otherwise awesome product idea.

For instance: Over the years I have had at least three hunters come to me with the idea of making a tree-stand with a lightweight injection-molded plastic deck, as opposed to the heavy steel stands available on the market. In each case I advised the clients to check into the cost of the molds required to produce such a product, knowing that the molds and tooling would cost upwards of $100,000 if produced by a reputable U.S. tool & die shop. None of those hunters has ever come back. No such product has appeared on the market. Such highly expensive tooling can be justified for products sold to the general public in the tens of millions. But hunters comprise only about 8% of the U.S. population so the market is much more limited; thus it would be very difficult to justify the cost of the tooling.

Saving Money on Expensive Tooling
It may be possible to have such expensive tooling produced overseas to reduce cost, but you would want this tooling to be contracted out by the production shop that you are using, so that you do not bear the responsibility if the shop later claims that the tooling is of poor quality.

Some types of tooling can be made less expensively for use in short initial production trials than what would be required for long-term production. For instance, plastic injection molds made of aluminum are much less expensive than those produced of D2 tool steel. However, the soft aluminum molds will not wear well under the abrasion of high-pressure molten plastics and can be used to produce only a fraction of the number of parts that can be produced using a hardened steel mold.

This has been a very brief discussion about determining your product cost. You should read further on this subject or seek out counseling from a qualified accountant or business consultant.

Product Liability Insurance
Of course it is usually advisable to purchase product liability insurance for your products to protect you if your product does harm to someone or if someone brings a suit against you alleging harm. If you plan to sell to any large distributors or retailers, this will not be optional, as they will require that you carry product liability insurance. They will also require that your policy

name their company as an *additional insured*, which means that the policy will protect them as well.

Wal-Mart for instance requires that its vendors carry insurance with a minimum of $2,000,000 coverage for each occurrence, and up to $10,000,000 per occurrence for products deemed high risk. Also, Wal-Mart requires that the insurance carrier(s) must be "A" rated according to A.M. Best or another insurance rating industry authority. For more information on Wal-Mart's requirements please refer to: http://walmartstores.com/Suppliers/9424.aspx.

You can usually find product liability insurance carriers by simply looking in the Yellow Pages or online. Be sure to get quotes from at least three carriers, as you will usually find that the rates vary considerably.

CHAPTER 9:
MANUFACTURING

So... now you have a functional prototype and are ready to get started on commercial production. This is a beautiful thing; there is nothing like the feeling of holding your first commercially produced product! It's definitely your "baby" and when it arrives there are well-deserved congratulations all around.

NO BUSINESS IS AN ISLAND

In this chapter I will discuss various means, methods, and strategies for producing your product or having it produced for you by others. Whether or not you do your own manufacturing, however, your business will be dependent on suppliers, either of raw materials or of finished products. You will also rely on vendors to provide your business with various operating and office supplies, etc. You always rely on others–sometimes this is good; sometimes this is bad.

Sorry about starting out on a "downer," but I want to talk first about the times that this is bad, because of the immense impact on your business if things do go sour in this regard.

It is typically in the manufacturing phase that Murphy shows his ugly face. He can really get in there and mess things up like a drunken jilted former lover at a wedding reception.

Pitfall: I cannot recall one client who was able to get his/her technology to market within the timeframe initially projected. Usually it is not even close.
Even after a client has one good production run the next run or perhaps the one after that often ends up going awry.

This is very important to understand, because if you cannot make your product you cannot sell your product, and if you cannot sell your product you cannot bring in sales revenue. Unfortunately, you usually have many expenses that cannot just be "turned off" to compensate for this lack of sales revenue–costs such as rent, loan payments, salaries, etc. The result of this situation is a financial death spiral at worst and dire straits at best.

WATCH YOUR BACK!

It has been my observation that the leading cause of delay in getting a technology to market within the expected timeframe is a lack of performance by one or more of the entrepreneur's suppliers.

You can avoid the financial devastation of this scenario by remembering the following credo–what I will call my

Overholt's Law of Supply: *Your suppliers will screw you.*

You can count on it. Although you can try to reduce it and manage it, it will happen. More than once I have had clients come back to me a year or so later and say: "You were totally right about suppliers."

Typical ways that your suppliers will screw you are of course late shipments, short shipments, and poor quality. Others include upward price adjustments, disputes over exactly what you wanted, and even going out of business. Each of these events has happened either to me or to clients I have assisted. You survive these crises by having enough cash in reserve to pay your expenses while you are working out the issues with your supplier(s) or finding new supplier(s).

YOUR PRODUCTION OPTIONS

Now that we have that little bit of unpleasantry out of the way, let's get to the meat of the subject:

There are several methods to consider in having a product commercially produced. Among these are:

- In-house manufacturing
- Domestic contract manufacturing
- International contract manufacturing
- Licensing agreement with an existing manufacturer/marketer
- Various combinations of the above

These options are discussed below.

In-House Manufacturing
In-house manufacturing (producing the product yourself on your own equipment) generally provides the most control over product quality and availability, but is the most capital-intensive method. In some cases, the cost of the required manufacturing equipment or the cost of the personnel with the expertise to operate it is prohibitive.

It is often possible to purchase good used equipment at considerable discount. The Internet is a valuable resource for identifying used equipment suppliers.

Although your per-unit cost may be less if you manufacture the product yourself, you should consider whether the capital and your time tied up in manufacturing is really worth it. There is normally quite a learning curve for understanding processes or industries. You may be better off concentrating on the marketing end of your business, especially at the outset. You can always bring the manufacturing in-house at a later date, even doing so incrementally.

If you do decide to do your own manufacturing, be sure to understand proper practices such as: just-in-time delivery; efficient manufacturing equipment layout; quality control procedures; workplace safety compliance; employee training; environmental compliance, etc.

There may be government-supported loan programs to assist small manufacturers in your area. A Small Business Development Center consultant usually can assist you with identifying and applying for these if so.

Domestic Contract Manufacturing
Domestic (in the U.S.) contract manufacturing is less capital intensive than in-house manufacturing, but the disadvantage can be less control over product quality and availability. Domestic contract manufacturers may be identified by consulting ThomasNet at

http://www.thomasnet.com/. Look up the manufacturing process of interest and contact the manufacturer. Not all will be interested in working with a startup, but many are.

Win-Win

It is important to set up win-win relationships with your manufacturers and vendors. Many books and other resources are available on this subject and it would be wise to understand this process. However, despite your best efforts, the fact is that win-win situations do not always develop between suppliers and customers.

Tooling

Be very careful in selecting the manufacturers that you will be working with, especially if you will be spending large sums on specialized tooling and/or molds. Even though you may own it, this tooling can be difficult to transfer to a different manufacturer if the first manufacturer is not working out. It could be that a new manufacturer to which you want to transfer the tooling does not like the way the tooling was designed or it is incompatible with the new manufacturer's existing equipment. It also could be that you end up in a payment or other dispute with the original manufacturer, who then refuses to transfer your tooling. You could be tied to the manufacturer you first chose unless you are willing to pay for new tooling at a new manufacturer.

One major problem with having one company produce tooling or molds and then having another company utilize them for production is that if there are quality or runnability problems, the two companies can point their fingers at each other as the source of the problem. You can be stuck in the middle with no good way out. It is best for you to be able to point the finger at only one entity!

It may be possible to negotiate an arrangement whereby the manufacturer amortizes the cost of the tooling into the price of the parts. For instance if the tooling costs $10,000, the manufacturer may spread this over the first 20,000 parts delivered, at $0.50 each.

Tooling for many manufacturing processes can easily cost into the tens of thousands of dollars. You may be able to identify less expensive initial alternatives until larger volumes are attained. For example: Laser-cutting of sheet metal parts instead of stamping them out with dies.

Typically, the manufacturer will specify minimum quantities of product that you must purchase, especially for the initial order. Full or partial prepayment of the tooling costs and initial order is normally required. These factors must be taken into account when calculating capital requirements for startup–if you have not planned for them, these costs will come as quite a shock.

Oversight

Some manufacturers will make claims regarding their capabilities that turn out to be exaggerated. Ask for references regarding the specific work you want to have done. You don't want to pay for a learning process on their end.

Be very careful to create clear areas of responsibility, leaving no "grey areas" that can be exploited by a manufacturer in the event of a dispute over quality, delivery, etc. Try not to allow a situation where one contract manufacturer can point the finger at another if the final product is not delivered to your satisfaction. Again, the risk of this is especially high if one company produces the tooling and another company produces parts with it.

Be very aware that quality control among small manufacturers can be *very poor.* Be sure to have a clear written understanding with the manufacturer regarding your expectations and the criteria for success. They may try very hard to get you to accept their poor quality and service. You must firmly stand your ground here.

It can take quite awhile until the manufacturer consistently produces a product that meets your needs, especially if you are attempting to do something innovative. You will usually need to "bird dog" everything, but you must not alienate the manufacturer in the process. You probably need them more than they need you! The manufacturer may have the option to just walk away if he gets frustrated or is losing money on the project.

If at all possible, be sure to physically be there during initial production runs—due, of course, to Overholt's Law of Supply.

Be sure to have written quality specifications for all important aspects of your product, including order lead time. Also be sure that both you and the manufacturer retain mutually approved *first article* quality references. These are production samples of your product made by the manufacturer, representing the expected quality. If a dispute later arises, you can use the first article reference to prove what was agreed upon.

International Contract Manufacturing

Generally, the same points apply in international contract manufacturing as apply in domestic contract manufacturing, but with the added issues of:

- Identifying qualified foreign manufacturers
- Language barriers
- Long lead times
- Currency fluctuations
- International money transfers
- Import/export procedures
- Import duties; customs brokers
- Dispute resolution
- Intellectual property protection, etc.

A full discussion of international contract manufacturing is beyond the scope of this document. Fortunately, many Small Business Development Centers have programs specific to international trade. For those seeking to evaluate international sourcing, this is a great place to start.

Yes You Can

International sourcing is relatively complex, but should not be viewed as so daunting that it is impossible for a small business. In fact it is very possible. I know of two entrepreneurs with no prior background other than being housewives who successfully had products manufactured for them in China. In one case, the middle-aged woman even went to remote parts of China on her own to visit potential manufacturers. She had some entertaining and some rather harrowing stories to tell of her experiences, but she got the job done!

A very good resource for identifying foreign sources of supply is http://www.alibaba.com/. In February 2011, Alibaba staffers in China were found to be falsely certifying suppliers as gold-level-quality suppliers and the CEO resigned as a result. Personally, I have had good luck with Alibaba and I know of others who have as well.

"Made in the USA" has a very nice ring to it, whereas "Made in China" falls flat. However, you must take an honest look at the economics of each option. In the case of the injection-molded tree-stand deck mentioned above, "Made in USA" would sink the product. In reality, American jobs would be created in the fields of logistics, transportation, marketing, retailing, and management if the product was made in China and became successful in the U.S. market. Support U.S. manufacturing if possible, but make a rational decision regarding foreign manufacture, not an emotional one.

Marking Country of Origin

You generally must mark your packaging and your product with country of origin if the value of the foreign content is above certain percentages. The U.S. Customs & Border Protection agency enforces these laws. Be sure you check with the agency to determine the requirements for your product. Information is provided at the following link: http://www.cbp.gov/linkhandler/ cgov/newsroom/publications/trade/co_origin.ctt/markingo.doc.

Licensing to a Manufacturer

There are many advantages to setting up a patent licensing agreement with an existing manufacturer that can both make and sell your technology such as with an *original equipment manufacturer (OEM)* of products related to yours. The most obvious are reduced cost to you and the potentially greater manufacturing and marketing ability of the existing company. Typically, in such an arrangement the OEM will both manufacture and market your product, paying you a *royalty* (a percentage of sales revenue) for the profit opportunity that this presents to them.

The Importance of Patents

Generally, in order to set up a licensing agreement with an OEM, you must have a patent that you can license to them. Remember that a patent grants an exclusive right to make, use, and sell something. If you have no patent, you have no exclusive right, and therefore the OEM already has the right to make, use, and sell your technology without having to go through you. You may get lucky and be able to make an arrangement in which an OEM signs an agreement to pay you for an unpatented idea that you bring to them, but since that OEM is wide-open to competition from everyone else on the planet, any such agreement is likely to be a very weak one.

Many OEMs will not even talk to you until you have applied for a patent on your idea. This is for their protection. Large companies have many product development and marketing personnel located around the globe and there is a reasonable likelihood that they already have thought of your idea, even though you may not be aware of this. If they agree to review your idea and then reject it because they are already working on it, they are open to the accusation by you that they stole your idea, even though they did not. However, if you have a patent or at least have applied for one, your documented date of invention vs. theirs is pretty clear cut.

Prospecting for Licensees

Some OEMs have a policy against accepting unsolicited ideas, but others have active programs to solicit new product ideas from the public. Many large companies have come to realize that they have historically been extremely poor at actual innovation, despite their large expenditures on R & D. Therefore they have begun to look to where the innovation has been occurring–out among the public and small businesses. One such company is Reckitt-Benckiser, at http://www.rb.com/Innovators, maker of various household products, cleaners, and health-related items.

Other companies reported to be proactive in accepting outside suggestions include: Clorox Co.; Kraft Foods Inc.; General Mills Inc.; Staples Inc.; Proctor & Gamble Co., and GlaxoSmithKline PLC.

There are many reasons why an OEM may not be interested in licensing your invention. One reason is known as the *not invented here syndrome*. This refers to a general human nature to reject ideas that come from the "outside." Other reasons include a lack of time on the part of personnel at the company from which you are trying to get interest and also the fact that the people at these companies have competing priorities–usually much higher priorities. Also, the OEM may feel that your patent is too narrow or otherwise weak.

Another issue that can work against you is the fact that people sometimes make bad decisions or are too lazy or biased to thoroughly investigate before making a decision. If you happen to be dealing with a person such as this, you should try to:

1) Recognize this fact
2) Not make an enemy of this person
3) Find a way around this person.

Of course the good news is that a person may make a "bad, lazy, or biased" decision in your favor, although this is much less likely to happen.

If you have determined that you want to pursue licensing, you must look at the process as a sales effort–a strategic sale for a complex product. It would be beneficial to study a book on strategic selling if you are not trained in making this type of sale. (Remember in Chapter 1 when I said that as a new-technology entrepreneur you are first and foremost a salesperson?)

A seasoned salesperson realizes that he/she must contact many prospects in order to make one sale. Many of the prospects drop out at various stages along the way, but the salesperson must keep working and not get discouraged too easily. You should adopt this attitude in licensing your technology.

Because of the very long time required to actually secure a licensing agreement, it may be wise to "have more than one iron in the fire" in your licensing efforts. This way, if your efforts come to nothing after a long period of working with one prospect, you may have a backup instead of having to start over at square one in the process. If you let the prospects know right from the beginning that you are giving more than one company the opportunity to review your invention, you should not have a problem in working with more than one. They usually understand that the company that responds to you most promptly and with the best offer will get the prize.

Another reason that you may want to approach several prospects at the same time rather than sequentially: If you are turned down by several companies in sequence, the word may get around the industry that you are shopping your invention around without success. This can cause the later prospects to be more leery of working with you. People from different companies within industry groups do talk to each other.

Of course a potential pitfall in having more than one iron in the fire is that you are exposing your technology more broadly, thus increasing the risk of being "ripped off." Like everything else, there is no absolute right or wrong approach and it is up to you to weigh the pros and cons.

Based on my experience, I would recommend having more than one iron in the fire. The odds of ultimate success with any one company are very low.

It is advisable to develop relationships with more than one department and especially with more than one person at your prospective companies; you do not want to have to start over at square one if your single contact leaves his/her position with the company. Typical departments that you should be in contact with include:

- Marketing
- Sales
- Product development
- R&D
- Your area's district office.

You need to develop a warm personal rapport with as many people at your target companies as possible. You also need to be patient and realize that these people have priorities that are not the same as yours.

<u>Inside Scoop:</u> **Be sure you have everything well planned out before you contact any prospect.**

Remain as consistent as possible from one company to another. One thing that competing prospect companies definitely will not understand is if you make a better offer to one than another.

A SBDC consultant can assist you with identifying companies to target for your licensing efforts.

Royalties

A *royalty* is the payment that a licensee makes to a licensor for the right to use the licensor's intellectual property. The ownership of the IP remains with the licensor. Royalties are typically earned as a percentage of the sales made by the licensee.

The royalty percentage that an OEM will pay varies depending on the product line and other factors, but 2 - 6% of net sales is a good ballpark figure. Net sales is basically total sales minus returns and non-payments (bad debt). This figure of 2 - 6% may sound like a very low figure to you, but remember what I said about the ratio of cost of goods vs. retail price: a 4X ratio. The royalty that the manufacturer pays you is part of their cost of goods. The dollar amount per unit that they pay you may need to be multiplied by four and then added to the MSRP. The manufacturer is obviously concerned about being "priced out of the market."

Avoid royalties based on the profit that the licensee makes on your technology. The licensee can easily manipulate or eliminate profits by paying inflated salaries, charging unnecessary expenses, etc., thus eliminating the need to pay you royalties.

The royalty percentage that a licensee will pay is related to the total value contribution that your invention makes to a product. If your invention essentially defines the entire product, then you can command a relatively high royalty percentage. However, if your invention merely improves an existing product, the royalty rate may be a smaller percentage of the net sales of the product.

An example of this would be someone who licenses a better engine mount to an automobile manufacturer. The auto manufacturer will not pay a 5% royalty on the entire price of the automobile for this contribution.

As mentioned, it can easily take up to six months or more to complete the process of contacting a company regarding licensing and then working through to a signed contract. It can take up to another year or more for the company to gear up for production and move the technology into the market. The latter is especially true if the product has a seasonal sales cycle.

Typically, royalty contracts stipulate that royalties will be paid quarterly, 30 - 60 days after the close of the quarter. (The OEM will try for 60 days and you will try for 30 days.)

It is often advisable to stipulate *minimum royalty payments* in your contract with a licensee. This is a minimum annual amount that the licensee must pay you in order to keep the license for the patent. The purpose is to allow you to receive income if the licensee for some reason–even if through no fault of their own–fails to sell enough product to cause significant royalty payments to you.

When all of the above is taken into account–and including the length of time it typically takes just to negotiate such agreements–it can take a very long time to realize any revenue from licensing efforts. For this reason, it is also advisable to request a *lump sum payment* upon execution of the contract, in addition to the royalty on net sales and minimum annual royalty payment.

Manufacturing Know-how

In the chapter on intellectual property I discussed manufacturing know-how as a type of trade secret. If you feel that you have developed manufacturing know-how as a trade secret, it is wise to separate this out from the patent license, either as a separate section of the licensing agreement or as a different agreement entirely.

The reason for this is that it is very possible that your patent could be found invalid, someone could "work around" it, or someone could blatantly infringe it. If any of these occur, but you have licensed your manufacturing know-how, you will still be left with a means to protect your development and to receive royalty income from an entity to which you license it. Patent license agreements are virtually always structured so that the license agreement terminates if the patent is found invalid. In this case the manufacturer no longer must pay you a royalty to make use of your formerly patented technology.

Typically you would want a separate royalty stream from the know-how, though you usually cannot command for this as great of a percentage as from the patent itself. For instance, if you want to receive an overall royalty percentage of 5%, you may specify 4% due from use of the patent and 1% due from use of the manufacturing know-how.

Be aware that it may be difficult to get a manufacturer to agree to pay a royalty on the manufacturing know-how, but it is not unheard of.

**Pitfall: If the manufacturer comes up with a better way to manufacture,
you may lose your 1% and thus your royalty stream may drop to 4%.**

As with most everything, there are pros and cons to consider; you cannot predict the future, and you must make your best informed decision on how to proceed regarding the licensing of manufacturing know-how.

Licensing to a Marketing Firm

One marketing company that has successfully commercialized mass-market new products for inventors is AllStar Products Group Inc. at http://www.allstarmg.com/. The Company receives about 10,000 submissions per year but only enters into licensing agreements for about 75 to 100 of these per year. This company, unlike many other companies claiming to help commercialize inventors' ideas, has commercialized products that have sold millions, among them the Topsy Turvy upside-down tomato growing system.

Risks of Licensing Efforts

You sometimes must take calculated risks regarding your invention. This is a very difficult concept for many inventors to understand. It is particularly true when you desire to license your idea to large companies. They will not sign a non-disclosure or non-compete agreement that gives you the protection that you would likely want when you submit your idea for consideration.

If you are considering licensing because you are unable or unwilling to create a company to make and sell your invention yourself, you may just have to take the risk that the large company may "rip off" your idea. However, most large companies are reputable and are not in the business of stealing ideas. You may need to take a serious look at what you end up with by protecting your idea from all possible chances of being ripped off, no matter how remote they may be, vs. allowing someone to take a look at your invention so that you at least have a *chance* of profiting from it.

To check out a particular company, you may want to check out the chat groups, etc. online, but of course you would want to thoroughly vet any information turned up in that manner.

As an aside, an analogous situation often develops when inventors are asked to give up a part ownership of their company in order to secure investments. The inventor must make a realistic assessment of the alternatives. Sometimes there are none. The inventor must then ask himself what he would rather have: 50% of *something*, or 100% of nothing.

Licensing Legal Advice

It is imperative that you receive competent legal advice from a qualified attorney in negotiating and signing any licensing agreement.

Combinations of Manufacturing Strategies

It is of course possible to create any combination of the above manufacturing strategies. However, be aware that a company to which you license your technology may not want you to make and market it in competition with them, so that combination may not be a viable one.

CHAPTER 10:
SUPPLY MANAGEMENT

Supply management, also called *supply-chain management*, is basically just what it sounds like–managing your suppliers so that they consistently provide you with timely delivery of quality products at competitive prices. Supply management has been recognized in recent decades as an extremely important aspect of business. The field has gained substantial respect as a profession as a result of the phenomenal successes of, for instance, Toyota and Wal-Mart due to their relentless focus on supply chain management.

The trade association for supply-chain managers is the Institute for Supply Management. Many resources, publications, and training materials are available from the organization, and it offers certifications such as: Certified Professional in Supply Management (CPSM), and others. Its Website is: http://www.ism.ws/.

LEVELING THE PLAYING FIELD

As a startup, you will almost certainly be initially much smaller than the suppliers with which you deal. This can have a tendency to lead to an asymmetric relationship. At first you may have little influence with your suppliers due to your lack of purchasing power, but you do not have to act subservient toward them. You must require from them the same respect that they would give a large company. However, arrogance and belligerence usually gets you nowhere with them.

As mentioned previously, it is probably the case that as a startup you need your suppliers much more than they need you, and you do not want them to call your bluff. Firmness and reason combined with offers to help are often much better tools to effect positive outcomes from suppliers. There are some, however, that do not improve under such management and then of course other means are merited.

No matter which manufacturing method that you choose other than licensing your patent to someone else, supply management will be very important to your success. Again, a full discussion is beyond the scope of this book, but a few points are pertinent.

SETTING UP WIN-WIN SCENARIOS

It is critical to set up win-win situations with your suppliers. If it is clear to them that they are benefiting from working with you, they will go the extra mile to keep the relationship going successfully. If you feel that your supplier is not going the extra mile for you, the reason could be that the supplier does not feel that he is winning.

Keep open lines of communication so that you can judge the sentiment of your suppliers toward your project. You may need to do as much of a sales job on your suppliers as you do on your customers if you hit a rough patch. You need to keep them focused on the big picture and on the long term, just as you must keep yourself focused on these issues.

Although it is admirable to want to be loyal to suppliers who started out with you and helped you get off the ground, you must not let a supplier's lack of development inhibit your growth. Remember that the relationship should be "win-win." One of those "wins" includes you!

An applicable adage is: "Dance with the one that brought you." But if the one that brought you can't learn the new steps, you must find another partner or you will stop dancing.

While management books and gurus extol the virtues of creating win-win relationships, the simple fact is that this utopia is not always achievable, as with any other utopia. You must work very hard to fulfill the slogan, but don't die by it. Sometimes you may just have to find another supplier.

One of the ways to create a win-win situation and avoid having to find another supplier is to adopt an attitude of trying to help out the supplier if possible. If they are having difficulty supplying you properly, see if you can suggest or provide resources to them to help them to help you.

YOUR HEADACHE IS READY FOR DELIVERY

Supply management will continue to be critical to your business as you grow. Even corporate giants such as Caterpillar Inc. can get into trouble by taking their eye off of this ball. For example, from 2006 to 2008, the market for mining equipment such as that made by Caterpillar saw explosive growth. The company saw booming sales but its profits actually declined over the same period. The problem? Caterpillar had trouble with its suppliers, which could not keep up with the increasing orders. The added costs for the "work-arounds" that Caterpillar had to implement to feed its manufacturing plants ate big chunks out of its profits.

Boeing had similar problems with its suppliers toward the end of the 2000s. The company had for over a decade aggressively outsourced the manufacture of components and systems previously produced in-house. This worked well as long as the company was simply producing more of the same thing–i.e. additional units of the existing airliner models. However, when Boeing tried to implement this strategy with its suppliers in the production of its dramatically new 787 Dreamliner the result was absolute disaster. The first delivery to an airline was more than three years late, costing the company billions. Boeing cited the inability of suppliers to produce quality high-technology components on time as a major reason for the seven announced delays in the completion schedule. In addition, Boeing found that it had to conduct extensive re-work on the planes that had been completed, including fixing problems with lithium ion batteries that overheated and caused the planes to be grounded for several months by the FAA in 2013.

In another example of the failure by even the largest of global corporations to properly perform even the most rudimentary of manufacturing-process-development work, airliner manufacturer Airbus in 2006 announced to the world the reason for its latest delay in delivery of its new A380 plane: Its design center in Germany was using version 4 of CATIA software, whereas its factory in France was using the incompatible version 5 of CATIA. This screw-up necessitated the complete re-design of the more than 330 miles of wiring in the A380. Airbus had to pay millions in compensation to its customers–various airlines–as the airlines re-learned the hard lesson of Overholt's Law of Supply.

MAY I TAKE YOUR HEADACHE?

In contrast stands Wal-Mart, which–as discussed elsewhere in this book–has become by far the largest corporation the world has ever known due primarily to its masterful management of its suppliers and supply chain.

Toyota Motor Corp. has become the world's largest automobile company largely through supply chain management and implementation of internal quality controls. Together, Toyota and Wal-Mart have re-invented business around the globe, with many other companies seeking to duplicate their success. You should too! (Focus on supply chain... the world's largest retailer and the world's largest auto company... see any pattern here?)

Throughout this book I have lauded Apple Inc. for its marketing prowess. But that is not the only reason the company is at the top of the heap as the world's most valuable technology company. Much credit is also given to Apple's superb manufacturing and supply management. Tim Cook–COO and later CEO of Apple–is given credit for having played a major role in turning around Apple's previous chronic supply problems, thus contributing mightily to the company's ability to accumulate $51 billion in cash and liquid assets. That massive war chest will allow Apple to keep its competitors reeling for many years.

IMPORTANCE OF BACK-UP SUPPLIERS

It is very important in supply management to prepare back-up plans. You may not have the money to actually have more than one producer for any certain part due to tooling costs, etc., but you should always have identified at least one backup supplier that you could turn to if necessary. Some of the larger companies that you want to sell to may require this of you.

INVENTORY MANAGEMENT

Inventory control is a very critical aspect of a new business since new businesses are typically short of capital. It is very easy to tie up capital in inventory that ends up sitting on a shelf. This capital is not working for the business.

Pitfall: Over-ordering

Be very careful not to order excess inventory simply to obtain price breaks. For instance, if your product will cost $10 each if you order 1,000 units from a contract manufacturer, but only $9 each if you order 5,000 units, you may be tempted to order 5,000 units to get the 10% cost reduction. However consider that the 1,000-unit order will cost a total of $10,000 whereas the 5,000-unit order will cost $45,000.

It is probably far wiser to take the $35,000 difference and use it for marketing to sell the more-expensive 1,000 units. At the normal 2X wholesale markup, you are earning $10,000 at a critical time for your business instead of purchasing 4,000 additional units that may sit on the shelf because you are left with insufficient funds to market them. This is wise financial management!

Nearly all entrepreneurs with new technologies are overly concerned that they will be unable to keep up with the expected raging demand for their new product. Therefore many of them ignore the above advice and order 5,000 units anyways. They reason that they want to provide "excellent customer service" and do not want to risk running out of inventory.

Consider this: Running out of inventory is definitely *not* one of the major reasons that new-technology businesses fail; but poor financial management *is*. If you go out of business, that is certainly the epitome of poor customer service!

You have to look at the likelihood of each risk actually occurring. One is an extremely remote possibility and the other is highly likely.

Inside Scoop: Another reason to refrain from over-ordering in your initial production runs is this: What if the product turns out to be poor quality?

Sometimes the quality of the product cannot be truly determined until after it is out in the market for a while. Think of all of the product recalls that you hear about after an item was shipped, even by major corporations that are known to focus on quality, like Toyota. There went a lot of money down the drain, certainly much more than you would save with a 10% quantity discount! It is usually best to start out walking before you run when producing new products. Believe me–I know this from personal experience and from seeing what happens to others.

CHAPTER 11:
INTERNATIONAL TRADE

W̶e live in an increasingly globalized economy and you need to take this into account right from the moment you start your business. Not only must you consider how international markets and events will affect your business directly, but you need to understand and keep on top of how international markets and events will affect your business more indirectly: issues such as: the price of oil; security situations; monetary exchange rates; trade agreements; trade barriers, and much more.

<u>Pitfall</u>: Shipping items out of the country or importing without knowing what you are doing

In this chapter we will review only those issues likely to directly affect your business. This is a good primer on international trade. Many of these issues may not affect you for awhile if you are a long ways from being ready to export your product, but you will be wise to review them anyways so that they will be in the back of your mind once you do become ready, thus avoiding potentially very costly mistakes.

IP ENFORCEMENT IN THE U.S.

We have previously reviewed how to obtain intellectual property registrations in foreign countries, but we have not covered how to respond if you find that someone is exporting products to the U.S. that infringe your trademarks or copyrights. Fortunately for entrepreneurs, the U.S. government will enforce trademarks and copyrights with regard to infringement by imported goods. Unfortunately for entrepreneurs, this enforcement is only for imported goods, not for goods produced domestically by a U.S.-owned business.

The U.S. Customs and Border Protection (CBP) agency enforces U.S. trademarks and copyrights primarily by impounding infringing products at the border. You should record your IP with the CBP to ensure efficient enforcement. The recording fee is $190 in 2010 for each copyright and for each class of goods for trademarks. Note that the IP must be previously registered with the Library of Congress (copyright) or the USPTO (trademark) prior to recording it with CBP. More information is available at: http://www.cbp.gov/xp/cgov/trade/priority_trade/ipr/

If an infringing product makes it past the border, you may contact the U.S. Department of Justice (DOJ) for enforcement of registered copyrights and trademarks. Start by contacting a local law enforcement agency and asking to speak with the "Duty Complaint Agent."

Unfortunately, CBP and DOJ do not enforce patents.

Also available to you for enforcing non-infringement by imported goods is the multi-agency National Intellectual Property Rights Coordination Center. Investigations are carried out by personnel from the FBI and Immigrations and Customs Enforcement office. More information is available and complaints of infringement may be filed on the Website at: http://www.ice.gov/iprcenter/

IP ENFORCEMENT IN FOREIGN COUNTRIES

The U.S. has international trade agreements with major foreign countries that require the countries to provide for means by which U.S. IP rights holders may enforce their IP. Of course the U.S. IP must first be duly registered in that foreign country.

The U.S. Commercial Service's Market Access and Compliance unit assists U.S. companies in the enforcement of their IP in foreign countries and will work with foreign embassies to resolve issues. More information is available at: http://trade.gov/mac/. The unit will also assist in resolving other issues in which U.S. companies are being treated unfairly in foreign markets in violation of trade agreements.

ASSISTANCE FROM THE U.S. COMMERCIAL SERVICE

The U.S. Commercial Service (USCS) is tasked with promoting and enhancing international trade. The USCS offers a broad range of services and has offices in locations throughout the country. If you plan to import or export, be sure to contact the USCS. The Website is: http://trade.gov/

The USCS participates in the STOPFAKES program to combat IP piracy from abroad. The Website is: http://www.stopfakes.gov/

The USCS also offers trade missions, which provide a "guided" and relatively low-cost opportunity to travel to a foreign country in an attempt to sell your goods or services. The USCS describes its trade missions as follows: "Department of Commerce (DOC) Trade Missions offer a proven cost-effective tool for helping U.S. companies learn first-hand about global markets. DOC recruits U.S. companies whose goal is to export their products and services. These U.S. companies travel together as a delegation on a trade mission where they attend market briefings, participate in site visits and networking receptions, and have one-on-one business matchmaking appointments with pre-screened potential buyers, agents, distributors, and joint venture partners.

"Trade Missions offer access, clout and the prestige of being part of a U.S. government trade delegation. DOC Trade Missions gain the attention of local/national government representatives, business leaders and media in international markets. Trade Missions help U.S. companies open markets, leverage opportunities in strategic industries, and expand U.S. trade relationships with our traditional trading partners, as well as in promising emerging global markets."

SMALL BUSINESS DEVELOPMENT CENTERS/SCORE

Many Small Business Development Centers and the SCORE organization can assist with importing and exporting compliance issues.

ASSISTANCE FROM STATE TRADE OFFICES

Many states have trade offices to assist businesses located within their borders to export their goods abroad. Be sure to check what is available in your area. Some states even provide financial incentives for exporters. For instance, the State of Pennsylvania provides the Market Access Grant to assist companies travelling abroad on trade missions. Some states have representatives in other countries to assist businesses with conducting business in those countries. For instance, the representative may be able to assist in vetting a foreign company with which you want to conduct business.

CUSTOMS BROKERS

If you plan to import or export, there are many regulations with which you must comply, including the payment of duties. A *customs broker* is a private business licensed by Customs to assist importers and exporters and to facilitate transactions with Customs in the U.S. and foreign countries. The broker can guide you through the process.

FREIGHT FORWARDERS

A *freight forwarder* is a company that takes care of the logistics of transporting your goods to their intended location in a foreign country or from their location in a foreign country. The freight forwarder can advise the best means of transportation, provide freight cost estimates and generally guide you through the transportation process between your door and that of the foreign business.

SECURING A CUSTOMS BOND

For import shipments over $2000 in value, Customs requires that the importer post a bond to ensure payment of duties, potential penalties, etc. This bond is purchased through a third-party private company and is basically an insurance policy so that Customs can recover from the bond company any amount due if the importer for some reason does not pay. There are two forms bond: a single entry bond covering only one shipment and a continuous bond, covering shipments for a period of one year.

DON'T GET BURNED–GET A LETTER OF CREDIT

Due to the difficulties of collecting debts across international boundaries, most businesses will require a letter of credit from an entity to which they ship goods on credit. This is a letter issued by a bank in which the bank guarantees to pay the amount of the invoice if the company does not. It is highly advisable that you require such letters of credit from any entity to which you ship goods on credit and verify the validity of the letter. It is also advisable that you require pre-payment from first-time customers.

FOREIGN-EXCHANGE RATES

If you are selling to a foreign customer, you should price your goods and require payment in U.S. dollars so that you are not affected by variations in currency exchange rates. If you are purchasing from a foreign supplier you should try to get the price and payment specified in U.S. dollars for the same reason. If you cannot, you must keep on top of the exchange rates and projected trends for them, as they will cause your costs to vary. A convenient currency exchange converter is offered at: http://www.xe.com/ucc/

FUNDING FROM THE EXPORT-IMPORT BANK OF THE U.S.

The Export-Import Bank of the U.S. (Ex-Im Bank) provides financing support for exporters and also offers information to assist them. The Bank describes itself as follows: "At Ex-Im Bank, we provide financing assistance for the export of U.S. goods and services to international markets because our goal is to make American exporters more competitive in the global marketplace. By offering the financing and insurance that most private institutions won't, we assume risk so you don't have to. Our insurance, guarantees and buyer financing help make selling internationally worry-free."

If you are selling to a foreign buyer you are well-advised to contact the Ex-Im bank to see what financial services are available as they can be very advantageous to you.

Working-Capital-Guarantee Funding

The Ex-Im Bank offers a working-capital guarantee that facilitates financing to allow you to purchase materials that you require to produce products for export. The guarantee also facilitates loans against accounts receivable resulting from export shipments. The loan is made by a private lender and the Ex-Im Bank provides a guarantee to the lender for 90% of the loan amount. This encourages private lenders to make such loans that they may not otherwise make.

DANGER: EXPORT CONTROLS AHEAD

Export controls are federal laws restricting the export of goods, services and technology or technical data to foreign nationals, banned countries, and banned entities. The definition of an export includes *actual exports*–the transfer of goods, services and technology or technical data from the U.S. to a foreign country, and *deemed exports*–the transfer within the U.S. of goods, services and technology or technical data to a Foreign Person. Violations can result in criminal and civil penalties.

International Traffic in Arms Regulations (ITAR)

The U.S. government restricts the export of information, services, and goods that may have strategic military value through the ITAR. Penalties for violation can be severe. If you are exporting anything that could be construed has having military value, it is best to check on compliance with ITAR well before export. The U.S. Department of State administers ITAR and more information can be found at: http://www.pmddtc.state.gov/regulations_laws/itar_official.html

Export Administration Regulations (EAR)

The U.S. Department of Commerce Bureau of Industry and Security administers the EAR. The Department defines the Regulations as follows: "The export control provisions of the EAR are intended to serve the national security, foreign policy, nonproliferation, and short supply interests of the United States and, in some cases, to carry out its international obligations. Some controls are designed to restrict access to dual use items by countries or persons that might apply such items to uses inimical to U.S. interests. The EAR also include some export controls to protect the United States from the adverse impact of the unrestricted export of commodities in short supply."

More information is available at: http://www.ntis.gov/products/export-regs.aspx

Office of Foreign Assets Control (OFAC)

There are certain countries and individuals to which it is illegal to export. The Department of the Treasury administers these laws through its OFAC. Treasury describes the controls as follows: "The Office of Foreign Assets Control (OFAC) of the US Department of the Treasury administers and enforces economic and trade sanctions based on US foreign policy and national security goals against targeted foreign countries and regimes, terrorists, international narcotics traffickers, those engaged in activities related to the proliferation of weapons of mass destruction, and other threats to the national security, foreign policy or economy of the United States. OFAC acts under Presidential national emergency powers, as well as authority granted by specific legislation, to impose controls on transactions and freeze assets under US jurisdiction. Many of the sanctions are based on United Nations and other international mandates, are multilateral in scope, and involve close cooperation with allied governments."

More information is available at: http://www.treasury.gov/about/organizational-structure/offices/Pages/Office-of-Foreign-Assets-Control.aspx

NAFTA COMPLIANCE

As Canada and Mexico are our immediate neighbors and largest trading partners, there is a likelihood that you will be subject to North American Free Trade Agreement (NAFTA) regulations. The primary regulation with which you must comply is the *Certificate of Origin*, which is a certification that an item being exported to a NAFTA country has a certain percentage of origin in a NAFTA country. The benefit is a lower tariff for the party importing the goods into a NAFTA country. More information can be found at: http://www.treasury.gov/about/organizational-structure/offices/Pages/Office-of-Foreign-Assets-Control.aspx or at: http://www.naftaworks.org

THE HARMONIZED COMMODITY DESCRIPTION AND CODING SYSTEM (HS)

The HS was developed to standardize (harmonize) the numerical coding system that countries use to categorize traded goods, thus facilitating their international trade. You must know the harmonized code for products that you intend to export. More information may be found at: http://www.export.gov/logistics/eg_main_018119.asp

MARKING COUNTRY OF ORIGIN

As you know, imported goods must be properly marked with their country of origin. However, there are specific rules regarding this marking. Information is provided at the following link: http://www.cbp.gov/linkhandler/cgov/newsroom/publications/trade/co_origin.ctt/markingo.doc

Be aware that any label indicating country of origin must be considered by CBP to be firmly affixed. If you simply put an adhesive sticker, for instance, on a surface on which it does not securely adhere–such as some types of fabric–CBP may decide that this is insufficient marking and hold your shipment at the border to be properly marked.

COMPLYING WITH FOREIGN REGULATIONS

Just as the U.S has quite a number of regulations regarding the safety and other aspects of products sold here, other countries have the same. In Europe, for example, the regulations are even more complicated. Be sure to do thorough research on requirements in each country to which you may want to export. For instance, products exported to Europe must comply with the CE marking and RoHS requirements.

CHAPTER 12:
FINANCING YOUR BUSINESS

Disclaimer: This chapter contains general information about soliciting investments, provided to help you understand various concepts of this complex and difficult process. The laws regarding solicitation are complex and subject to change. <u>Do not rely on the information in this book as legal counsel</u>. You must obtain competent legal counsel prior to making any investment solicitations.

CONCEPTS AND TERMINOLOGY OF FINANCING

<u>Funding Mantra</u>: **People pay for passion.**

<u>Inside Scoop:</u> **Determine how much money you need to achieve your goals and then go get it.**

In this chapter I will focus primarily on financing your business by securing capital from equity investors, although other means will also be discussed. I will start with some general overview material and provide more detail further in. As some of these concepts are complex, I will repeat some of them or try to explain them in different scenarios or in different contexts. Please bear with me if you get it the first time; I figure you can always skip past certain parts if you desire.

In order to understand the financing of your business you must understand the meaning of the words *capital*, *capitalize*, and *capitalization*.

Capital, as used in this chapter, means wealth in any form (typically monetary, but including property) that can be used to create more wealth.

Capitalize refers to the process of establishing a capital base for the company, such as seeking and receiving *equity investment* into a company. In turn, equity investment refers to money provided to a company in return for an ownership stake in the company. For instance: "He is looking for angel investors to capitalize his company."

Capitalization can be used in reference to the amount of capital that the company has under its control, as in: "The company has $1 million in capitalization." It can be used to refer to the stock-market value of a company, as in: "The company has a stock-market capitalization of $5 billion." The word can also be used to denote a status, such as: "The company is in the capitalization phase," which means that the company is currently seeking capital.

A great glossary of private equity financing terms is provided at: http://mba.tuck.dartmouth.edu/pecenter/resources/glossary.html

<u>Inside Scoop:</u> **The most important concept in capitalization is undercapitalization.**

THE EVILS OF UNDERCAPITALIZATION

Undercapitalization refers to an unfortunate condition in which a company has underestimated the amount of capital that it will require to start up and therefore it ends up with too little capital to meet its needs. The company did not seek sufficient capital investment to get it through to the point at which it is making money. This is an extremely common condition for a young company attempting to commercialize a new technology. It is probably the number one reason that a company fails. Undercapitalization is actually a symptom of company failure–not the cause of it– but try telling that to the bank.

Pitfall: Under-appreciating undercapitalization

Absolutely every entrepreneur I have ever worked with who is developing financial projections states that he is being "very conservative" in estimating his projected sales and "very liberal" in estimating his projected expenses. The entrepreneurs are therefore quite confident that the amount of capital they are projecting they will have to raise will give them a very comfortable margin for error. However, despite this confidence, I have rarely seen a company that did not get itself into a condition of undercapitalization. I will address several reasons for this later in this chapter.

HOW DO I KNOW HOW MUCH MONEY I WILL NEED?

All entrepreneurs I have worked with are perplexed by the need to forecast the amount of money that they will need to borrow or raise in order to avoid undercapitalization. After all, it is just a guess–a prediction of the future. But it is a life-or-death estimate, as we have just seen.

The number representing the amount of capital you must secure comes from your cash flow pro-forma statement, which in turn is generated from your business plan. In your business plan you will lay out what it is that you want to do, how you are going to do that, how much that will cost and how much revenue that will bring in. From this you will develop cash flow projections, monthly for the first year, quarterly for years two and three, then annually for years four and five if you choose to project out beyond three years.

A good description and example of a cash flow statement can be found at: http://en.wikipedia. org/wiki/Cash_flow_statement

Your cash flow projections will show how much cash you have "in the bank" at the end of each period. This figure can never be allowed to go negative in the actual operation of your business. However, you may see that the figure goes negative at some points in your cash flow projections. If so, you must decide to then put into your projections the receipt of cash through a loan or investment to raise the cash inflows to the point that your period-ending cash is positive. Alternatively, you could project higher revenues or lower expenses, but you cannot just do this arbitrarily to achieve positive period-ending cash position!

In this manner you will see not only how much money you need to bring in, but when you need to do so.

WHERE TO FIND MONEY AND HOW TO SECURE IT

There are six basic options to choose from in funding your company. Virtually all entrepreneurs use a combination of these options. Basic funding options are:

1) Loans
2) External equity investments
3) Partnerships
4) Crowdfunding/Peer-to-peer funding/Microfinancing
5) Self-funding
6) Government research grants

Below are some highlights on funding options, but for more detail, a Small Business Development Center or SCORE business consultant is a great resource.

Loan vs. Investment

A loan must be repaid and involves no ownership stake in the company by the entity loaning the funds. An entity making a loan will typically require collateral as a means of recouping its funds if the company cannot repay the loan.

In contrast, an investment does not need to be repaid and it involves an ownership stake in the company by the entity investing the funds. If the company is unable to generate sufficient cash flow to pay dividends to investors and the investors cannot sell their shares for at least the price they paid for them, the investors may lose some or all of their money. If the company goes bankrupt the investors may lose their money.

In a bankruptcy proceeding, an entity that has invested in a company is typically last in line behind entities that have loaned to a company when it comes time to divvy up any of the company's remaining assets such as equipment, intellectual property, etc.

Many entrepreneurs wonder which they should pursue for their business: loans or investments. Like nearly everything else, there are pros and cons to each. You must evaluate these and make your own decision.

LOANS

Types of Loans

There are two basic types of loans: a term loan and a line of credit. A *term loan* has a defined amount and repayment plan. For example, car loans and home mortgages are term loans. Term loans are meant for the purchase of capital assets such as land, buildings, and equipment. A *line of credit*–also known as a *credit line*–is a type of revolving credit. The lender sets an upper limit on the amount that can be borrowed and the borrower taps that amount as needed. The borrower repays the borrowed amount as cash is available to do so. A line of credit is for short-term needs such as the purchase of inventory prior to a busy sales season. After the busy season the lender would expect the borrower to pay the line of credit down to zero. The credit line remains open for future borrowing as needed. Lenders expect a line of credit to be paid down to zero at least once per year.

Loans for Startups

Loans for business startup and product development efforts often come from family and friends, as banks normally will not loan solely for these purposes. Be sure to prepare written documents for loans from family and friends, at the very least. If the amount is substantial, it is best to consult an attorney to draw up a loan contract.

It may be possible to secure a bank loan for a new company that will conduct product development in the early stages as part of its overall business plan. In this case, the majority of the loan would need to be for purposes such as purchasing land, building, or equipment and a minority would be for working capital needs such as product development efforts. The reverse is very highly unlikely when dealing with a bank or even with a government loan program.

Entrepreneurs with equity in a house may be able to get a home equity loan or home equity line of credit. In some cases you may have much more discretion in how to spend the proceeds of these loans that you would the proceeds of a commercial loan.

The U.S. Small Business Administration (SBA), the U.S. Department of Agriculture (USDA), and other government entities have loan programs available for small businesses, including startups. Many of these loan programs are executed through a bank or must include bank financing. There are stringent requirements for obtaining these loans. Part of the mission of the USDA is rural development, so if you live in a rural area (i.e., not a metropolitan area) you may be surprised by what you may be eligible for. For instance, in addition to loan programs, the USDA has the Value Added Producer Grant, which provides money to match on a 1:1 ratio market-research funds expended by startups that produce an agricultural product and convert it into a higher-value product. Be sure to check with your local economic development agencies to see what may be available in your area.

What the Lender Will Want

When a person or entity provides a loan, they typically want collateral. If the borrowed funds are used to purchase land, buildings, or equipment, those items can be the collateral. If the money is going toward inventory purchases, the inventory may be the collateral. If a lender is making a loan to a company for working capital for which there is no collateral, that lender may require a lien on assets such as the above items. Alternatively the lender may require the commitment of, for instance, a home, bonds, stocks, retirement accounts, etc.

An institutional lender and a wise individual providing a loan to a business will want you to address the following issues so that they may make their decision:

- What is the credit history of everyone owning 20% or more of the company?
- How much does the company want to borrow?
- What will the company do with the money?
- How will the company repay the money?
- What is the collateral?
- How much money are the company owners committing to the project?
- How can I get it out of the owners' hide(s) if the company cannot repay?

Your Personal Guarantee

The way a lender addresses that last question is by requiring anyone with 20% or more ownership in the company to sign a *personal guarantee*, which is a document that states that the signer will pay the debt if the company cannot. This will be a *joint and severable guarantee*, meaning that the lender can recover the full amount equally from all guarantors or in any other ratio the lender chooses, including all from one guarantor. If the lender sees that it will be much easier to collect from one guarantor than others, they may go after that person solely, because of the ease of so doing.

The reason for the personal guarantee is that the owners of a corporation or LLC are not legally responsible for the debts of the corporation or LLC. A savvy lender knows this, so they require the personal guarantee to get around this fact.

A savvy lender will not accept a personal guarantee from someone not able to pay the amount guaranteed. For instance, if the company is trying to borrow $300,000 and the lender looks at the income of one of the large-percentage owners and finds that they would not be able to "make good" on the guarantee, they will typically not make the loan. Of course the best way to avoid this scenario is to be sure that any large-percentage investors you bring on are able to guarantee large loans.

This personal guarantee requirement can work to your benefit if a potential investor is demanding a large ownership percentage in your company. Point out to that person that they may be required to personally guarantee loans if they own more than 20%. Of course you run the risk of scaring them off, but you must disclose everything fully to potential investors, so you should not try to hide this information in any case.

I have more than once seen situations in which a company was not able secure a loan because one of the large owners was unwilling to provide a guarantee. You may be wise to secure from any individual that will end up with more than 20% of the company an agreement in writing that they will personally guarantee loans up to a certain amount. This can prevent problems later down the line. You may not now think that you will need a loan, but you cannot predict the future and a loan may at some point be the difference between life and death for your company.

SECURITIES & COMPLIANCE ISSUES

It is very important to understand the concept of a *security* if you plan to seek investment into your company. The following is a great definition from the *Yahoo Small Business* Website: "A security is an investment in a profit-making enterprise that is not run by the investor. Here's another way to think about it: If a person invests in a business with the expectation of making money from the efforts of others, that person's investment is generally considered a "security" under federal and state law. Conversely, when a person will rely on his or her own efforts to make a profit, that person's ownership interest in the company will not usually be treated as a security."

<u>Federal Laws</u>
There are strict laws governing the solicitation of security investments into businesses. When you solicit investment for your business you may be selling a security and fall under securities laws. A *security*, in this context, is a share of stock or sometimes an ownership interest in a LLC or LP. Securities laws are set by the U.S. Securities Exchange Commission (SEC) and by state governments. There are severe penalties for violations of securities laws.

BE SURE TO CONSULT A QUALIFIED ATTORNEY BEFORE MAKING ANY INVESTMENT SOLICITATIONS OF ANY TYPE!

General information regarding federal regulation of the solicitation of investment is available on the SEC website, http://www.sec.gov and at http://www.seclaw.com

The SEC maintains an ombudsman's office that you may call with questions regarding small-business-related securities issues. The phone number is 202-551-3460. The SEC maintains a Website specific to small business issues at: http://www.sec.gov/info/smallbus.shtml

<u>State Laws</u>

As previously mentioned, states also regulate the sale of securities, so be sure to check on this in your state. **Do not proceed with an investment solicitation without knowing the rules and regulations of each state in which you are making a solicitation.** State securities regulations are usually administered by the State Securities Commissioner of the state's Department of State.

Note that state regulations regarding the sale of securities are generally known in the business as "*Blue-sky laws.*" This probably stems from a reference to unscrupulous operators who over the years have fleeced people by selling "blue sky" investments in which every day was sure to be a sunny day and there was no chance of dark clouds on the horizon.

<u>Pitfall</u>: Forgetting about state securities laws when raising investments

Do not dismiss the states! State securities regulators can and do issue large fines and even send offenders of their state's securities laws to prison. In one recent case in Alabama, an offender was convicted and sentenced to a 10-year suspended prison sentence primarily for promising to triple investor's money on an investment of only $10,000. The Alabama Securities Commissioner even pursued prosecution of the offender after he fled the state to avoid prosecution.

A private group, the North American Securities Administrators Association (NASAA), has developed the Small Company Offering Registration (SCOR), which is touted as a "simplified question-and-answer registration form that companies may also use as the disclosure document for investors." It was primarily designed for state registration of offerings under SEC Rule 504 for sale of securities up to $1 million. NASAA has compiled an *Issuer's Manual* to assist in completing the form. Although the SCOR form is touted as "simplified," the *Issuer's Manual* instructions for it is 103 pages long. The forms are available at: http://www.nasaa.org/Industry___Regulatory_Resources/Corporation_Finance/564.cfm.

A number of states have formed regional reciprocal agreements to coordinate SCOR or Regulation A filings. These regions are: New England; Mid-Atlantic; Midwest; and Western.

<u>Registration of Securities</u>

The federal government–through the SEC–and the various state governments, require that securities offered for sale within their jurisdictions be registered with the governing body unless certain very specific conditions are met which may exempt the offering from registration. The rules covering these exemptions are, for the uninitiated, quite complex and confusing.

Every offer or sale of securities by a company either has to be registered with the SEC under the Securities Act of 1933 or an exemption from registration has to be available. The most popular exemption to registration is Regulation D, and in particular Rule 504 or 506.

For more information about the SEC's registration requirements and common exemptions, read its brochure Q & A: Small Business & the SEC at: http://www.sec.gov/info/smallbus/qasbsec.htm. **Be sure to do this!**

SECURING EQUITY INVESTMENTS

Importance of Company Structure

In order to secure equity investments into your company, you must first form an entity in which someone can invest: typically an S-corporation, C-corporation or Limited Liability Company (LLC). Following is a brief discussion of how company structure affects equity investment.

Sole Proprietorship/General Partnership

A sole proprietorship or a partnership can receive a loan, but these entities cannot receive an equity investment through the sale of securities. You can recruit a general partner into a business partnership with you, but if that partner brings money into the business it is not via the sale of securities such as stock. This is because you are jointly establishing a company, not selling off portions of it to someone.

In a general partnership, your partner will by definition have substantial management rights and will share direct control of the company. For this reason the SEC does not regulate general partnership financial transactions. The SEC recognizes that the partner can protect him/herself– via direct management control–from being victimized by unscrupulous management. In contrast, a stockholder has very limited means to protect him/herself, therefore the SEC has set up many regulations to protect that person.

Limited Partnership (LP)/Limited Liability Partnership (LLP)

Sales of ownership interests to the limited partners in a LP or a LLP will typically be considered to be a sale of a security due to the lack of management control by the limited partners.

Corporation/LLC

Once a corporation is formed, its ownership is apportioned among owners through the sale and/or distribution of securities in the form of shares of stock, which are considered to be securities.

In the case of an LLC the ownership interest that is apportioned to owners may or may not be considered a security. The test is whether the purchaser of the interest will have an active management role in the company. If not, the interest will be a security and you will fall under securities laws when you attempt to sell it to the investor.

Facing the Realities of Financing

Talk is Very, Very Cheap

The hard fact is that an entrepreneur with little or no history of prior success has very few options available when it comes to funding product development and the startup of a company. The even harder fact is that the process can often be unbelievably frustrating, primarily due to the fact that talk is cheap. Many people will express interest, but far fewer will actually invest, and often at a far lower dollar amount than you expected; almost always much later than promised.

I saw one recent study by a reputable group (I unfortunately cannot recall which) that stated that only 50% of purported "investors" actually invest in companies. Couple that with the very large number of investment options that the actual investors have to pick from and an entrepreneur's odds can be very long indeed.

In your plans, you must take the above into account. If you do not, you run a great risk of running low on or out of money while you are waiting for your capitalization efforts to come to fruition.

You First!

You must be willing to put your own money in first and to then ask your family, friends, and acquaintances for their financial assistance. Approaching family, friends and acquaintances is often difficult and is fraught with risk if things go sour, but it is often the only viable option.

Deductibility

You are rightfully concerned about what would happen if you do not succeed and your friends and family lose their investment. You may take some solace, however, in knowing that such an investment loss is normally tax deductible. The rules for deductibility change from time to time, but historically the ability to deduct losses from investments into companies that have raised less than $1 million in capital are particularly lenient. Other investment losses are deductible, but perhaps over a longer period of time. It may be that the entire amount of the loss cannot be recouped. Be sure to consult a competent tax advisor and recommend to your investors that they do the same.

It's a Sales Process

Soliciting funding is a sales process. Therefore, you must conduct a well-orchestrated sales campaign in order to be successful over the long term. If you do not have the knowledge, personality, time or desire to do this, then you must find someone to partner with who does.

Pitfall: "Here's my great technology, give me money."

Inside Scoop: You are selling an *investment opportunity*, not a technology.

If you do not approach the process with the above wisdom you will flail away in vain once you start pitching to sophisticated investors. Remember that these people have a revolving door of entrepreneurs coming in and out with their whiz-bangs and Oh-my-Gods, each more brilliant than the next. You are competing directly with these other entrepreneurs for the investor's attention and money. The investor does not care if he makes a killing on your technology or the next guy's; he just wants to see the brightly lit pathway by which he is going to make a killing.

Give a Little

Another important concept to grasp–obvious though it is, but so quickly forgotten–is that you cannot get something for nothing. You must be willing to give up something to get funding, usually something substantial.

You may believe in yourself and your technology and "know" that the world will come rushing to your door. But others will not be so sure and they will want protection for their risk. This is sometimes a very difficult concept for entrepreneurs to grasp.

Pitfall: "Pay me for my dream."

The bottom line is that the more validation you have due to assets such as:

- A strong management team
- Signed contracts
- Actual sales
- Defined manufacturing costs
- Protected intellectual property
- Solid marketing plans
- Validated market size, etc.,

the less you will have to give up for a given amount of financing.

Inside Scoop: Only a fool will pay you for a dream that has done little but bounce around inside your head.

"Tough love": If your dream cannot even motivate *you*, how the heck do you expect it to motivate others?

Accredited Investors and What They Mean to You

As previously mentioned, the reason for securities laws is to protect unwary investors from scam artists. The laws were set up over the years after "little old ladies" were fleeced out of their life savings by investing in get-rich-quick schemes. However the SEC does recognize the difference between a little old lady on a pension and a wealthy businessman. For this reason, the SEC has developed the concept of an "*accredited investor.*"

A wealthy businessman or a substantial organization, for instance, is expected to have enough financial sense to avoid being scammed; they are deemed accredited investors. Federal securities laws define the term accredited investor in Rule 501 of Regulation D as:

- A bank, insurance company, registered investment company, business development company, or small business investment company;
- An employee benefit plan, within the meaning of the Employee Retirement Income Security Act, if a bank, insurance company, or registered investment adviser makes the investment decisions, or if the plan has total assets in excess of $5 million;
- A charitable organization, corporation, or partnership with assets exceeding $5 million;
- A director, executive officer, or general partner of the company selling the securities;
- A business in which all the equity owners are accredited investors;
- A natural person who has individual net worth, or joint net worth with the person's spouse, that exceeds $1 million at the time of the purchase, excluding the value of their primary residence;
- A natural person with income exceeding $200,000 in each of the two most recent years or joint income with a spouse exceeding $300,000 for those years and a reasonable expectation of the same income level in the current year; or
- A trust with assets in excess of $5 million, not formed to acquire the securities offered, whose purchases a sophisticated person makes.

The concept of accredited investors is important, because if you are soliciting investments from someone who is not an accredited investor, the rules are often more strict as to the amount and type of information that you must provide to that person regarding the investment opportunity.

Depending on which exemption from registration that you claim, it may be up to you what information about your business you choose to give to the accredited investor—that is, as long as the information is not false or misleading. The accredited investor, of course, may choose not to invest if he feels that you are not providing sufficient information.

Promise of a Return on Investment

Pitfall: *"You will be able to at least double your money in three years."*

If you go around telling this to investors, that may be good practice for later telling this to your cellmates.

Be aware that no matter to whom you are selling, it is illegal to promise a return on investment or to promise that the stock price will increase in the future. It is permissible to state that the technology, management team, opportunities, etc. are wonderful, but you cannot extend this into a promise of a return on investment. In fact, you must clearly state that all investment is at risk of loss and you must detail the risks involved.

Risk Assessment

When raising capital it is very important for you to remember that an idea is nearly worthless without the money behind it to fuel the development, intellectual property protection, and sales efforts required to profit from it. Also, a person who puts in money is taking an actual, clearly defined, and high risk.

An entrepreneur with an idea but no money believes that he is taking a high risk when he takes investments—the risk that by giving up ownership percentages of his company, he will profit less than if he does not give this up. However, this risk is very vague and abstract—the cold hard fact is that odds are very high that there will not be any profits to forfeit. Remember, the U.S. Patent and Trademark Office has done studies that show that only 2% of persons that receive a patent ever make a profit from it.

Therefore, the person putting up actual cash investment can and should command ownership positions relative to their risk. It is true that "a fool and his money are soon parted," and you may find a fool who will put in a significant chunk of change for a tiny ownership stake, but if you need to eventually "move up the food chain" to more knowledgeable investors with bigger money, you will find that these persons rarely make such mistakes.

Sophisticated Investors—A Critical Distinction

This gets us to the concept of a *sophisticated investor*—the polar opposite, obviously—of a fool. It is very important to understand that investing in technology commercialization companies that expect to enter huge markets and create large companies is a highly specialized endeavor. Only those persons who have previous experience under their belt on one side of the equation or the other (entrepreneur or investor), and perhaps business consultants that have assisted several companies all the way through the process will truly understand the many complexities, variables, and considerations that must be taken into account.

The key here is the phrase "all the way through the process." This means through to the anticipated end point of VC capital, IPO, M & A with a large corporation, etc. Just because someone has previously invested in a business, a startup, or even a technology startup does *not* necessarily mean that they know what they are doing. They need to have been through the several rounds of investments and to have seen first-hand what happens to early investors once VCs step in, when a company goes public, etc.

Again, you may find a person with money and with great business experience in some field–maybe even experience in owning and operating several companies. However, this alone does not give them knowledge of issues such as:

- How to properly set a pre-money valuation
- SEC Regulation D rules 504, 505, and 506
- The due diligence criteria to which the company will be subjected by VCs and later potential acquirers
- Full-ratchet anti-dilution protection
- Warrants
- Cram-downs
- Drag-along rights
- Convertible debt
- Participating preferred stock
- Liquidation preferences
- Pari passu
- Escrow periods
- Put options
- Earnouts
- Reverse vesting
- And many other concepts that will affect the early investor, whether he knows about them or not.

I refer to those investors who understand these aspects of investing in startup companies as *sophisticated investors* (my definition here does not exactly match the SEC's). When I refer to an *un*sophisticated investor, it does not mean that the investor is unsophisticated in general, or even that he is unsophisticated in making certain types of investments (publicly traded stocks, bonds, etc.). It means that he is unsophisticated in the field of early-stage private-equity capitalization of companies that plan to go on to the "big time." The term that I normally use to refer to an unsophisticated investor is *naïve investor*. Again–no disrespect intended!

Note that a person could meet the SECs definition of an accredited investor but not meet my definition here of a sophisticated investor.

It is incumbent upon you to learn about private equity capitalization if you intend to raise money for your company. This will take time and effort. It is actually an entire "field of study" for you as an entrepreneur. However, remember this: You are an investor in your company as well, and you will find out the very hard way how all of this works if you do not understand it.

Inside Scoop: Knowledge is power... don't be the one without it!

Retaining Control of Your Company

For most entrepreneurs seeking capital, there is always tension between bringing in money and giving out ownership stakes in their company. Entrepreneurs want the money, but they don't want to give up anything of any real value for it. Mostly, entrepreneurs are worried about loss of decision-making control or being shoved aside in their own company. In fact, these things can and do happen to entrepreneurs if they are naïve, not careful, or not effective in their jobs.

Nearly every entrepreneur I have worked with is highly and irrationally concerned about losing control of their company if they bring in investors. They have heard horror rumors about entrepreneurs being left out in the cold by greedy VCs. I used the term "horror rumors" instead of "horror stories" because the latter term would imply that there is even a wisp of truth behind them, which there is not.

You heard that right: There is absolutely no truth to the rumor that *effective* entrepreneurs routinely get pushed out by sophisticated investors.

To prove this point, here is a challenge I throw down to all readers of my book:

Name one instance of a startup company that reached national prominence through outside investment and in which the original entrepreneur was pushed out before the company "hit the big time."

To help you out, I will list a few of the cases in which the original entrepreneur(s) *did* remain at the helm (CEO, President, Chairman, etc.) as the corporation grew monstrous, went public, etc. These are the biggest names in entrepreneurial business success, creating some of the world's richest men, starting with a couple of examples going back over 125 years. VCs were involved in many, but not all of those companies listed below, although massive outside investment was always involved. I have included a range of industry sectors and scenarios for your reading pleasure.

<u>36 Colossal Entrepreneurs That Retained Control</u>
1) F. W. Woolworth (Woolworth's/Foot Locker)
2) S.S. Kresge (Kresge's/K Mart/Sears Holdings Co.)
3) Henry Ford (Ford Motor Co.)
4) Paul V. Galvin (Motorola)
5) Will Hewlett and Dave Packard (Hewlett Packard)
6) Sam Walton (Wal-Mart)
7) Ken Olsen (Digital Equipment Corporation)
8) Ray Kroc (McDonald's)
9) Bill Gates (Microsoft)
10) Larry Ellison (Oracle)
11) Howard Schultz (Starbucks)
12) Philip Knight (Nike)
13) Howard Schulze (Best Buy)
14) Andy Groves (Intel)
15) Rob Glaser (RealNetworks)
16) Steve Jobs (Apple)
17) Michael Dell (Dell)
18) Jeff Bezos (Amazon.com)
19) Len Bosack (Cisco Systems)
20) Mike Lazaridis (Research in Motion [Blackberry])
21) Chris Sullivan (Outback Steakhouse)
22) Dr. Irwin Jacobs (Qualcomm)
23) Ted Turner (Turner Broadcasting System)

24) Scott McNealy (Sun Microsystems)
25) Marc Andreessen (Netscape)
26) Jim Clark (Silicon Graphics)
27) Fred Smith (FedEx)
28) John Mackey (Whole Foods Market)
29) Jerry Yang (Yahoo)
30) J. Darius Bikoff (Energy Brands/Glaceau [Vitaminwater, Smartwater])
31) Larry Page & Sergey Brin (Google)
32) Tom Anderson (MySpace)
33) Chad Hurley & Steve Chen (YouTube)
34) Mark Zuckerberg (Facebook)
35) Jack Dorsey (Twitter)
36) Andrew Mason (Groupon)

How's THAT for a list of who's who in the world of rock-star entrepreneurs?

Note that Jerry Yang was forced out of Yahoo more than a decade after the company hit the big time, but the CEO position is never a lifetime guarantee at any major company. Also, Steve Chen and Chad Hurley left YouTube two and four years, respectively, after it was sold to Google in 2006. Considering that the two were at the helm when the company was sold for $1.65 billion, I can bet that you would not mind having been in their position.

And for every one Jerry Yang that I am aware of, I am aware of three instances in which the original entrepreneur was brought back to the top after having earlier given up his slot to a more "seasoned" executive. These three are Steve Jobs, Howard Schultz and Larry Page.

Between 1985 and 1997, Apple struggled to perform under the leadership of three CEOs brought in with big-shot credentials. Steve Jobs came back and the rest will be corporate-America history for decades, if not centuries to come.

In early 2011 Google CEO Eric Schmidt stepped aside in favor of Google co-founder Larry Page as the company began to feel itself under attack by newcomers like Facebook. Page was the original CEO in 1998 but had turned over the reins to the more-experienced Schmidt in 2001.

I expect that someone will successfully reply to my challenge and find a founding entrepreneur that was pushed out of a massively successful company prior to it "hitting the big time," but no matter how I rack my brain I cannot come up with one. It really appears to me that this is the measure of what it takes to get to the top of the global heap: A founding entrepreneur whom the future investors want to remain at the helm.

The key is to be a dynamic leader and competent businessman that no investor in their right mind would want to see pushed aside, thus ruining their investment. If you are not, you are toast, and this is as it should be.

So what are you afraid of? Go out and get the money!

Critical Components of Company Valuation

I have been asked by entrepreneurs many times how to determine what percent ownership to give to an investor for a certain amount of investment, but there is really no set formula for this. However, the ending point for the negotiation is to determine *company valuation*, or the monetary value of the company. For a startup, this is an extremely difficult number to determine, as it is almost entirely dependent on uncertain future events.

For a well-established company, the valuation can be–for instance–the *book value* of the company. This is the value of the company's assets minus liabilities as given in the company's accounting books. Little or no provision is made for the future growth prospects of the company. For a publicly traded company the valuation also could be the company's *market value*, which is the number of shares the company has issued, multiplied by the share price. For publicly traded companies the book value and the market value are often de-coupled. A hot company such as Apple will have a market value far in excess of its book value because the stock price is very high. A company such as General Motors just prior to bankruptcy will have a market value far below its book value because the stock price is very low.

In the case of Apple, people are willing to pay more for the company than the value of its assets because they are speculating that the stock price will continue to rise and they can sell the stock at some point in the future for more than they bought it.

Book value is a relatively straightforward number to determine and is calculated by accountants. In contrast, stock prices are largely determined by human sentiment, speculation, and predictions of a company's future prospects–how wishy-washy is *that*?

The de-coupling between book value and stock price occurs for startups as well and is typically much more pronounced than for a public company. You can see that for a startup neither book value nor market value make much sense. The first is because startups typically have very few assets and the second is because the stock is not publicly traded and so it is very difficult to determine the true value of the shares. At least with a publicly traded company there is a very large group of people who all agree on the value of the stock; if you were to argue against this value you would just be a voice in the wilderness. This is not the case with a start-up; everyone has their own opinion and there is no large market to look to for guidance.

This leaves the entrepreneur and the investor wide latitude to claim polar opposite positions regarding company valuation and therefore ownership percentages.

How Pre-Money Valuation Affects Ownership Percentage
Here is a little scenario to help you understand how the assignment of ownership percentage is based on company valuation: If I own a piggy bank with $100 in it and I take $100 from you and put it in the piggy, it will then have $200 in it and we will each own 50% of the piggy. Alternatively, if I own a piggy bank with $400 in it and I take $100 from you and put it in the piggy, it will then have $500 in it; but after this transaction I will own 80% of the piggy and you will only own 20%. Your investment was the same in dollars, but the resulting ownership percentage varied depending on the initial value of the asset into which you contributed your money.

This is the big issue in securing investments: determining the value of the company prior to the investment, which is known as *pre-money valuation*. You try your hardest to justify a high pre-money valuation and the investor holds out for a low pre-money valuation.

If the investor has $100,000 to invest, and you promise to give him 25% of the company for it, then the valuation of the company before the investment would be $300,000 (pre-money valuation) and the valuation would be $400,000 afterward (*post-money valuation*). Valuation is explained in more detail further below.

In the end, the amount of the company you give up really comes down to how strong of a case you can make that you can build a successful business. After that, it is a matter of negotiating skill. You and I would probably each come out of a particular investment negotiation with differing percentages, because we have differing negotiating skills. (Hopefully, yours are better than mine!)

There is one basis from which some entities may want to start in your negotiations, however. This is *discounted cash flow (DCF)*. The DCF analysis basically looks at the money the entrepreneur is asking for and how much return that investment is expected to produce in the future vs. the projected inflation rate and how much the investor could expect to receive from extremely safe investments. Is the risk worth the difference?

A good laypersons' explanation of DCF is provided at: http://www.experiglot.com/2006/06/06/how-to-calculate-discounted-cash-flow-dcf/

Since the company's future cash flow is just an educated guess, so is any company valuation derived exclusively from it. However, the future cash flow that is used in the DCF analysis should be that from the mutually agreed-upon cash flow pro forma statements for the company. In turn, these will be based on the business plan. The business plan should take into account the strengths, weaknesses, opportunities, and threats related to the business venture. When all of these factors are taken into account, the DCF method of setting the valuation will be based on a thorough analysis of the business opportunity.

Related financial terms with which you should familiarize yourself if you intend to raise equity capital (so that you don't look like a country bumpkin) are: *internal rate of return (IRR), net present value (NPV), free cash flow, and time value of money.* The Investopedia Website has definitions of these terms available at: http://www.investopedia.com/terms/d/dcf.asp

There are several services such as VentureSource, available at: http://www.dowjones.com/privatemarkets/venturesource.asp that track actual private equity transactions, including company valuations, but they charge for their information–usually substantial money for the services that provide truly useful information. If you want to spend the money, you may be able to show to an investor several recent transactions that back up your position regarding your company's valuation. VCs and some angel groups will normally access this information before making investments.

How Sophisticated Investors Will Evaluate You

It is very important for you to study and understand the perspective of sophisticated investors if you intend to solicit them for investment. To do otherwise is wasteful of your valuable time and foolhardy. I have found that there are in the world two general categories of people when it comes to startup-company equity investing: Those who know (e. g. the sophisticated investors) and those who do not know (e. g. the newbie entrepreneurs).

When the two groups collide, sparks usually fly.

Here, though, is the problem for entrepreneurs who do not know: You will not get the money unless you meet the needs of and conform to the rules set by those with the money. So... save yourself an awful lot of time and agony by learning and conforming to the needs and rules, or else just go away.

For instance, know that a savvy investor will automatically cut your revenue projections at least by half before they even talk to you. Why would they do this? Because they are not stupid! They have over the years seen swarming ant-farms of money-pleaders filing through the office with their meaty projections, ten times their own weight and held high by sheer force of vanity.

Meanwhile, the anteater is so fat it can no longer get in the building. No problem though; it has a very long tongue.

I can tell you what my criteria would be in deciding whether to invest in a company that is commercializing a new technology. I would ask these two questions:

1) Is the CEO or another empowered senior member of the management team thoroughly familiar with effective sales processes, extremely diligent in pursuing them, and tenaciously hard working?
2) Does the company's product kill its customers outright?

If the answer to #1 is "yes" and the answer to #2 is "no," I will consider investing. If I instead wanted to depend on raw luck to receive a return on my investment, I would buy a lottery ticket.

Of course the above is greatly over-simplified in order to drive home the following:

Inside Scoop: **If you can sell and you have a product that is at least viable in the market, you can succeed. Lacking these, _you will fail._**

Unfortunately, in the real world, savvy investors are much, much more needy creatures than I. They are all about risk identification and mitigation and do not accept one iota of known risk. They even hair-split risk into various sub-categories and analyze each separately: Technology risk, market risk, etc. In nearly every regard they are much more like bankers than entrepreneurs. (_You_ are the entrepreneur, not them.) The vast majority of VCs want an absolutely structured approach to absolutely everything. They are completely absorbed into pie charts; ratios; analyses; Gantt charts; milestones; pedigrees, and ironclad-proven concepts, strategies, or approaches.

Pitfall: **Believing a VC who tells you initially that this is not true**

If you want to truly innovate, you will be on your own!

A Sophisticated Investor's Criteria for Investment
The following list details many of the top criteria that sophisticated investors actually use in establishing whether to invest and at what valuation if so. I have placed the first several of these in approximate order of importance, but understand that each situation is unique and every investor is has different opinions and needs, so no such list can be completely authoritative. After about the first dozen listings it gets very difficult to list the items in any real order of priority, but I have taken a stab at it for you, nonetheless.

- Recent deal flow, valuations, and "exits" for similar businesses. Is your sector hot and trendy or has it already run its course? If you are trying to sell into a "down" market, get ready for heartache; you can be like the plague to an investor. You must learn how investors view your market and business model. Sophisticated investors have a very strong herd mentality because they are aware of which sectors are making money for investors and which are not. Their sentiment can turn 180 degrees in as little as several months, so keep on top of it.
- Likelihood of a lucrative exit event (especially for VCs)
- Clean records, honesty, and good reputations of company executives

- Previous entrepreneurial experience level of the management team
- Current amount of sales revenue
- Total available market size and reasonably expected revenue growth rate for the business and its market
- Clearly defined, attractive business model and revenue model (How will you do business and how will you make money?)
- The level of "pain" that the product relieves for its users
- The company's demonstrated ability to actually sell into the relevant market
- Does your revenue model provide recurring revenue from an end-user?
- Amount of investment requested and planned uses
- The passion of the entrepreneur (It is hard to rank this one on a priority list.)
- Physical location of company headquarters within a day's travel or less for the investor is strongly preferred
- Excellent business plan with a concise executive summary
- Number of board seats the investor will control, compared to total seats available
- Amount of funds previously invested by the entrepreneur and other investors (The more the better.)
- Number of existing investors (The fewer the better; this can be a deal-killer.)
- Number and quality of patents actually issued to date
- Number and quality of patents pending (These are of much lesser value than issued patents.)
- Is the technology disruptive to the market? (Disruptive is good.)
- Number and quality of strategic partnerships with signed agreements in place
- Demonstration of effective use of previously invested funds
- Product development status or plan
- Professional-quality financial pro formas
- Well-researched and innovative marketing plan
- How "scalable" is the business? (More is better.)
- Short innovation and implementation cycles
- Is FDA approval required and what will be the process for that if so?
- The ability of the entrepreneur and management to take advice (coachability)
- Length of the sales cycle (shorter is better)
- Advisors (patent attorney, SEC attorney, CPA) with solid relevant experience
- Will the customers have to change their behavior to benefit from the technology?
- Clean tax payment history of the company (required up-to-date prior to investment)

I want to reiterate that the order of the above list is approximate, especially as you go further down the list. I have tried to show, for instance that some investors will only invest within a certain geographic region, so no matter how great of a business plan you come with you will be rejected. For this reason I have listed location within a day's travel as higher priority than an excellent business plan. Virtually all of the above bases must be covered before a sophisticated investor will part with his money. Sophisticated investors will check out these factors <u>and much more</u> in their process of *due diligence*. I have only "hit the high points" here as an illustration and a general guide. I cannot predict what each and every investor will evaluate in each and every situation; nor can I predict what priority every investor will put on each criterion.

Note that an initial pitch to a sophisticated investor does not have to, nor should it attempt to cover every one of the above issues. Full detail on developing a pitch to investors is beyond the scope of this book, but in general you must cover the following issues:

What do Sophisticated Investors Want From You?

In your initial pitch to a sophisticated investor you normally must present a business plan executive summary of three pages or less covering the following:

- What exactly will your business do?
- How big is the market and how fast is it projected to grow over the next five years?
- How will you make money?
- Who is your management team and what is their prior relevant experience?
- Who is the competition and how will you out-compete them?
- What is your stage of development?
- How much money are you asking for; what will you do with it, and what are you willing to give up for it?
- What is your exit strategy?
- A five-year summary financial projection (Sometimes this can be an attachment in addition to the one-to-three-page executive summary.)

Note that an *exit strategy* is a strategy for creating a liquidity event, which is discussed further below.

How to Make Your Pitch to Investors

If you plan to make a pitch to sophisticated investors it is absolutely imperative that you receive competent coaching from a qualified advisor. You also must rehearse your pitch repeatedly. Record your presentation and review it for presentation skills. In your presentation be sure to make eye contact, stand relatively still, omit the "ums" and "uhs," speak with authority but not arrogance, and do not turn your back when looking at a projector screen.

You will usually be given 8 to 20 minutes to make your pitch. Following this will typically be a question and answer session. *It is here that many entrepreneurs bite the dust!* They have their nice little presentation all worked out and rehearsed, so that goes smoothly. However, they are thrown for a loop by wacky questions from "out in left field" lobbed by an investor who may not have been listening or may just like to see an entrepreneur do the dance. Get ready to get shot at, because this is what will happen. Prior to your pitch you and your team should have thought up all of the skeptical and even the ditzy questions that may be shoveled your way.

Pitfall: Not listening

Your key to success in the Q & A session will be to *listen to the question* and ensure that you understand it, perhaps by repeating it back. I find that very often the entrepreneur fails in this most basic aspect of the Q & A session; they have not even understood what the investor was asking!

After understanding the question, take your time to come up with the *best* answer; do not just throw out *any old* answer. If you do not know the answer, do not attempt to make something up, and especially do not dismiss the question offhand as irrelevant, etc. If you do not have a powerful answer, gracefully acknowledge the validity of question and offer to get back to the inquirer within 24 hours.

Be sure to roll out your "big guns" in response to the questions. By this I mean, respond with your strongest answer. Several times I have watched as a spectator while a client of mine makes a perfect pitch to investors, only to squirm in my seat during the Q & A session wanting to jump up and explain: "No, no, the answer is_____." I guess that is the benefit of not being in the harsh glare of the spotlight, but please take your time to thoroughly consider your answer. An investor who feels that you are pensive and thoughtful will probably be more impressed than if he thinks you shoot your answers from the hip.

When you go in front of sophisticated investors you will hear every reason under the sun why your business model, revenue model, technology, market space, management team, timing, or ability to control the phases of the moon and the coming and going of the seasons is somehow lacking. Each new investor may raise new and different objections, but often there is some commonality as you make pitches to different investor groups, and if so, you should diligently try to discern and address any such issues.

Inside Scoop: You are always ugly in some way

Often, after a long and arduous search, you may be like Goldilocks and find an investor group that is just right for you, but sometimes you just may not be a fit for any sophisticated investment group. This does not, however, automatically mean that you would not be a fit as an acquisition target or as an investment opportunity for a corporation.

Inside Scoop: Corporations often invest for very different reasons than do investment groups, so be sure to "turn over these rocks" if necessary.

What is Scalability and Why is it so Important?
When a sophisticated investor talks about *scalability* or talks about whether a business is *scalable*, he or she is referring to an all-important aspect of a business when it comes to profitability. The best way to explain the concept to you is to give the following examples.

First, however, it is important to understand the concept of *incremental cost*, also known as *marginal cost*. This is the cost associated with producing and delivering to the customer one additional unit of a product.

A software business is highly scalable in part because once the cost of developing the software has been borne by the company it can then sell that software many times over at virtually no additional direct cost of goods, since the goods are simply intellectual property. The company can also typically distribute that software online at very low cost and especially at relatively little incremental cost as the business grows.

Also, businesses based on online delivery of software or software as a service (SaaS) are able to grow extremely quickly. Witness Facebook and especially Groupon–the latter of which posted $1 billion in revenue faster than any other company in history. For these reasons, software or SaaS businesses are highly scalable.

In contrast, a company producing a hardware product must spend additional money for each unit produced, forever. Sure, the company may improve efficiency, but it will never get its per-unit cost near that of software. Worse yet, that company must build ever-larger manufacturing and/or warehousing and physical-distribution systems to handle its growth. These factors greatly inhibit the ability of a hard-goods company to grow as fast as a software company and when it does grow, it will require large cash infusions and will make lower profit margins.

Service businesses fall into basically the same realm as hard-goods businesses. Take consulting for example. There is some upper limit on the amount of work that an individual consultant can do. At some point as the business grows, new consultants must be hired. When this is done, new office space and equipment must be purchased, additional wages and commissions must be paid, etc. The incremental cost of a billable hour of consulting is not nearly as low as the incremental cost of distributing over the Internet an additional copy of a software product or an additional unit of a largely automated software service.

Of course all companies will have certain overhead costs, whether their business is highly scalable or not. The issue of scalability looks primarily at the incremental cost and the ability to grow rapidly with relatively little capital infusion.

If you were an investor, in which type of business would you rather invest? If you said the hardware or service businesses then you are a contrarian to the market, for the market definitely prefers the software or especially the SaaS business models. I once knew an entrepreneur that went out to angel groups and VCs soliciting investment into a business comprising both hardware and software products that were related to each other. The gentleman was repeatedly told: "Get rid of the hardware part of the business and we will consider investing." Not one angel group or VC said anything different.

This does not of course mean that no sophisticated investors will invest in a hard goods or a services business; such investments happen all the time. I am talking here about preferences.

Cash Flow Position–The Driving Force
The reason that startup companies must seek outside capital through loans or investments is because they initially spend far more money than they take in through sales. They have *negative cash flow from operations*. Quite simply, *cash flow* is the cash that flows into and out of a business. This cash includes investments. However, when people talk about a business becoming cash flow positive they are ignoring investment or loan receipts in this analysis. The term *cash flow positive* means that the business is able to sustain its operations through its revenues (virtually always this means sales revenues).

The business could have outstanding loans or even be receiving loans for capital assets such as land, building, and equipment and still be cash flow positive as long as the company can cover all of its expenses and make the loan payments from its revenues.

It is very important to prepare realistic projections of your future total expenses and income so that you can develop a realistic figure for the amount of capital you will need in order to carry you through to the point at which your business is cash flow positive. Once your business is cash flow positive you no longer need to seek loans or investments simply to maintain business operation. Projections of income and expenses are often called *pro forma financial statements* or simply *pro formas*.

As mentioned previously, one of the most common ways new-technology entrepreneurs fail is through undercapitalization. A business that is undercapitalized can run out of money before it becomes cash flow positive.

Undercapitalization takes its grim toll when a business' expenses come in at the projected level or higher but the revenue does not. The business is left with thin reserves on which to draw in order to make it though the unexpected rough spot. Typically, the first spending cuts are made in advertising and marketing, sending the business into a death spiral that is very difficult to pull out of.

Deep Pockets to Sustain You

Of course the best way to avoid undercapitalization is to raise sufficient capital. However, all financing sources are not equal. You want to find financing sources with "deep pockets" that can provide additional funding if needed. It is usually less desirable to receive investments from individuals who are "tapped out" after their initial investment.

The reason for this is that it is often much easier to go back to current investors for additional investment than it is to go to new investors when you need more money, because the current investors have an interest to protect, whereas new investors do not. You can then see why it is desirable to have investors who are not "tapped out" after their initial investment!

Entrepreneur, Meet Murphy

Huge Pitfall: Forgetting about Murphy when projecting capital needs

As we learned above, positive cash flow occurs when your revenues exceed your expenses. Your company can then be self-sustaining, without further cash infusions from investors just to stay in existence. The typical error that entrepreneurs make in projecting the date that their company will become cash flow positive is that they do not take Murphy's Law into account. The problem is that they are virtually never able to get their product on the market within the timeframe that they initially project–something *always* goes wrong.

When "Murphy" steps in and delays product sales, the company must have a cash cushion to sustain itself during the delay. Additionally, it usually requires unanticipated funds to correct the problems causing the delay. Therefore you must secure enough initial investment to survive the onslaught of Murphy.

Inside Scoop: *It's called: "Murphy's Law," not: "Murphy's Theory," and it applies to you!*

Please take the time now to re-read the preceding three paragraphs because this is not a pitfall, but a *certain deathtrap*.

Escrow and Tranche: Two Tools of Savvy Investors
Escrow Accounts

Many sophisticated investors will require a form of protection for their investment known as an *escrow account*. This is a bank account into which money may be placed and from which the money may not be withdrawn until the account balance reaches a pre-determined dollar amount.

For instance, if you were to come to me and state that you need to raise $250,000 to start your business and you wanted $50,000 from me, I would tell you to set up an escrow account at a bank into which I could put my money. Other investors would do the same. Once the account balance reached $250,000 the money would be released to you.

The reason I would do this is because I would not want you to spend my $50,000 to get part way to your goal and then be unable to raise the other $200,000 that is required to get all the way to your goal. The escrow account ensures that you do not get access to my money unless you have raised enough money to fully reach the goal toward which you asked me to invest.

Tranche

Another tool that savvy investors use to protect their investment is a tranche. A *tranche* is the infusion into a company of a portion of a larger commitment of funding. For instance, an investor may agree to invest $300,000 in three tranches of $100,000 each. The investor will typically in the investment agreement designate certain milestones that the company must achieve with the funds provided in one tranche in order for the company to be eligible to receive the next tranche.

This has the obvious effect of protecting the investor from putting $300,000 in all at once and watching it all evaporate due to poor management, etc.

This concept is extremely important for you because you must be very careful to ensure that the milestones are actually achievable and allow for the unexpected.

Climbing the Investment Ladder
The process of securing investments for a company is analogous to climbing a ladder–when climbing a ladder you do not attempt to start out on the top rungs. Instead, you start at the bottom and work your way up, building on the success of each prior step. In the same way, it is typically unreasonable for most entrepreneurs of modest means to expect to get a $1 million or even a $100,000 investment as the first investment from an external source.

The very first rung on the investment ladder should start with your own money invested into the company. After you form the corporation or LLC, you can purchase shares in order to personally invest in the new company. This show of faith and acceptance of risk on your part will go a long way in convincing others that the company is worthy of their own investment.

The next rung on the ladder is to raise small amounts of capital from others. Typical initial outside investment amounts secured by most first-time inventor-entrepreneurs range from a few thousand to a few tens of thousands of dollars, depending on the amount that they need and how many wealthy people that they know. After you have raised $50,000 - $100,000 or so in small chunks, you should have established enough credibility to be able to solicit investments in $25,000 - $50,000 increments or higher, although usually still from among your circle of family, friends, and acquaintances.

Don't forget to include your business advisors such as attorneys or CPAs in this list of "acquaintances." They may either be persuaded to invest cash or to provide their services in exchange for an ownership stake in your company, which is nearly as good to you as cash. If they will do neither, see if they will defer payment until a certain goal for your company is reached, such as a certain level of sales revenue.

It is important to note that the best place to look for your early investments (up to a total of about $50,000 - $100,000) is your circle of family, friends, and acquaintances. It is extremely unlikely that someone who does not know you in any way will invest thousands of dollars into your company, although this does very rarely but sometimes happen.

Typically, after $50,000 - $100,000 of investments, you should be able to seek larger amounts from outside your circle. Often, the first ring outside of your circle will be the networks of your current investors–their family, friends, and acquaintances.

As of September 2013 it became legal for entrepreneurs raising investment capital to publicly advertise the offering, which had been previously illegal for those offering unregistered securities. However, as of November 2013, the SEC had not issued final regulations regarding the constraints on doing so, such as disclosures that must be made, etc. Be sure to check into these regulations before making any public investment solicitations.

Next in line for your search you may want to consider persons who are involved in the industry that your technology serves. For example, if you are developing a new technology that will be used by home builders, you may want to approach successful local home builders or owners or managers of building supply stores, etc. for your early funding. You may even be able to identify other entrepreneurs that made significant money in the industry and may have since sold their business.

I know of a number of entrepreneurs who raised early money from persons in the related industry and whom they had not previously known. It would of course typically be inappropriate to ask for an investment before you get to know the person. A good introduction may be simply to ask the person for their opinion and advice regarding the product and its marketing. After a substantial amount of time and after you have gauged the person's interest, you may want to broach the subject of investment by asking the person if they know anyone who may be interested in investing.

The key to funding strategy is to use the early small investments to achieve real results that make you attractive for larger investment amounts–each step builds on prior successes. Investors want solid validation of your claims that you will be able to achieve greatness. The more money *you* ask for, the more validation *they* will ask for. That validation will be the success you achieved with your earlier investments.

You must ramp up the investment increments as rapidly as possible (made possible by achieving results) so that you do not end up with myriad investors, each with a small chunk of the company. Remember that each investor has the right to sue you if something goes wrong... how much do you want to charge someone for that right? Initially, you may have no choice but to charge a low amount for it, but later you should have the leverage to raise that price substantially.

As you achieve significant results, you are usually able to raise the stock price as you bring on later investors, thus giving up a lower percentage of ownership per dollar invested. This increase in stock price has two benefits: it reduces dilution and it reduces the number of shareholders.

The latter is critical because sophisticated investors do not like to invest in a company with numerous shareholders; they have no idea who all they will be forced to deal with. If a company has too many shareholders it can kill an investment deal unless a way can be found to reduce their number before or during the investment process. It is hard to define the term "too many" in this regard, but fewer than a dozen shareholders may be considered manageable in most cases. It is not uncommon, however, for startups to accumulate much larger numbers of shareholders.

Note that sophisticated investors typically will not purchase stock directly from existing shareholders because this money benefits the shareholders and does not work toward advancing company goals.

In summary, the investment ladder typically looks like the following. Of course no such list is exact and you may be able to jump around a bit.

Steps on the Investment Ladder

1) Your own money
2) Your family and friends
3) Your acquaintances
4) The family, friends, and acquaintances of your family, friends, and acquaintances (and so on down the line*)
5) People in the industry to which your technology pertains
6) Individual angel investors
7) Angel groups
8) Venture capital groups
9) Initial public offering, merger, or acquisition

*Note that if you get too far removed "down the line" with your investment solicitations, the SEC may claim that this constitutes a public advertisement. Be sure to seek competent legal counsel on this point.

Pitfall: Being shy about asking others for money

I know many entrepreneurs who are reluctant to ask for money for a number of reasons, some due to shyness, lack of confidence, fear of failure, and some with reasons that I just cannot figure out. Some entrepreneurs feel that by asking for money they will convey a message that they or their business is weak or that they are somehow desperate. However, it is well known that startups must seek outside capital and nobody with a lick of sense would be shocked to learn that you need to raise capital. In fact, anyone who knows anything about startups would be shocked if you did *not* try to raise capital.

Bridge Loans
Often a company will get a loan from one of the above entities during the stage in which the company is seeking an investment from an entity further up the ladder. This is known as a *bridge loan*. The purpose of a bridge loan is to provide the company with operating capital while the often drawn-out negotiations are taking place for the new investment. Sometimes the bridge loan is provided by the entity from which the company is seeking the investment.

How to Put Your Money in Like a Pro
If you have established a corporation or LLC, it is very important that any funds that you intend to invest into the company (as opposed to loan to the company) are put in via the purchase of the company's shares.

Pitfall: Spending your own money for the benefit of a corporation or LLC

Do not simply write checks from your personal bank account to cover company expenses. Doing so leads to many undesirable financial complications down the road, especially if there are multiple "owners" doing this. Instead, purchase shares of the company to fill the company coffers and then spend from the company's bank account. Buy more shares if the company needs more money or sell shares to others.

I have seen an instance in which three guys formed an S-corporation using an easy online service and then started using their own credit cards, cash, and personal checks to do things like travel, buy supplies, etc. for the company. Nearly a year after forming the corporation they had not issued any stock to themselves. The three of them had spent varying amounts of their personal funds. One of the guys owned the technology, but had put in far less money than the others. Because nobody had purchased any stock, technically nobody owned any of the company. What a mess to try to clean up after the fact!

Also be very careful in loaning money to the company. It is unrealistic to expect that later angel investors or VC investors will allow the company to pay this loan back to you from out of the proceeds of their investment. Sophisticated investors will not allow this. They want their money to work toward the future success of the company, not pay for past activities. They get their return from what the company will do in the future. Your loan will be repaid from the operating proceeds of the company, which can be a long time coming.

Pitfall: Arguing with sophisticated investors about how all of this should work

Naïve Investors
Again, it is important to realize that there are many people who have money but who have little knowledge of how investing in early-stage companies works; it is completely unlike any other type of investing activity. These are naive investors. Just because someone meets the qualifications of an accredited investor does not mean that they truly understand the dynamics of early-stage-company investing.

You may be able to get rather good deals for yourself in terms of company valuation and stock price when you are dealing with naive investors, but once you are dealing with angel groups or VCs, you will find that the rules rapidly change. These new rules apply not only to you, but they apply to the earlier investors that you recruited. At this point, your naïve early investors may be in for quite a shock and for this you may take the blame.

Securing Funds in Investment Rounds
As you move up the investment ladder you typically do so in discrete investment rounds. A *round of investment*–also known as a *capital round*–is an offering of a set amount of stock at a set price and company valuation. An investment round is typically denoted by a letter and an amount of capital being raised. For instance: $250,000 Round A capital raise. In this A Round, the pre-money company valuation may have been set, for instance, at $1 million. If so, the investors in Round A would collectively own 20% of the company after their $250,000 of investments.

Here is how that scenario is figured: $1 million pre-money valuation plus $250,000 in Round A investment equals $1,250,000. After the investment the Round A investors own $250,000 divided by $1,250,000, or 20%, of the company.

Any of the entities listed in the above *Steps on the Investment Ladder* could invest in this round, but not all would be interested in so doing. For instance, VCs typically will not invest in capital rounds of less than about $3 million.

After the A Round is closed and the company achieves significant progress with the money, it may want to go out for a larger B Round. The company would typically set a higher pre-money valuation, such as perhaps $4 million. The B Round may be set to raise perhaps $1 million. If so, the investors in Round B would collectively own 20% of the company after their investments. Note that the Round B investors paid $1 million for their 20% stake, whereas the Round A investors only paid $250,000.

Down Round/Cram Down

With the above section title I have just struck terror in the heart of any reader who has gone through such an event.

The above scenario of increasing pre-money valuation assumes that the company has achieved significant results with the funds invested, so everything goes along merrily. If the company has not achieved significant results with the funds invested and the company is bleeding and struggling when it goes out for another capital round, it may be seen as shark bait. In this case savvy investors will force a *down round*, also known as a *cram down*, and it won't be pretty for the bait.

What happens is that the investors will force a pre-money valuation that is lower than one or more of the previous rounds (thus the name down round). This means that the new investors receive a higher percentage of the company for their amount of investment than did previous investors. This causes severe dilution of existing stockholders. (Dilution is explained further below.) However, the existing stockholders may be staring at the option of losing everything if they walk away from the deal and have no choice but to take a shellacking.

Oops–Who Owns the Technology?

Many inventors want to continue to own the patents for the company's core technologies even after they form a corporation or LLC and bring in investors. Naïve investors may allow this but sophisticated investors typically will not. The company must have control of the technology upon which it depends, not one particular individual. Sophisticated investors will typically require you to sell (assign) your technology. You may attempt to cut a deal in which you merely license your technology to the company, but do not count on being able to do this.

Investment Negotiation Strategies

One of the biggest concerns that entrepreneurs have with accepting investment capital is the need to give up partial ownership of the company.

The amount of ownership that you must give up for a certain amount of investment is partly a function of your negotiating skill. If you are a strong negotiator, you will likely end up with more in a given situation than if you are a weak negotiator, as there are really no absolute formulas. Each situation is unique and it is a game of give-and-take.

You should have a sound basis for your position regarding what you will give up and you need to be consistent from investor to investor unless you have good justification for making changes.

On a side note: One of the first ways in which naïve investors are naïve is a lack of understanding of proper valuations for startup companies.

Of course, entrepreneurs can be naïve as well, and they typically assign a far higher valuation to their company than will a savvy investor who "knows the ropes." The valuation dollar amount is important because it is the means by which the ownership percentage that you have to give up for a certain investment amount is determined.

In particular, and to reiterate in case it did not make sense to you the first time through, it is typically the pre-money valuation that sets this percentage. Pre-money valuation is the value of your company just prior to receiving the investment. Post-money valuation, in contrast, is the company valuation just after you receive the investment–that is–the pre-money valuation plus the amount of the investment.

If you want $10,000 from someone and you agree to give up 10% of the company in return, then the pre-money valuation you are setting is $90,000. That is because after the investment–as promised–the investor will have 10% of a company worth $100,000. It is a simple math problem of "$10,000 equals 10% of ___." The "blank" gives you the post-money valuation. You subtract the investment from the post-money valuation and that equals the pre-money valuation. For purposes of future discussion, let's call this $10,000 "investment 1." After investment 1, you and any prior investors would own 90% of a company worth $100,000.

The standard share price for stock in a startup company is $1.00. Therefore, in the above scenario for investment 1, you would issue 10,000 shares to the investor. (This assumes that you and any prior investors owned 90,000 shares before the investment.)

Dodging Dilution
This is a good time to more fully discuss the concept of dilution. In the field of equity investment, *Dilution* refers to a condition in which the percent ownership stake in a company is diminished among earlier investors after later investors come in. For instance, it would be common to set up a corporation that is authorized to sell 10,000,000 shares, and also common to sell those shares initially at $1.00 each. The company founder may initially invest $90,000 into the company by purchasing 90,000 shares. At this stage the founder owns 100% of the company. The remaining authorized shares are just vapor at this point.

Let's say that the founder's uncle then agrees to invest $10,000 for 10% of the company. The company would issue 10,000 shares at $1.00/share and the founder's ownership would fall to 90%.

As long as the share price stays at the same price that the earlier investor paid, the dilution ratio for each additional dollar of investment stays the same. However, if the share price is increased to $2.00, then the dilution ratio to the earlier investor is only half as great as if the stock was sold for $1.00. This is because dilution is based on percentage ownership of the total shares outstanding, not on the percentage or amount of money invested or the total company valuation. Of course when the stock price is raised to $2.00, an investor gets half as many shares for his investment as he would have if the price remained at $1.00. This is the primary reason that companies attempt to increase the stock price in each successive round of capital raised.

Note that before investment 1 in the example above, original investors in total had a 100% ownership (equity position) in the company that was worth $90,000. After the investment the original investors only have a 90% equity position, *but their investment is still worth $90,000.* This latter point is very important for the prior investors to realize! Their ownership percentage has been diluted, but the value of their investment has not changed.

Now, let's say that you have achieved some real results with that $10,000 from investment 1 that we just discussed and are ready to solicit another investment (investment 2), this time for $25,000. However, you are not willing to give up 25% of the company this time, but only another 10%. This situation, in which you are giving out the same percentage of the company as before–but for 2-1/2 times the money–recognizes the fact that you have built up the value of the company since the previous investment came in. The pre-money valuation is then set at $225,000, so that investor 2 will end up with 10% of a company worth $250,000 for his $25,000 investment.

Here is what the situation looks like after completion of investment 2: All of the investors who were in prior to investment 2 (original plus investment 1) collectively have 90% of the company, but the original investors in turn only have 90% of that stake, or 81% of the company. After investment 2 the original investors have an 81% stake in a company worth $250,000. This equals $202,500. The original investors, who put in only $90,000, have a smaller piece of a much bigger pie and came out quite nicely in the deal!

It is sometimes important to keep in mind the size of the pie and not so much your percentage of it when conducting investment negotiations.

Where dilution really starts to matter for the original founder(s) is in control of the company. Typically, voting rights are commensurate with percent ownership of the company. Once the founder's ownership percentage sinks below 50%, that person can lose the decision-making authority that he previously held. Depending on corporate structure, there may be ways around this by setting up different classes of stock such as non-voting stock, etc. but those methods are beyond the scope of this book. Note, however, that an S corporation can issue only one class of stock.

Angel Investors–Miracles for the Deserving
Angel investors are individuals or groups of individuals that may invest for reasons other than those for which venture capitalists (VCs) invest. For instance, they may not place such a focus on cashing out through mergers, acquisitions, or taking the company public, relying instead on dividends or increase in stock value for their return on investment. Angel investors may also invest in companies that have more limited market potential. Angel investors generally do, however, want to minimize their risk and make a substantial return on their investment.

In reality, an individual "angel investor" could be thought of as anyone outside of your family and friends who invests into your company. Some "angels" do not even know that there is a term for what they are doing, whereas others are members of formal angel investing groups.

Angel groups are sometimes loose affiliations of individual investors. In this case the group meets together and individuals may co-invest alongside one another, but each member of the group makes his or her own decision whether to invest and each invests their personal funds. Other angel groups take investments from members and then pool the funds from which the group as an entity makes an investment.

Many angel groups have as a goal securing future investments from VCs. If you accept money from such a group this will obviously expose your company to VC issues. Before you accept money from an angel group you should know their expectations in this regard, or else be comfortable with dealing with VCs.

Angel investors typically do not invest amounts of money as large as do VCs or investment banks. Typically an angel group may invest up to several hundred thousand to a million dollars, with each individual angel in the group investing a fraction of that amount.

Venture Capital–Feast or Folly?

Venture capital is typically only available for companies that have a demonstrated potential for high growth to sales in the billions of dollars. VCs will require that the company plan to have an *exit* within several years. This means that the VCs will want to cash out of their investment by selling the company to a larger firm, merging it with another firm, or conducting an initial public offering of stock (IPO).

Venture capitalists usually invest in companies that have several years of significant sales history. If you or your company has little prior record of success or yours is a niche product, it is virtually impossible to receive investment from a venture capital firm. If this is the case, you should think long and hard before spending your time chasing VC capital, no matter how "gee-whiz" your technology is or how certain you are that it will sell in the billions.

If you feel that you are a candidate for venture capital investment, the process of trying to secure venture capital should be approached with the same "strategic sale" philosophy as described above for trying to secure a licensing agreement.

Specialization

VC firms specialize in various ways. Some may invest only in more mature companies and some may invest at earlier stages, known as *seed stage* investing. When you see a VC firm that says it invests in seed stage companies, take that with a huge grain of salt. True seed stage investing entails investing in a company for feasibility studies, market research, product development, and strategy refinement. Do not expect this to happen to you.

Another way VCs may specialize (and some angel groups as well) is by market sector. For instance, one group specializes in medical devices and another specializes in telecommunications. You would be well advised to study any target VC firm to learn whether they would even consider an investment into your market segment. Picking a good investment is so incredibly difficult that many firms simply will not stray outside of their area of expertise.

Getting Attention

VCs get literally inundated with investment pitches, most coming in *over the transom*. This term refers to the small window over the doors of older office buildings. In the days before air conditioning, these windows would often remain open even though the door was shut. An unsolicited submission to the editor at a publishing company could be thrown over the transom. The VCs I have spoken to state that this is a highly ineffective way to get their attention. The effective way to get their attention is by having someone they respect refer you to them.

State of Incorporation

If you live in one of the less populous states and you plan to seek venture capital investment, you should consider setting up your corporation in the state of Delaware rather than in your home state. This does not mean that you have to have your headquarters in DE or locate any operations there. The reason for this is that VCs like to have certainty and uniformity regarding the governing laws among the various corporations in which they invest. Because the corporate laws in Delaware are business-friendly, there are a great many companies that have chosen to incorporate in that state, and thus it has become a type of de facto standard for the VCs.

I found out the hard way about incorporating in a small state when I started a technology business and incorporated in the state of Montana. That was fine for the first year until we went on a *road show* to make presentations to VC firms. They said flat-out that they would not invest unless we re-incorporated in Delaware, which we did at a cost of over $2,500 including attorney fees.

Sympathy for the "Devil"

Despite the misconceptions of naïve entrepreneurs, VCs are not the "Devil." If you get the chance to sit down and make a pitch to a VC, remember that the money that you are asking for typically does not belong to the VC. A VC firm goes out and raises a fund, typically receiving the money as investments from large institutional investors such as insurance companies, pension funds, etc. This is the money that they may or may not invest in your company. If the VC makes a bad investment, they will have their own investors breathing down their necks.

> **Pitfall**: Many people believe that VCs expect to make a "home run" on only one out of every ten of their investments.

Believing the above, many entrepreneurs figure that they should be able to get a VC investment even though they don't have a home-run scenario; after all, the VC expects that nine out of ten will fail anyway. Although it is true that VCs achieve a home run on only about one out of every ten of their investments, they do not *expect* anything less than a home run from any company into which they put their money.

They understand Murphy's Law and the fact that they cannot predict the future. If they invest in companies that are questionable from the outset, they are really setting themselves up for failure.

Many entrepreneurs feel that VCs are better called *vulture capitalists*, and I have heard significant animosity expressed toward VCs for being vultures that swoop in and pluck all the money from entrepreneurs through the deals that they make. Here's a little sympathy for the "Devil": I have seen several studies contending that over the long term, investing in a VC firm is not a very lucrative way for large institutional investors to make money. Many VCs have short bursts of money-making during bubbles followed by long periods of languor during the hangovers.

The above has been a general overview of angel and VC investors and you are encouraged to learn more about these entities as there is of course a lot more to know if you actually plan to seek capital from them.

The Secret World of Corporate Investors

Most entrepreneurs I have met think only of angels and VC firms when they are looking for money. Yet there is often a huge elephant in the room that they ignore. Many larger corporations, particularly those in technology fields, have venture funds from which they invest in smaller companies, or they may also invest directly. At other times, of course, those larger companies may buy a smaller company outright.

The former would be considered by the small firm to be an equity investment, whereas the latter would be considered an "exit."

As of 2013, American corporations were sitting on immense record-level piles of cash, a hoard so huge that many stockholders started to rebel against the waste of assets. (The amount was estimated at $2,000,000,000,000). Well guess what? You just may have the solution to all of their troubles!

Receiving an investment from a large company can often bring far more value to your company than receiving an investment of equal dollar amount from a VC firm. This is because the large firm has a direct stake in the success of the smaller firm and also has the marketing horsepower to ensure that that stake pays off, and pays off handsomely.

An example of this effect is the local-deals business, LivingSocial Inc. In 2010, LivingSocial received a $175 million investment from Amazon.com Inc. In early 2011 LivingSocial offered a $20 Amazon gift card for $10 and sold 1.3 million of them in 24 hours. This phenomenal success garnered national media attention for LivingSocial that was likely worth far more to the company than the $13 million in revenue from the deal.

Not long before, LivingSocial's much-larger and much-better-known competitor, Groupon, had been prominently in the news because it had turned down a reported $6 billion buy-out offer from Google Inc.

Prior to the Amazon deal, LivingSocial was barely known. I suspect that some brilliant marketer at either Amazon or LivingSocial figured out how to muscle their own way into the national news!

Who's Using Who?
This is a great time to address an attitude common among entrepreneurs that is extremely bass-ackward thinking and highly arrogant. I have heard this quite a number of times.

Pitfall: "I don't want somebody else getting rich off of me."

This attitude can crop up when an entrepreneur does not have much money of his own and must raise equity capital, thus selling a portion of the company. The attitude is that the entrepreneur came up with the idea and also has to do all of the work while the investor sits back and collects profits.

**Inside Scoop: Well, this is how it works and it is the entrepreneur's tough luck.
Tough luck for them!**

How's that for some tough love?

In fact, the entrepreneur is asking the investor for real cash money that the investor has already worked for and had the fortitude to put into savings or other investments instead of blowing it on toys and other goodies.

[Here is a good time to tell you about a great bumper sticker regarding spending money that I once saw when I lived in Montana. It stated: *"I spent most of my money on women, whiskey, and fast horses. The rest of it I just wasted."*]

The entrepreneur is asking for the investor's money <u>so that the entrepreneur can get rich</u>! The entrepreneur is trying to get rich off of the investor, not the other way around! If the business goes bust, the entrepreneur loses little hard cash while the investor loses a bundle.

Think about it: Who's using who here?

Private Placement
Each of the above investment scenarios are *private placements* that are exempt from registration under the Securities Exchange Act of 1934. Private placements are generally regulated by the SEC under Regulation D. In a private placement the company may issue common stock, preferred stock, membership interests, warrants, promissory notes, and/or convertible promissory notes (convertible debt).

Pitfall: Being indiscrete regarding your solicitation of investments

Virtually all startup businesses solicit investment as a private placement. However, it is important to note that you must be very careful about making general solicitations if you are relying on the private placement exemption to registration of your securities. If you for instance send solicitation emails to general lists of potential investors with whom you have had no prior ties, you may be required to provide certain disclosures and to ensure that all investments accepted are from accredited investors.

If you for instance send solicitation emails to general lists of potential investors with whom you have had no prior ties, you could run afoul of the law. If you for instance send solicitation emails to general lists of potential investors with whom you have had no prior ties, you may be required to provide certain disclosures.

The SEC has not considered entrepreneur presentations at angel fairs, venture capital fairs, etc. to be a public offering, even though the events are usually broadly advertised. You are also generally safe in making contact with persons or entities who list themselves as angel or venture capital investors, but again, seek competent legal counsel.

Where to Find Angels and VCs
Some states, such as Pennsylvania, have angel capital associations. If so, it is usually efficient to find angels through these associations. For instance, the Pennsylvania Angel Association (PAN) has a Website through which an entrepreneur may submit a request for funding to several angel groups at once.

The national angel investor organization is the Angel Capital Association (ACA) and its Website is: http://www.angelcapitalassociation.org/. Note that ACA does not have a submission mechanism similar to that of PAN.

The *Angel Capital Education Association* has a list of many angel groups at: http://www.angel capitaleducation.org/listing-of-groups.

The trade association for venture capitalists is the *National Venture Capital Association (NVCA)* and its Website is at: http://www.nvca.org/. The NVCA has many resources for entrepreneurs including a listing of many of the venture capital groups in the country.

There are a number of investment fairs and events around the country. Each normally solicits submissions from entrepreneurs wishing to present to angels or VCs (as the case may be) for funding. A search for the terms *angel fair, venture fair* or the like will bring up these opportunities.

ACE-Net

The following information is from the ACE-Net Website at: http://acenet.csusb.edu/faq.html. "*ACE-Net* is a non-profit initially set up by the U.S. Small Business Administration that conducts networking, educational, training and research activities for entrepreneurs and investors. Companies seeking equity capital can apply to list on ACE-Net. Companies who apply answer a basic set of questions derived from their business plan. Once accepted, they are listed in the ACE-Net database.

"By using ACE-Net's pre-screened database, investors in angel groups, Small Business Investment Companies (SBICs), and individual accredited investors and intermediaries can deal directly with entrepreneurs instead of having to find investment opportunities through brokers or finders. They do so by locating entrepreneurs listed in ACE-Net's secure database and then contacting them as their interest dictates.

"ACE-Net is the simple, secure and low-cost way for investors and small companies to find each other. It is an Internet-based listing service for securities offerings of small, growing companies located throughout the nation that are viewed anonymously by accredited investors."

Pratt's Guide to Private Equity and Venture Capital Sources details 4,000 entities that invest in companies. Information is available at: http://thomsonreuters.com/products_services/financial/financial_products/a-z/pratts_guide/

Corporate Capital

As mentioned above, some larger corporations–particularly those in technology fields–have venture capital funds. It would be useful to contact companies in your market space and inquire.

Syndication

Both angel groups and VCs will often *syndicate* their investments. What this means is that they try to bring in partners to invest alongside them. For instance, if you need $1 million and approach a certain angel group for that amount, they may tell you that they can raise $500K from among their members and then bring in another $500K from a different angel group that they trust and have worked with in the past.

Source of Market Research: You

> **Pitfall**: Some angel or VC groups may bring you in to make an investment pitch, but primarily to learn all about what you are planning to do in the market space in which they have investment interest.

> **Inside Scoop**: You can try to have potential investors sign confidentiality agreements, etc., but you cannot remove what you put in their head. If you want to solicit investment, this is just the risk you will have to take.

Caution: Shady Characters Ahead!

Be very careful in dealing with persons or entities that claim to be angels, angel firms, or VC firms. There are a lot of shady characters out there seeking self-fulfillment by pretending to be hot-shot investors. At a minimum they will waste a lot of your time, and you do not have time to waste. There are also financial predators looking to scoop up companies in order to facilitate fraudulent activities. Additionally, never forget that if it sounds too good to be true...

<u>Convertible Debt</u>
One of the methods by which a sophisticated investor may want to fund a company is through *convertible debt*. This is basically a hybrid between a loan and an investment. It is an arrangement in which money is loaned to the company at interest but the lender/investor has the option at a later date to convert the loan to stock (equity) in the company.

This generally gives the lender/investor the best of both worlds. To someone providing funds to a company, the best aspect of a loan is that it must be repaid and it collects interest in the meantime. A loan, unfortunately for the lender, cannot rise substantially in value. The best aspect of stock is that it may rise in value astronomically. Equity, unfortunately for the investor, may lose all value and the company does not have to repay the investor. Additionally, a holder of debt (lender) is ahead of a holder of equity (investor) in the line to recoup assets should the company go bankrupt.

From the perspective of someone funding a company, convertible debt hogs to itself most of the best aspects of a loan and the best traits of an equity investment but sheds the worst perils of each. The funder avoids the downside potential but participates in the upside potential of the funding. If this sounds unfair, that is because it is. But if the company needs the money badly enough, its owners just have to take it. (Ever hear of the Golden Rule?)

Perhaps the best part of convertible debt for the entrepreneur (other than the infusion of money) is that before the debt is converted to equity, the lender/investor does not hold stock in the company and as such is not entitled to voting rights.

<u>Liquidity Events–Bane or Bonanza?</u>
Nearly all investors make their investment in order to receive a larger amount of money back at some point in the future–a *return on investment*. There are three primary ways of receiving a return on investment:

1) The company makes a profit and distributes it to the owners of the company
2) Individual shareholders may independently sell their shares
3) All or a large part of the company is sold in a single transaction and the proceeds are distributed to the initial owners.

A *liquidity event* is a transaction that provides an opportunity for investors to "cash out" of their investment in bulk. This name stems from the fact that an asset that is cash or easily converted into cash is known as a *liquid asset*. When a company's stock is privately traded, it is relatively difficult for individual owners to sell their stock in it to others; the company's stock is *illiquid*.

However the owners can convert their illiquid asset into a liquid asset by selling all or part of the company for cash. Another way to convert to a liquid asset is to sell all or part of the company to a larger company for cash and/or the larger company's stock. The larger company's stock is typically much more *liquid* (easy to sell for cash).

Another type of liquidity event is an initial public offering of stock (IPO). This provides existing owners of the stock with a much larger market into which they may sell their stock, thus allowing them to turn their stock certificates into cash.

226

The goal in a liquidity event is not only to convert illiquid assets into liquid assets, but to receive more value from the transaction than the amount that was initially invested into the company being sold or merged. A common target is a *10X multiple*, which is a ten-fold increase in value received vs. amount invested.

Many investors–VCs in particular–make investments solely on the condition that there will be a liquidity event, also known as an *exit*, within a few years of their investment. VCs do not invest in companies in order to make money through the profitable operation of the company. They want to "flip" it in a liquidity event and take the proceeds to invest in another company. This may seem bad for the entrepreneur, but it is *definitely not*. This is how the mega-gazillionaire hotshot entrepreneurs got rich.

Pitfall: *"Those nasty VCs want to flip my company."*

There are several types of liquidity events. I will further review here the two most common types of liquidity events, which are:

1) Initial public offering (IPO) of stock
2) Acquisition by a larger company or a financial entity

An *initial public offering* is the means by which a small privately held company puts its stock up for sale to the general public as a way to raise very large amounts of capital. An IPO is an extremely complicated maneuver regulated by the SEC and requiring a host of professional advisors. IPOs occur very rarely. An IPO offers a company the opportunity to raise very large amounts of capital since any person or entity may purchase the stock.

When a company "goes public" its stock may be sold through entities such as Pink OTC Markets (Pink Sheets), Over-the-Counter Bulletin Board (OTCBB), NASDAQ, the New York Stock Exchange (NYSE), or other stock exchanges. Note that companies that have not registered with the SEC as public companies also may be traded through Pink OTC Markets and OTCBB.

The *IPO market*–which is the demand among large institutional investors for stock from companies issuing stock in an IPO–varies considerably with differing economic conditions. During bubble economies IPOs can be issued and gobbled up at a rapid pace, although only a very tiny fraction of all small corporations "go public" in any given year. After the inevitable bubble-burst the IPO market can decline to the point that no IPOs are completed for a year or more. As IPOs are a primary means by which VCs liquidate their investments, the decline of the IPO market can cause a backup of investor enthusiasm back through angel investors. Remember that the flow is from angels to VCs on that investment ladder. If VCs aren't buying, it sometimes slows down the angels.

An acquisition is a much more likely type of liquidity event. From the moment that you start your company you should be thinking about this possibility and keeping track of possible acquisition partners. Of course, just because you are thinking about this does not mean that you have to sell your company. As a matter of fact, you may be tracking these potential partners because you plan to buy *them* some day! Acquisition activity varies in the same way as IPO activity and this variation causes similar changes in investor interest back up the chain.

227

You may be wondering what VCs do with their money when the IPO and M&A (merger & acquisition) markets are bottled up. They typically hunker down and invest in currently owned companies to keep them afloat through the difficult environment until things start to flow again in the IPO and M&A markets.

The Complex World of Company Stock
Stock in Lieu of Pay

Your company may decide that it wants to give employees–particularly founders or top management–stock in lieu of pay in order to conserve cash. Be very careful about doing this, as the IRS does not like it if the company avoids paying payroll taxes or if the employee avoids paying income taxes by this arrangement. Generally, the stock would be considered income to the employee receiving it and the employee will owe taxes in real cash dollars although all he/she got was a lousy piece of paper–stock in startup companies is typically very difficult to sell and may even have time restrictions on its sale.

Stock Options

The proper way to reward employees by using company stock is via stock options. A *stock option* is an arrangement by which the company grants an employee the right to purchase a certain amount of stock at a set price (typically the price at the time of option grant) during a specified future time period. The theory is that the stock price will rise and the stock will be worth more in the future time period than the price it was at the time of grant–the price that employee has to pay for it in the future. During the specified future period the employee can buy the stock at the lower price and at any time sell it for hopefully a higher price, making a profit that is taxed at a rate lower than ordinary income. The company must develop a stock option plan and put it up for approval by the shareholders prior to offering stock options. Consult a qualified attorney for details.

Restricted Stock

Restricted stock is stock that cannot be sold until certain conditions are met. Restricted stock may be granted to employees for various reasons. The employee cannot sell the stock until it vests–typically three to five years after grant. This creates an incentive for employees to stay with the company, as they will not receive the stock if they leave employment prior to expiration of the vesting period.

Another type of restricted stock is stock that sold by startup companies such as S-corporations. The purchaser cannot sell the stock for a period of at least one year from the date of purchase. This is to ensure that the purchase is for investment purposes and not as a means to get rich quick by immediately re-selling the stock. This protects the company from having to deal with unknown shareholders.

Restricted stock may also be issued to corporate directors.

Stock Warrants

The following is excerpted from a definition at optiontradingpedia.com regarding warrants and their difference from stock options: "Stock warrants are contracts between investors and the financial institution issuing those warrants on behalf of the company whose stocks the warrants are based on. When you buy warrants, it is these financial institutions selling it to you and when you sell warrants, it is these financial institutions buying and not another investor. Companies issuing warrants do so to encourage the sale of their shares and to hedge against a reduction in company value due to a drop in their share price. Therefore, when you buy a warrant, you are helping the company no matter if it gets exercised or not. However, in a stock option transaction, the company itself does not receive a direct benefit at all. It is the winning investor who enjoys the profits."

Fully Diluted

We saw earlier that the term dilution refers to a decrease in percent ownership in a company–as more stock is issued, the previous shareholders hold a lower percentage of the total shares outstanding. However, the company can commit itself to issuing shares in the future through stock options, restricted stock, warrants, and convertible debt. The term *fully diluted* refers to the dilution that would exist if all of these commitments were executed. For instance if I own 1,000 shares comprising 10% of the 10,000 total issued shares, but the company has committed 1,000 shares available to be issued if all of the options, warrants, restricted stock, and convertible debt is exercised, my fully diluted percent ownership would be only 9.1%. (1,000/11,000)

Capitalization Table

It is very important as the company sells stock and issues options, warrants, and the like to keep accurate track of all of this. This is done by maintaining a *capitalization table (cap table),* that lists, for instance, the stockholders and their contact information as well as: the number of shares owned, type of shares owned, date purchased, and the price paid. Options, warrants, and restricted stock are tracked in the cap table as well.

Required Tools for Soliciting Investments

As with any endeavor, you must have the proper tools if you are to attempt the complex process of soliciting investments into your company. Although you may not be required by law to provide all of the below-listed items to an accredited investor, no sophisticated investor will invest without them. These items may not all be necessary for your initial contact with a potential investor. Be sure to find out what they do and do not want. Many of them are very busy and do not want to receive excessive amounts of information to wade through on their first look at an opportunity.

Business Plan and Executive Summary

First, you must have a professional-quality business plan as per the section above regarding building a business plan. Many investors may initially only want to see the executive summary.

Financial Statements

You will need to provide historical data as well as projections of the financial statements detailed below. If you are already in operation, provide as many years of historical data as you have, up to three to five years. Include this historical information even if you have no significant revenues. Regarding projections, a VC firm will typically require five years, whereas some angels, etc. may be satisfied with three years. The pro forma statements that you must provide are:

- Income Statement (also known as a Profit and Loss Statement or P & L)
- Cash Flow Statement
- Balance Sheet

In addition you will typically need a *Breakeven Analysis*, which considers your expenses and selling price to determine how many units per year you will need to sell to generate sufficient revenue to cover your expenses, or *break even.*

You will also typically need to prepare a *Sources and Uses of Funds Statement* showing where you anticipate your startup capital will come from and what you intend to spend it on.

Depending on a number of factors, the SEC sometimes requires that these financial statements be certified by an independent public accountant. I would recommend that you get this certification whether required or not if you are approaching sophisticated investors. Do not, however, give financial statements to a potential investor that are not of professional quality. If you are not thoroughly skilled in preparing and understanding these statements, get help.

Also, be prepared to intelligently discuss the numbers and their ramifications. Be sure that you understand how your numbers compare to similar businesses, especially regarding management ratios such as gross margin, net margin, return on investment (ROI), return on equity, various expenses as a percent of revenue, inventory turns, etc. A free resource to find some of this information is: http://www.bizstats.com/.

Some investors may want to see your tax returns.

Capitalization Table

You may be asked to include a capitalization table.

Company Valuation

You may need to submit a professionally prepared company valuation. This will be more and more necessary as you approach investors who are more and more sophisticated or as you ask for increasing amounts of money. There are many firms which will prepare valuations, including many accounting firms. Before you pay for a valuation, ask whether it will be prepared by a credentialed individual, such as a Certified Valuation Analyst. If not, you may not receive a very useful result, as a sophisticated investor will require this. You may be able to negotiate with an investor to get them to pay for a professional valuation, although they may not share the result with you.

Private Placement Memorandum (PPM)

A *private placement* generally is the sale of securities without SEC registration, typically made under Regulation D. In many cases you will be required to provide a PPM to those from whom you are soliciting an investment in a private placement. Along with other information, a PPM explains how the offering complies with SEC Regulation D exemptions. A PPM must contain a complete description of the security and the terms of sale. It must also contain information about the issuer's financial situation and a clear and complete description of the risks to which an investor will be subjected if they invest, including market risk, etc.

Prospectus

In certain instances you may be required to submit to an investor a prospectus rather than a PPM. A prospectus is a more detailed document. Consult a qualified attorney to determine what you must submit in your particular circumstances.

Investor Suitability Questionnaire/Form

Early in the process of actually soliciting an investment from an individual, you need to determine whether the person whom you are soliciting is suited to make such investment. One very good means of doing so is to have the prospect fill out an *investor suitability questionnaire* or investor suitability form, in which the investor provides information relative to his/her financial position and sophistication. I recommend that you have your attorney provide you with such documents, but you may also purchase them online, for instance from the National Law Foundation at: http://www.nlfforms.com/investment-suitability-questionnaire-6-pages.html

PowerPoint Presentation

You will often be expected to make your presentation using a presentation tool such as PowerPoint (Or you can get free presentation software from Openoffice at: http://www.openoffice.org/. This also includes a word processor and spreadsheet program). Typically this will comprise 10 –20 slides and last 8 –20 minutes. Be sure to inquire with your investor what will be expected of you.

Term Sheet

If you get an angel group or VC interested in investing in your company they will offer you a *term sheet.* This is a rather complex document that lays out the terms of the investment, if one were to be made. A term sheet is not an actual offer to invest. Negotiating the final terms in the term sheet can take months and cost thousands of dollars in attorney fees. The reason for this is the protective provisions that the investors will attempt to stuff down your throat that give them the upper hand in just about every aspect of the investment. Some of these provisions are negotiable and some really are not, and you will just have to take them or leave the investment opportunity on the table.

Some of these provisions have names like: Full-ratchet anti-dilution adjustment; liquidation preferences; preferred stock; reverse vesting, and drag-along rights. Be sure that you hire a *competent* attorney to help you through this process.

Due Diligence

If you come to terms regarding the deal, the angel group or VC firm will then conduct due diligence on your company and its principals. *Due diligence* is the process by which the VC checks out the veracity of everything you have told them and much more. If they find out you have been less than honest you are toast, so think about this right at the start of your search for investment. I have been told by one prominent VC firm that about 80% of the companies on which they conduct due diligence "wash out" in the process.

Inside Scoop: It is as important for you to conduct due diligence on your potential investors as it is for them to perform due diligence on you.

Be sure that you ask for references from the VCs of other companies that they have funded, but do not stop there. Try to interview companies not on the list that they provide, for obvious reasons. Also, be sure to get to know the partners of the firm to the greatest degree possible, as it is *people* you will be dealing with, not an inanimate entity. You may be able to conduct some of this due diligence on the Website: http://www.thefunded.com

Stock Subscription Agreement

Okay, once you have gone through all of the steps of finding investors and enticing them with all of your tantalizing (but fully legal!) solicitations, you will then provide to investors one last document: the *stock subscription agreement*, which is a contract with an investor for the investor to purchase stock in your company. The agreement should include the PPM as an attachment and should establish that the offering is a private placement. It should also ask for certain information and protections from the investor, such as an acknowledgement and acceptance of the investment risks involved and, if appropriate, an assertion by the investor that he is an accredited investor.

This agreement may be structured such that the purchaser will make a number of purchases at a given price in the future and over time, thus the name subscription agreement.

You must provide this document to all of your individual investors, starting with your initial investors.

Time

You can probably see from all of the above that it takes a very long time to actually receive an investment from an angel group and especially from a VC firm, from the point at which they decide they like your company. For a VC investment, six months is considered the bare minimum (for instance, if you just cave-in to the VC's terms), and it can stretch on much longer for various reasons.

Early on in my experience with VCs I attended a training session for entrepreneurs that had been invited to present at a venture fair. There were over a dozen VC firms represented in the audience of the session I was attending. In the Q&A session after the speaker concluded, I asked how long it would take after a presentation to actually receive funding from a VC if one were interested in the company. I posited "six months" as the potential timeframe, thinking I was probably being overly pessimistic. This was met with a round of snickers and some outright laughter, with the speaker kindly informing me that it would probably be longer than that.

PARTNERSHIP ENTITIES

Another method of securing financing is to form a legal partnership (such as a general partnership or limited partnership) with a person or persons who are interested in you and your technology and who have the financial resources to help you succeed.

A general partner will have an ownership stake in the company and will be entitled to substantial control. For this reason, a general partner's investment is not treated the same as a stockholder's investment by government regulators. This means that you will not be subject to the same securities laws as you would be in selling stock to a stockholder. Of course you must still be careful not to make any misrepresentations to a potential partner.

A limited partner's investment into a limited partnership (LP) is typically treated as a security and falls under securities regulations.

It is unwise to set up a partnership in which two owners have 50/50 ownership, as this may lead to gridlock if the two cannot agree on a course of action. A 51/49 split will avoid this gridlock. If this is not possible, you may consider in your partnership agreement setting up a board of advisors which may provide input on critical decisions and perhaps act as an arbiter if the partners deadlock on an issue.

A couple of other important considerations are that one general partner can commit the company to a loan without the other general partner's knowledge. The "other partner" is fully responsible for repayment. Also, the partnership may dissolve upon the death of one of the partners.

CROWD-FUNDING: A HOT NEW SOURCE OF MONEY

Crowd-funding, micro-financing, and *peer-to-peer financing* are all terms that refer to a means of funding a project, typically via the Internet, in which many individuals contribute small amounts toward a project. Although this type of funding source has been around for many years to fund theatre and other art projects, it has more become more popular to fund entrepreneurial projects. There are quite a few websites that can help you find money through crowd funding. I will list some of them here, but cannot vouch for them.

The JOBS Act made it legal to raise equity capital in limited amounts from non-accredited investors through crowd-funding. However, it is highly undesirable to have a large number of small investors in your company. As of this writing, the SEC has not issued final rules regulating crowd-funding, so be sure to do your legal homework before proceeding down this path.

Another, less dangerous method of crowd-funding your business is by pre-sales of your product. In this method, you take orders with payment and then use that money to fund the business. You do not give up part ownership of your business and have no potential legal issues with the SEC. However, you of course must actually be able to deliver the product using the money raised. It is almost unheard of for an entrepreneur to be able to launch a product in the anticipated timeframe and within the anticipated budget, so you could still run into difficulties regarding your obligations.

Among the hundreds of crowd-funding facilitators are:

- http://www.kiva.org/ Note that Kiva has a special micro-lending program for women.
- http://www.kickstarter.com/
- http://www.crowdcube.com/
- http://peerbackers.com/
- http://www.rockethub.com/
- http://www.sponsume.com/

Some tech startups have reportedly raised over $100,000 via services such as Kickstarter in little over a month.

SELF-FUNDING A COMPANY

Instead of bearing all of the hassles and headaches of trying to get money from others, you may decide to just fund your company all by yourself.

Self-funding is very high risk because it puts all of the risk on you. Of course, it can be very high reward because if they materialize, you will get all of the benefits. (Oh—except for Uncle Sam—he may get a little bit too!)

Some entrepreneurs start out as a sole proprietorship and fund the business themselves. Others form a LLC or corporation at startup and fund that entity themselves. If you choose either of these scenarios, be sure to clearly document the financial transactions between your personal assets and your company as to the type and amount, etc. For instance, you could purchase stock in your company to inject funds into it or you could loan money to your company for that purpose, or of course a combination of both.

Pitfall: Trying to sell damaged goods

Considerations of Self-Funding

One point to realize in considering whether or not to self-fund your startup: Be very certain that you will be able to go it alone successfully. If you cannot do so, struggle, and later seek outside investment capital, you will be marketing an investment in a company with a poor history. It is generally much easier to market a startup company with no track record–a dream–than an existing company with a poor record–a nightmare. In the latter case, investors will view you as a bigger risk–damaged goods–and will require ownership percentages, etc. commensurate with this.

If you ever find yourself in the position of selling what could be considered damaged goods, remember that it is not only immoral, but it is illegal to do anything less than fully divulge the true state of your company's finances and its financial outlook when soliciting any and all investments.

If you will need to get a loan such as a home equity loan to cover your product development, startup costs, etc., you may need to do so before quitting your job if you are employed. Once you quit your job, you may be unable to get a home equity loan, personal loan, etc.

Don't Lose Your Money

Again, it is very important that any funds that you intend to invest into your corporation or LLC (as opposed to loan to the entity) are put in via the purchase of the company's shares.

Do not simply write checks from your personal bank account to cover company expenses, even if you are operating as a sole proprietor. Doing so leads to many undesirable financial complications down the road. Instead, purchase shares of the corporation or LLC to fill the company coffers and spend from the company's bank account. Buy more shares if the company needs more money. If you are a SP, write a check from your personal account and deposit it into your business account.

If you loan money to the company, do not expect that any later angel investors or VC investors will allow the company to pay this loan back to you from out of the proceeds of their investment. Sophisticated investors will not allow this. They want their money to work toward the future success of the company, not pay for past activities. They get their return from what the company will do in the future. Your loan will be repaid from the operating proceeds of the company, which can be a long time coming.

RESALE OF STOCK

As mentioned elsewhere in this book, it is typically difficult to re-sell stock in small startup companies. One of the primary reasons for this is that it is difficult for the holder of the stock to find someone interested in purchasing the stock. Two services that provide a market for such stock are Second Market at: http://www.secondmarket.com/ and SharesPost at: http://www.sharespost.com/. Note that SharesPost bills itself as a market for venture-backed securities, which are securities in a company that has received VC investment. Be sure that you and any investors in your company that may want to use such services thoroughly vet them and understand the SEC regulation implications of using the services.

FINDING GOVERNMENT GRANTS

Before you get too excited by the words in the above title, let me assure you that there are no federal government grants that provide money for the general purpose of starting up a business. However, there are a very few federal grants that can be used by a startup company for very tightly defined purposes.

Some federal-government-sponsored research grants are available for new product development that is of interest to the government. Contact a SBDC business consultant for details on the following programs. Contact information for various programs is given in the Resources section near the end of this book.

Federal Research Grants
At the federal level, the Small Business Innovation Research (SBIR) Program and Small Business Technology Transfer (STTR) Programs provide research grant funds through various agencies, focusing on technologies relevant to that agency's mission. Such agencies include: Dept. of Defense; Dept. of Transportation; Dept. of State; Dept. of Health and Human Services; Dept. of Homeland Security, etc., so the range of research efforts that can receive grants is quite diverse.

However, these grants are very competitive and typically go to well-established companies or educational institutions. In particular, these grant programs do not operate on the scenario of you approaching the government and convincing them of what a great idea you have and that they should fund your research. Instead, they operate under the scenario of the government putting out solicitations for solutions to problems that it has identified and wants to have solved. If you can propose a solution to their defined problem, you can submit a response to their solicitation.

There is an exception to every rule, however, and there is an exception to the one I just stated about you approaching the government with your idea. The rules and qualifications for these programs are very complex and beyond the scope of this book, but you can learn about the programs, the rules of which vary somewhat by agency, at the SBA Website at: http://www.sba.gov/aboutsba/sbaprograms/sbir/index.html.

About 8% of first-time applicants to the SBIR/STTR programs are successful in securing a grant. It may take up to a year from the date of application to receive the funds. The funds are not to be used for pure research, but for development of technologies that will be commercialized, and a plan for commercialization must be included in the application.

Zyn Systems maintains a Web portal for the SBIR/STTR programs at: http://www.zyn.com/sbir/. Search services are provided at the right side of the page. Be sure to search the closed solicitations as well as the open solicitations. The purpose of this is to see which agencies may have in the past put out a solicitation for technology such as yours. You should call the program manager and discuss your technology if so.

The federal government maintains a Web portal for all federal grant programs at http://www.grants.gov.

State Programs

Many states have loan and/or perhaps grant programs for new technology development. Be sure to check what is available in your state or perhaps even in a neighboring state if the deal is good enough to make it worth re-locating.

Consultants

There are a number of private consultants that specialize in the SBIR and STTR grant programs. Be sure to thoroughly vet anyone that you hire as a consultant, as there are a lot of scammers out there! DO NOT pay anyone a fee to find you a government grant. The only thing you should pay anyone for may be the actual preparation of a grant application for a grant for which you have independently determined that you are a highly qualified candidate. To do anything else is a sure way to lose your money.

I have seen people in tears because they were scammed out of as much as $5,000 by entities they found over the Internet that told them they would secure government grants for the person. In the case of the $5,000 loss, the unfortunate person was a housewife and the scammer said he would find her SBIR grants of up to $750,000 to develop a new medical technique that she had conceived. The problem is, the government will not give $750,000 to a housewife to develop a groundbreaking new medical technique. This fact did not bother the scammer one bit, however, and he took her money.

The story of the housewife has a happy ending, however! She had come in to see me after she had sent the money but had received no real assistance. She had already told the scammer that she wanted her money back, but the scammer skillfully browbeat her, saying that lack of success was her fault, she was not holding up her end of the bargain, etc. I told her to do the following: Call the scammer and tell him that in two business days one of two things will happen:

1) She will open her mailbox and find a cashier's check for $5,000 or

2) She will call the Better Business Bureau, the Federal Trade Commission, the Attorney General in her state, and the Attorney General in the scammer's state.

I told her to then hang up and do not answer the phone for two days. Guess what was in her mailbox two days later!

Small Business Administration

An excellent, more detailed overview of financing is available at the SBA Website at: http://www.sba.gov/financialassistance/borrowers/index.html

CHAPTER 13:
DO YOU HAVE IT IN YOU?

This process of technology commercialization is ultimately not about the technology or even that all-important market. It is about you. It is about your leadership, your ability to be realistic, your optimism, your resilience. Train yourself to be successful and happy–it's a choice. Connect to others. Be a dynamic inspiration. Determine who around you cares and who doesn't. Bond with the caring and help the uncaring to care.

If others are not helping you, then help them to help you–and that includes yourself. Get the training you need, whether for tactical or for more innate or emotional issues. Learn to cope with stress; it will try to pile on. The best way to cope with stress is to ignore it. Take things in stride. Realize that difficulties are what you signed up for and that getting stressed only hurts.

Many entrepreneurs become Mr. Mom, as I was for a time. I occasionally took my young son to short informal meetings if I had no other option, figuring that if the other person was so narrow minded that this was a big issue to them I did not want them in my life or in any way associated with my business.

PERSONAL CONSIDERATIONS

Sacrifice
If you are to be successful, you will need to sacrifice short-term pleasure for long-term gain. Unfortunately, that includes family life, unless you somehow have the luxury to take your family on the road with you.

Stamina
The commercialization process requires massive amounts of what I call *mental stamina*. This is the mental toughness that causes you to keep going; keep pushing; keep on smashing against the daunting odds that are sometimes stacked against you. This is where you need to grab the sleek handle of that 12-pound sledge hammer and "hold on to your dream!"

Sleep
If you are like me, your mind often goes 100 miles an hour in 20 different directions. It can be very difficult to slow down, relax, and get that much-needed sleep. When things are going poorly–as they surely will at some point–one of the worst things that can happen to you is to lie in bed tossing and turning. For me in the middle of the night my problems always seemed magnified. I even had a term for the event: "night terrors." After awhile I noticed a pattern that when I got up in the morning, things were not as dire as they seemed the night before. I learned to tell myself in the middle of the night not to listen to myself. Yes, I actually consciously told myself that it was the middle of the night, I should ignore my tormented mind, and things would be fine in the morning. This actually worked for me. Another thing that worked was to turn on the TV to distract my mind from grinding on all of the issues.

Organization
It is no surprise to you that it is important to be organized. Don't just know it; please just do it.

Speaking
The CEO of a company that is raising capital from sophisticated investors is expected to be a powerful public speaker, especially if that CEO is presenting at venture fairs, etc. Be sure to hone your skills in this regard. You will find that even if you are not afraid to get up in front of an audience, this does not mean that you are a powerful speaker. You must, like everything else, learn about effective public speaking and then practice, practice, practice!

I one time asked a VC: "What if the CEO just is not an effective speaker?" He said: "Find a new CEO." That may be a little bit harsh, but I think you get the point.

Arrogance
Arrogance will kill off your friends and helpers, leaving you standing stark naked and all alone in the cold, cruel world. If you think that you might be arrogant, ask several people whom you suspect may feel that you are arrogant. See what they say. To do this will take great *bravery*. If you are afraid of what you might hear from them, then you can safely assume that you are indeed arrogant. If so, good luck with that.

Coachability
The opposite of arrogance is *coachability*–the ability to accept and act upon the advice of experts. This trait is quite important to an entrepreneur.

I have heard evaluations of entrepreneurs by funding entities in which the entities' personnel label an entrepreneur as "un-coachable." Once this happens, that entrepreneur is in a box as far as those funders are concerned–*a pine box*!

Work
Not getting where you want to go? Work harder!

Whoever said: "work smarter, not harder" definitely did not know what they were talking about. You must work smarter *and* harder. I would bet on a whole bunch of hard work versus a little bit of "smart work" (what is that, anyways?) any day. *Nothing* of value can be accomplished without hard work.

You should be in motion. Get out from behind your desk, out of your office, out of your city, out of the country. It's a big, big world out there and you will be swimming in it. Go out and get it!

I once saw on top of a salesman's desk a placard facing the chair with this nugget of insight: "If you can read this, you are not out selling."

Credit
A good credit score is very important. Having a poor credit score will be like dragging an anchor as you proceed. Be sure to start working on improving your score, if necessary, the moment that you get the inkling that you may want to start a business someday. This is obviously very important if you seek loans for your company from a bank or government entity, but it may also be important for sophisticated investors who may want to check your credit score as part of their evaluation of whether to invest in your company.

Expectations

Pitfall: Unrealistic expectations

Previously in this book I mentioned the importance of managing expectations. I was talking about your need to manage the expectations of others, but you should apply that advice to yourself as well. You must understand (if somehow you do not already) the difficulty and disappointment that you will face in your journey to successful technology commercialization. Here's a bit of paradoxical thinking for you:

Inside Scoop: *If you expect disappointment you will be less disappointed.*

That tidbit of wisdom is important because I have seen that disappointment often leads to dejection. Dejection greases the steep slope to failure.

Here is an illustration of this reality: A couple of years ago I spoke with two entrepreneurs–both of them MBAs with extensive business experience–as they were in the early stages of launching a company to develop and market an innovative software product. At some point deep into the conversation I told them that if they woke up in the morning expecting that things were going to go wrong they would go to bed "not disappointed." However, if they woke up every morning expecting everything to be just peachy, then they would likely have a bad day when that did not happen.

Two years later, one of those entrepreneurs said to me: "I thought you were the biggest pessimist when you said that, but now I see why you said it." This was despite the fact that the entrepreneurs had experienced significant overall success. Each step toward success is difficult. There are many shoves backward; the trick is to not stay there.

Greed
Greed is one of the worst enemies that an entrepreneur will face. Not the greed of others, but the entrepreneur's own greed. It can overpower common sense and torpedo relationships that are crucial to success.

Many inventors feel that because they came up with an idea and struggled mightily in developing it, they are entitled to the vast bulk of the profits, while others are simply trying to "horn in" on their efforts or steal what is rightfully the inventor's.

It is nearly impossible for an inventor to be successful while lugging around the weight of this attitude. It is usually very obvious to others and is perceived for what it is–selfishness and greed.

The inventor must consider which he would rather have: 50% of *something* or 100% of *nothing*. Read that statement again and consider it carefully, because it is one of the most important issues for your success!

Creativity
Creativity in all you do–that is the only way. Remove barriers that get in the way of creativity, such as: avoiding risk; not listening to others; arrogance; self-criticism, and not being observant of what is going on.

Work (Yes, Again–It's That Important!)
After reading this book you may have the idea that commercializing a new technology is a lot of hard work. However hard you think it will be, I can tell you that it will be harder than that. Until you have done it you cannot possibly imagine it. This is the most common comment I receive from entrepreneurs several years into the process: "You told me it was going to be very hard,

239

but I didn't know it would be this hard." If that is unnerving then you need to seriously consider whether you are up for this.

The sweet little side note is that victory feels like victory when you have to work for it. Successfully commercializing a new technology is like making it onto the starting line-up of a professional sports team and maintaining that position. It really is! How hard do you think those men and women worked to get there and stay there? They have their talents; you have yours. Talent is useless unless it is used.

Inside Scoop: *If you can compare yourself with everyone in the world and see someone else working harder, you are losing.*

Everything
Entrepreneurship is not about one thing. It's not about two things, ten things, or even 100 things; it's about *everything*. Recall the illustration I used earlier in this book to compare business to life. In life you cannot take care of four out of the five essential inputs and just ignore the one that's left. You will DIE! Success in business is not just about all of the things that you do, it's also very much about the things that you *don't do*, because these omissions can kill your business regardless of how great you are doing everything else.

This is a major reason why the colossal entrepreneurs work much, much harder than everyone else–they know what needs to be done and they don't stop until they get every essential item taken care of.

Open-Mindedness
With all that there is for you to do, it is easy to get in a hurry and not take the time to properly consider the ideas, suggestions, or comments of others. If you have had a streak of successes it is also hard to bury the hubris that sometimes results. Always, always take the time to really consider viewpoints and suggestions; don't be dismissive. Take a look from the other point of view. Make a thorough analysis.

It is vital as a leader to be decisive, and some people feel that quick decision-making demonstrates that quality. But there is a huge gulf between decisive and dismissive.

I have a personal saying that goes like this: "Most of my best ideas were not my own ideas." This does not mean that I tried to take credit for those ideas! It means that I saw the value in the ideas and suggestions of others, followed up on them, and benefitted greatly from them, along with the idea-generator.

Passion
Envision success. Envision the shining path to success. It is your dream that drives you. It is your passion that persuades others.

Aggressiveness
One result of true passion is the aggressive pursuit of ambitious goals. You must set ambitious goals and then pursue them extremely *energetically* and *aggressively*!

Discipline
Discipline is doing what you do not want to do when you do not want to do it.

Fear
Fear is the most excellent of all substitutes for discipline, for fear is the most powerful of all motivators.

Humans–and indeed most animals–have an inborn, "pre-wired" response for dealing with intensely scary situations, called the *fight or flight response*. When activated, this response prepares all bodily systems for rapidly, effectively, and efficiently dealing with danger.

Inside Scoop: Keep a close watch on your competitors because hopefully they will scare the crap out of you.

Fight for your life!

Assessment
It is important to truly assess your fitness for the job. Step outside yourself and take a good look. Think about what traits or training you would set as a requirement if you were to hire, for $100,000 a year, someone else to do what you are planning to do. Write a job description for your own position. Write the help-wanted ad. Interview yourself. Then ask: "Self, would I hire me to do this?" Or would you recommend that you go get more training and then come back and apply again? Maybe you need to find mentors or partners to fill in the gaps. Your ability to find helpers will depend on your ability as a salesperson. You must "sell" others on your dream and especially on your ability to achieve it with help.

There are a number of online self-assessment questionnaires and I strongly recommend that you take some. A very nice free suite is available on the University of Pennsylvania Website at http://www.authentichappiness.sas.upenn.edu/questionnaires.aspx. These measure everything from "grit" to character strengths, to happiness.

One self-help guru (I do not recall whom) recommends that a person write down, at the end of every day, three good things that happened and why they occurred or why they felt good. Sounds like a good idea to me. I have also heard it put this way: "Find out where happiness lies and start marching in that direction."

Capitalize on your strengths and build on them; use them to their fullest. You are what you do. How often are you kind? How often are you a leader?

Inside Scoop: Succeed or not in your epic endeavor, you will have explored deep inside the universe of you. Trite but true, this will for the rest of your life stand you taller.

Others
It may be more of a help to others around you–this self-assessment and realization–than it is to yourself. When you concede your limits, others will fill your gaps, and in this they feel valued. When you understand your substance, you will offer it to others, and in this too they feel valued.

Responsibility
The world is depending on you and many others like you to prevail. You have a responsibility to succeed! With a few notable exceptions like Apple Inc. and pharmaceutical companies, large organizations do not innovate. Progress comes from the grinding hard work of small teams working together and guided by a dynamic, inspirational leader. The innovations developed and

delivered by start-ups and small companies provide not only the devices and services to make lives more viable or simply more enjoyable, they also provide the new jobs that provide a living for countless families around the world. Please don't let us down!

Future
"The best way to predict the future is to create it."

This is one of the most powerful quotes in human history, attributed to various authors including Abraham Lincoln and Peter Drucker. No matter the sage, it is salient because it is your only hope. Get out there and take charge of your destiny. Do not just drift along wherever the currents and eddies may shove you. Grab an oar; buy a motor; build a jet-boat!

Isolation
I hope that in the process of me writing this book for you and you reading it, you and I have formed some type of connection or bond, even though we have not met. If you are an independent inventor or otherwise working on your own, it can sometimes get very lonely. I know this because I have lived it.

Prior to starting my first company I had worked for over 15 years in large organizations where there was always someone with whom to joke around, go to lunch, or to discuss the latest technical problems. When I went off on my own this suddenly stopped. Although I had a partner, we worked out of our homes across town from each other and saw one another only about once a week. On Monday mornings after my wife went off to work and the kids to daycare I was left alone in the quiet–many times facing monumental business, financial, or technical challenges filling the spaces that only hours before had been alive with love and companionship.

Come the weekend I made sure to invite friends over for dinner, visit friends, or go to other social events to fill this newfound void in my life.

Inside Scoop: We are not robots. We need human interaction.

Do not forget this as you follow your own path to success.

Overview
So what have we learned? Passion. Persistence. Ambition. Hard work. Optimism. Seek help. Avoid the pitfalls.

Here are several other little gems that I have saved for last:

In this book I have in several cases lain out two or more parallel routes that you may trek to your promised land. This is particularly true of manufacturing strategies: In-house, domestic contracting, licensing, etc. You may be bewildered and wonder which path is the *best* to pursue.

Here is my answer: All of them.

That's right: Each path is the best one for you to follow.

By this I mean that at the end of each of those roads other entrepreneurs have built massive mansions. Why can't you do so as well? There is no cosmic reason. The trick is to look ahead so that you know what lies down the chosen path and how to flourish along the way. Conjure now those "early explorers" we came across in this book's Introduction with their valuable maps!

As we now come to the end of our journey of exploring this commercialization process, I would like to present two final "wisdoms" as guiding lights. In all situations keep these in view. One is given below and the other in the section immediately following.

<u>Inside Scoop:</u> Do it well or don't do it at all.

It sounds so obvious but it is not. "This is what I want to do" must be immediately followed by: "Do I know how to do it?" and more importantly: "Can I excel?" Will anyone argue against the assertion that steadfast adherence to this philosophy yields the greatest chance of achievement? Grow great or go home.

LUCK

One factor that will play an important part in your endeavor is plain old luck–both bad and good. This is where my favorite adage comes in.

<u>Wisdom of the Ages:</u> The harder you work, the luckier you get.

The more things you do and the longer you do them, the more you put yourself in a position for good luck to act upon you and your endeavors.

Good luck!

ENTREPRENEUR RESOURCES

Small Business Development Centers
The U.S. Small Business Administration has set up a number of Small Business Development Centers across the U.S. These centers provide free and confidential business assistance to entrepreneurs and owners of small businesses of all types. Areas of assistance may include:

- Accounting/Finance
- Business and strategic planning
- Environmental management
- Marketing
- International business
- Government procurement procedures
- Technical issues

You can find the small business development center nearest you by going to: http://www.sba.gov/aboutsba/sbaprograms/sbdc/index.html

SCORE
The U.S. Small Business Administration has also set up the Service Corps of Retired Executives (SCORE) organization, a nationwide network of chapters comprised of retired business executives. These individuals provide free business consultation to entrepreneurs and small business owners. These are individuals who have actually lived in the same trenches that you will find yourself in. You can find the SCORE chapter nearest you by going to: http://www.score.org/index.html

U.S. Patent & Trademark Office (USPTO)
The Website is http://www.uspto.gov. Note that the USPTO hosts an annual Independent Inventors Conference at its headquarters in Alexandria, VA. If you can afford it, this is a very informative conference. More information is available at: http://www.uspto.gov/inventors/independent/aiic_main.jsp

U.S. Small Business Administration (SBA)
http://www.sba.gov

U.S. Securities Exchange Commission (SEC)
This is the federal entity that regulates the sale of securities. A good overview of how SEC regulations affect small businesses is available at: http://www.sec.gov/info/smallbus/qasbsec.htm

SBIR/STTR Programs
The SBA's information center for federal SBIR and STTR research grants is available at: http://www.sba.gov/aboutsba/sbaprograms/sbir/index.html. Grant information may also be found at http://www.zyn.com and http://www.grants.gov

National Technical Reports Library

The National Technical Reports Library at http://www.ntis.gov/products/ntrl.aspx provides access to a large collection of historical and current government technical reports that exists in many academic, public, government, and corporate libraries. NTRL provides a comprehensive offering that delivers high-quality government technical content in all subject areas directly and seamlessly to the user's desktop.

Community of Science

COS, at http://www.cos.com/ is the leading global resource for hard-to-find information critical to scientific research and other projects across all disciplines. It aggregates valuable information so you spend less time and money searching for the information you need. You can find funding with COS Funding Opportunities: search the world's most comprehensive funding resource, with more than 25,000 records worth over $33 billion. Identify experts and collaborators with COS Expertise: search among 500,000 profiles of researchers from 1,600 institutions throughout the world. Discover who's doing what—current research activity, funding received, publications, patents, new positions and more. Promote your research with a COS Profile: showcase your research and expertise among researchers and scholars from universities, corporations and nonprofits in more than 170 countries. Use convenient tools to keep your CV updated and accessible.

American National Standards Institute (ANSI)

Provides standards and links to standards sites, available at: http://www.ansi.org/

International Organization for Standardization (ISO)

International standards available at: http://www.iso.org/iso/home.html. ISO also produces Publicly Available Specifications, Guides, Technical Specifications, and Technical Reports.

Department of Defense Single Stock Point (DODSSP)/ Acquisition Streamlining and Standardization Information System (ASSIST)

The DODSSP for Military Specifications, Standards and Related Publications is available at: http://dodssp.daps.dla.mil/. The responsibilities of the DODSSP include electronic document storage, indexing, cataloging, maintenance, publish-on-demand, distribution, and sale of Military Specifications, Standards, and related standardization documents and publications comprising the DODSSP Collection.

The DODSSP also maintains the Acquisition Streamlining and Standardization Information System (ASSIST) management/research database at: http://dodssp.daps.dla.mil/assist.htm. ASSIST is a database system for DOD-wide standardization document information management. The ASSIST database resides at the DODSSP. The ASSIST-Online is a comprehensive Web site providing access to current information associated with military and federal specifications and standards in the management of the Defense Standardization Program (DSP), managed by the DODSSP. ASSIST-Online provides public access to standardization documents. ASSIST-Online includes many powerful reporting features and an exhaustive collection of both digital and warehouse documents. ASSIST is the official source of DOD specifications and standards.

Internal Revenue Service

IRS small business resources are available at: http://www.irs.gov/businesses/small/content/0,,id=98864,00.html

US Department of Agriculture Office of Small and Disadvantaged Business Utilization

Assists USDA in achieving its Small Business Procurement Goals for prime and subcontracts awarded to: Small, Small Disadvantaged, 8(a), Woman-Owned, Historically Underutilized Business Zone (HUB Zone), and Service-Disabled Veteran-Owned small businesses. It also lists contracting opportunities. The Website is: http://www.dm.usda.gov/smallbus/

Federal Laboratory Research Partnerships

Through partnerships with federal research laboratories, entrepreneurs may set up joint research projects or access technologies developed by the labs. You can learn about current federal research projects at http://www.osti.gov/fedrnd/. The federal labs offer their technologies for use by the private sector through their *office of technology transfer*. The best portal to access technologies across the spectrum of laboratories is through the Federal Laboratory Consortium for Technology Transfer's Website at: http://www.federallabs.org/locator/

A useful site for information about how to access Department of Defense research and research capabilities is: http://www.dodtechmatch.com/DOD/index.aspx

The Center for Technology Commercialization (CTC) at: http://www.ctc.org/ describes itself as follows: "Focusing on state and local public safety communities and those government agencies and suppliers who support them, CTC, Inc.—a private non-profit 501(c)3 company—provides quality advice and assistance as it relates to public safety and homeland security activities."

The National Technology Transfer Center (NTTC) at: http://www.nttc.edu/ facilitates transfer of technologies from federal labs to private sector commercialization.

Private companies can partner with federal laboratories through a *Cooperative Research and Development Agreement* (CRADA). The Argonne National Laboratory Website has a good description of the CRADA program on its Website at: http://www.anl.gov/techtransfer/ Information_for_Industry/CRADA/

Inventors Associations

Many regions have inventors' associations and it may be useful to join one if you can. Simply search the term and region to see what is available near you.

Small Business Technology Council (SBTC)

The SBTC helps members to take greater advantage of the SBIR program, ensure protection of company data rights, and create new business opportunities through Phase III commercialization of SBIR technologies. It also provides great networking opportunities. Information is available at: http://www.sbtc.org/

National Association of Seed Venture Funds (NASVF)

NASVF is a membership-based organization of entities that fund seed-stage ventures. It may be useful to review their membership list of 175 entities and determine if any may be a good fit for your company. The organization's Website is at: http://www.nasvf.org/

Kauffman Foundation

This is a non-profit foundation dedicated to promoting entrepreneurship and it provides a number of programs for entrepreneurs, either directly or indirectly. For more information see: http://www.kauffman.org/

Visa Business Network

The Visa Business network provides a Q & A forum for business questions affecting small business, as well as networking opportunities, a tool to find mentors, information on credit cards and finance, and more. The address is: https://www.visabusinessnetwork.com/

American Express Open Forum

This site provides a entrepreneurial, finance, and networking information. https://www.open forum.com/?cid=inav_home&inav=open_forumhome

Discover Card Small Business Resources

See: http://www.discovercard.com/business/resources/

MasterCard Small Business Resources

See: http://www.mastercard.com/us/business/en/smallbiz

Investopedia.com

A useful dictionary of equity capitalization terms is available at: http://www.investopedia.com/categories/ipos.asp

Young Presidents' Organization (YPO)

If you meet the criteria–a company executive under 40 years of age with 50 employees under his/her control, for instance–I strongly encourage you to join YPO for its many training and networking opportunities. More information is at: http://www.ypo.org

Innovation Institute

The Innovation Institute will, for about $200, perform an assessment of the viability of your idea. The firm does not sell marketing services. This eliminates the conflict of interest that causes invention promotion firms to tell you that you have a great idea even if you do not, so that they can sell you more services. The Web address is: http://www.wini2.com/

United Inventors' Association (UIA)

The mission of the UIA, as presented on its Website is as follows: "The United Inventors Association is the Inventor Industry's national membership foundation dedicated to inventor education and support. Our mission as a 501(c)3 non-profit is to offers educational outreach programs to inventors and Certification to local support groups and invention service providers who comply with UIA professional and ethical standards." More information is at: http://www.uiausa.org/

ACKNOWLEDGEMENTS

I would like to thank those who through the years helped me to learn about and survive in the wonderful world of startups, not least of which is my family, whose support helped me more than they can know when the going sometimes got tough. Then there are my two original business partners, Tyler Waylett and Arne Jacobsen, both of whom were indispensable and awesome teammates. Thanks, gentlemen, for all of your help.

I am also deeply indebted to Kathy Misunas and Terry Jones, both of whom took time out of their very busy schedules to assist me by reviewing my book and giving me great advice on certain style elements that needed improvement.

APPENDIX: INVENTOR PROTECTIONS

The American Inventors Protection Act of 1999 gives you certain rights when dealing with invention promoters. Before an invention promoter can enter into a contract with you, it must disclose the following information about its business practices during the past five years:

- how many inventions it has evaluated,
- how many of those inventions got positive or negative evaluations,
- its total number of customers,
- how many of those customers received a net profit from the promoter's services, and
- how many of those customers have licensed their inventions due to the promoter's services.

This information can help you determine how selective the promoter has been in deciding which inventions it promotes and how successful the promoter has been.

Invention promoters also must give you the names and addresses of all invention promotion companies they have been affiliated with over the past 10 years. Use this information to determine whether the company you're considering doing business with has been subject to complaints or legal action. Call the U.S. Patent and Trademark Office (USPTO) at 1-866-767-3848, and the Better Business Bureau, the consumer protection agency, and the Attorney General in your state or city, and in the state or city where the company is headquartered.

If a promoter causes you financial injury by failing to make the required disclosures, by making any false or fraudulent statements or representations, or by omitting any fact, you have the right to sue the promoter and recover the amount of your injury plus costs and attorneys' fees.

In addition, although the USPTO has no civil authority to bring law enforcement actions against invention promoters, it will accept your complaint and post it online if you complete the form, **Complaint Regarding Invention Promoter**, at http://www.uspto.gov/web/forms/2048.pdf. The USPTO also will forward your complaint to the promoter, and publish its response online.

To read complaints and responses, visit Inventor Resources at http://www.uspto.gov/web/offices/ com/iip/index.htm.

To order a copy of the American Inventors Protection Act, call the USPTO toll-free at 1-800-PTO-9199, or visit http://www.uspto.gov/web/offices/com/speeches/s1948gb1.pdf.

Source: Federal Trade Commission Website

ABOUT THE AUTHOR

Steve Overholt has spent the last eight years as a technology commercialization consultant, mentoring more than 100 entrepreneurs and existing companies through the arduous process, helping his clients secure millions of dollars in investment capital, and grooming them for successful exits.

Steve has presented seminars on the topic at the U. S. Patent Office's Annual Independent Inventors' Conference; the national Association of Small Business Development Centers' Annual Conference; the PASBDC Fall Technology Conference, and others.

Steve has conducted R & D at Fortune 500 and other large corporations, where he received three U.S. patents for his inventions.

He also has invented products on his own and formed companies to manufacture and market them, receiving two patents in these efforts and winning several international awards for product innovation.

His inventions have been licensed to one of the largest corporations in the relevant industry.

Steve has started up and run companies with international reach, written and co-written business plans for his entrepreneurial ventures that have received over $2 million in angel and VC investment. One of his startups was sold to a NASDAQ-listed company. His products have been on the market in major retailers for over 10 years.

Mostly, though, Steve enjoys applying his knowledge and experience toward assisting other entrepreneurs like you. ☺

CPSIA information can be obtained
at www.ICGtesting.com
Printed in the USA
LVOW03s0106010716
494862LV00005B/30/P